The REVELATION Of JESUS CHRIST

THE REVELATION OF JESUS CHRIST

The End Times

"Thou sawest till that a stone was cut out without hands, which smote the image upon his feet that were of iron and clay, and brake them to pieces" Daniel 2:34.

DR. ODELL FURTICK, JR.

Ordering Information:

For orders and inquiries, please contact:
1-888-404-1388
www.goldtouchpress.com
book.orders@goldtouchpress.com

Printed in the United States of America

DEDICATION

This humble work is dedicated to: CRU Military Ministry
My parents, Mr. Odell Sr., and Juanita Furtick,
My Lovely wife, Bernadette Porras Furtick, and
Most of all to my dearly beloved children and grandsons
(Pierre, Dominique, Brandon, Liam and Ayesha)

-Odell Furtick, Jr.

CONTENTS

Introduction ix

Chapter 1   Prologue: Christ In Glory 1
             Part I: Write The Things Thou Hast Seen.....................1

Chapter 2   The Letters To The Seven Churches Of Asia Minor 13
             Part II: Write The Things Which Are........................13

Chapter 3   The Letters To The Seven Churches Of Asia
             Minor (Con't) 29

Chapter 4   The Throne Room Scene................................42
             Part III: Write The Thing Which Shall Be Hereafter...42

Chapter 5   The Scroll With Seven Seals 53

Chapter 6   The Four Horsemen Of The Apocalypse 58

Chapter 7   An Interlude: the Sealing Of The 144,000 Jewish
             Servants 71

Chapter 8   The Seventh Seal/Silence In Heaven/Seven
             Trumpets Judgment (1-4) 79

Chapter 9   The Fifth & Sixth Trumpets Judgment (5-6) 87

Chapter 10   The Mighty Angel And The Little Scroll 94

Chapter 11   The Two Witnesses And The Last Trumpet..............100

Chapter 12   The Woman And The Dragon In Heaven 111

Chapter 13   The Two Dreadful And Terrible Beasts....................123

Chapter 14   The Final Hours To A New Beginning....................136

Chapter 15   Prelude To The Last Seven Plagues 148

Chapter 16 God's Wrath Resume With The Final Seven
Bowls Judgment.. 155

Chapter 17 The Destruction Of Babylon The Great:
Ecclesiastical 165

Chapter 18 The Destruction Of Babylon The Great: Commercial ... 177

Chapter 19 The Transition Of Power: The Battle Of
Armageddon And The Second Coming Of Christ..... 185

Chapter 20 The Millennial Kingdom On Earth: The Reign
Of The Son Of God 203

Chapter 21 The Eternal Age: A New Heaven, A New Earth
And A New Jerusalem 214

Chapter 22 Epilogue: Warnings And Promises...........................229

Bibliography...237

INTRODUCTION

The New Testament revealed the mysteries that was concealed from the prophets in the Old Testament.

John has exiled to an isolated Greek island in the Aegean Sea called the Isle of Patmos as an old man circa 95 A.D. by the decree of Emperor Domitian (Revelation 1:9). "I, John... Was in the isle that is called Patmos, for the word of God and the testimony of Jesus." The island is about 10 miles long and 6 miles broad along the northern coast. It is known as a rocky island where John had not seen Jesus in about 63 years since this Revelation.

The Three Main Divisions of Revelation:

1. Chapter 1, "WRITE THE THINGS WHICH THOU HAST SEEN"
2. Chapters 2-3, "WRITE THE THINGS WHICH ARE"
   - The letters to the seven churches of Asia Minor.

3. Chapters 4-22, "WRITE THE THINGS WHICH SHALL BE HEREAFTER":
   - The opening of the seven seals, in chapters 4 to 7 and 8:1.
   - The seven Trumpets Judgment, in chapters 8 to 11.
   - The beginning of the end, in chapters 12 to 14.
   - The seven Bowls Judgment: The destruction of the Antichrist's religious system and régime, in chapters 15 to 19.
   - The Millennial Kingdom, the final war, and the Great White Throne Judgment, in chapter 20.
   - A new beginning and eternal future with God and the Word of God in chapters 21-22.

Three critical things when reading the Bible:

1. Who is the orator?
2. What's the purpose of the book?
3. Who is the beneficiary?

Four Views on the Book of Revelation:

1. **The Idealist View** [Catholic Church]: This view uses a non-literal or allegorical approach to interpreting Revelation's book. It is not to be taken literally. This idea was developed in Alexandria, Egypt. The Idealist view also teaches that good will triumph over evil in the end. Robert Mounce argues the Idealist view, saying, "Revelation is a theological poem presenting the ageless, struggle between the Kingdom of Light and the Kingdom of Darkness. It is the notion that Christ's forces are continuously meeting and conquering the demonic forces of evils." [1]

2. **The Preterist View-** *Preter*, which means "past," is derived from the Latin. The preterist view is divided into two groups (1) Partial/orthodox Preterist (2) Full/Radical Preterist. The Partial Preterist teaches that part of the prophecies found in Revelation 1-19 was fulfilled in the first century of John's days. Specifically, after the destruction of the Temple and the fall of Jerusalem in 70AD under the hand of Emperor Titus-Domitian. Their defending argument comes from the prophecies of the Olivet Discourse in Matthew 24. Revelation 20-22 will be fulfilled in the future. Full Preterists believe that all the prophecies found in Revelation have been fulfilled in 70 A.D. We are currently living in the new heaven and the new earth now. Their view denies the second coming of Christ.

---

1   Mounce, Robert, *The New International Commentary of the New Testament*: The book of Revelation (Grand Rapids: Williams Eermans Publishing Company, 1977), p43.

3. **The Historicist approach** [Protestant Reformers/ the Seventh - Day Adventist]. This view teaches that Revelation is symbolic of the church's history and the apostle's life through the end of the ages. The symbols in the Apocalypse correspond to events in the history of Western Europe, including various popes. Most interpreters place the events of their day in the later chapters of Revelation. [2]

    - Chapters 1-3: seven periods in church history.
    - Chapters 4-7: the breaking of the seals and denote the fall of the Roman Empire.
    - Chapters 8-10: The Trumpet Judgments represent the Roman Empire's invasions by the Vandals, Huns, Saracens, and Turks. According to Protestant historians of the Reformation Period, the Antichrist in Revelation was believed to be the Papacy.
    - Chapters 11-13: represent the true Church in its struggle against Roman Catholicism.
    - Chapters14-16: The Bowl Judgments of Revelation represent God's judgment on the Catholic Church, culminating in the future overthrow of Catholicism depicted in chapters 17-19.
    - Chapter 20-22: the final thing that we are waiting for, the Second Advent of Jesus Christ.

4. **Futurist View** [Evangelical Christian] This view teaches that the Olivet Discourse and Revelation chapter 4-22 will occur in the future. The Futurist divides the book of Revelation into three sections as indicated in 1:19: (1) write the things which thou has seen (2) write the things which are (3) write the things which shall be hereafter. Futurists apply a literal approach to interpreting Revelation.

---

2   Pate, C. Marvin, ed. Four Views on the Book of Revelation. Grand Rapids: Zondervan, 1998.

Replacement Theology:

Replacement theology teaches that the church is the replacement for Israel and that the many promises made to Israel in the Bible are fulfilled in the Christian church, not in Israel. So, the prophecies in scripture concerning Israel's blessing and restoration to the Promised Land are "spiritualized" or "allegorized" into promises of God's approval for the church. There are significant problems considered to exist with this view, such as the Jewish people's continuing existence throughout the centuries and the revival of Israel's modern state. If God has condemned Israel, and there is no future for the Jewish nation, how do we explain the Jewish people's supernatural survival over the past 2000 years despite the many attempts to destroy them? How do we explain why and how Israel reappeared as a nation in the 20th century after not existing for about 1900 years?

The Type of Language in the Book of Revelation: Pictorial Language

The language is often called "Apocalyptic." This term describes the language because the first Greek word in this book is *apokalupsis* [translated in our English versions as "The Revelation"]. The word means "an uncovering, or unveiling."

The language is designed to uncover [reveal] "things which must shortly come to pass" (Revelation 1:1). This is its purpose, but this does not describe the language. The message of this book was signified to John. This indicates the abundant use of signs (symbols) in its presentation. The words and phrases are used to signify, symbolize, and reveal what is otherwise hidden in the text.

CHAPTER ONE

PROLOGUE: CHRIST IN GLORY

PART I: WRITE THE THINGS THOU HAST SEEN

The Revelation of Jesus Christ (vv. 1-3)
Christ in Glory-The Revelation of Jesus Christ is the unveiling of the incarnate person of Christ in the past, present, and future. The primary focus of this book is on the Second Coming of Jesus Christ. God wanted Jesus' servant, John, to know His plans for the future for humanity.

Here, John receives the glorious Revelation of Christ. Possible this oracle was given to Jesus Christ by the Father, or Christ signified it by His angel (Gabriel or John's guardian angel) to communicate or reveal to John "the things that must shortly come to pass." The Gk. word "signified" means to communicate to.

About 710 years before writing the book of Revelation, the Archangel Gabriel had spoken to Daniel concerning future events. Its prophecies speak with increased meaning to a future generation. The angel Gabriel specifically told Daniel to "seal up" these prophecies until the "time of the end." (Daniel 12:4).

His angel could also be the Archangel Michael; the prince of Israel had shown John the things he saw in Heaven and recorded these visions in his book.

John describes that what he saw was the Word of God. John's calling was to bear witness and make a record of what he had seen and all the things he witnessed Christ doing during His earthly ministry. While banished to the Isle of Patmos, John was transported to Heaven to gaze into the future. He records all things the Word of God communicated to him. He writes, in John 1:1, "in the beginning was the Word, and the Word was with God, and the Word was God."

> "There was a man sent from God, whose name was John. The same came for a witness, to bear witness of the light that all men through him might believe. He was not that light but was sent to bear witness of that light. That was the true Light, which lighteth every man that cometh into the world. He was in the world, and the world was made by him, and the world knew him not" (John 1:6-10).

> "That which was from the beginning, which we have heard, which we have seen with our eyes, which we have looked upon, and our hands have handled, of the Word of life; (For the life was manifested, and we have seen it,

and bear witness, and shew unto you, that eternal life, which was with the Father, and was manifested unto us). Blessed is he that readeth, and they that hear the words of this prophecy, and keep those things which are written therein: for the time is at hand" (1 John 1:1-3).

The LORD promises a special blessing to the readers and hearers of this prophecy. Not everyone in the first century would have a copy of the manuscript of Revelation. There was no printing press available in those days to manufacture copies and circulate them to the churches throughout Asia Minor.

The Lord promised that *"the readers and hearers of this book they will be blessed."*

Here in this passage, John warns his readers that Christ's return is imminent and needs to be ready. According to the Justinian Martyr, A.D. 167, he confirms the early church communities read passages from the four Gospels and the Old Testament writings.[3]

The Church adopted the public reading of the scriptures in a synagogue (Luke 4:16, Acts 13:15, Colossians 4:16, and I Thessalonians 5:27).

Greetings and Doxology (vv. 4-8)
John addresses the seven churches in Asia. There were probably other churches within the same region.

The Lord uses these churches to reveal Himself to all churches present in John's day and throughout the church age.

"Grace be unto you, and peace," John identifies from the Triune God as the source of grace and peace.

---

3   Justin Martyr, Dialogue, chapter 81.

The Doxology: *"From Him which is, and which was, and which is to come"* God the Father *"Yahweh"* is viewed as eternal, existing in the past, present, and future.

The Doxology: *"From the seven Spirits which are before His throne"* This is a complicated expression here in context referring to the Holy Spirit.

The opinion held by Albert Barnes "It is difficult to perceived in what sense *"seven spirits"* could ascribed to God, or how he could be described as a being of "Seven Spirits." At lease, if he could be spoken of as such, there would no objection to applying the phrase to the Holy Spirit."

The Scriptures give us three views for interpretations of the seven Spirits of God.

1. The first view recorded in the writings of Isaiah 11:2, which says: "And the Spirit of the LORD will rest on him, the Spirit of wisdom and understanding, the Spirit of counsel and might, the Spirit of knowledge and the fear of the Lord." The Bible does not indicate what the seven Spirits are but gives references to His works.
2. The second view concerns the seven angelic beings found in Revelation 4:6-9, 5:6-14, and 1:5.
3. The number 7 in biblical terms refers to completion and perfection. The "seven Spirits of God" specified the perfection and completeness of the Holy Spirit.

vv. 5-6 The Doxology: *"From Jesus Christ, who is the faithful witness,"* Jesus is above all the witness; He was a martyr (Isaiah 53) and a faithful witness unto death. All praise to Our Lord and Savior Jesus Christ for His finished work. It is was through His work on the cross that we are made blameless.

"First begotten of the dead" Jesus was the firstborn from the dead, in His resurrection (Acts 2:24, 26:23, 1 Corthinians15:23,1 Peter 1:3, and Revelation 14:13). "Who is the image of the invisible God, the firstborn of every creature" (Colossians 1:15). Jesus had risen from the dead unto

glorify and was given a resurrected body. This was the reason that John did not recognize Christ in His glorified form.

"Made us kings and priests" In the Millennial Kingdom, this would refer to selected duties for some of the saints. The kings of the earth will be subordinate under the kingship and authority of Christ. In chapter 22, we are given detailed descriptions of the Millennial Kingdom. Jesus will reign as King of kings and king David as His co-regent. The saints will reign with The Messiah in His earthly kingdom as kings and priests of the Most High God (cf. Daniel 7:27, Zechariah 14:9-20, Isaiah 11:1-9, 1 Corinthians 6:1-3, Galatians 3:29, 2 Timothy 2:12, and Revelation 5:10).

"But ye are a chosen generation, a royal priesthood, a holy nation, a peculiar people; that ye should shew forth the praises of him who hath called you out of darkness into his marvelous light," (1 Peter 2:9).

v. 7 *"He cometh with clouds"* This one of most important themes of this book is *"Christ will return."* The Heb. meaning for *"clouds"* is "to cover." The cloud plays a symbolic role as a recurrent theophany of God, His slender Glory or presence concealed from humanity (cf. Exodus 16:10; 33:9; Numbers 11:25; 12:5; Job 22:14 and Psalms 18:11). The cloud is associate with Christ second coming in (Acts 1:9-11, I Thessalonians 4:17, and Matthew 24:30).

The LORD called Moses from a pillar of cloud and told him that His Shekinah Glory would be with the Israelites (cf. 13:21-22, 24:16-18, Exodus 33:9-11, 40:34-38 and Leviticus 16:2).

"When he had spoken these things, while they beheld, he was taken up; and a cloud received him out of their sight. And while they looked steadfastly toward Heaven as he went up, behold, two men stood by them in white apparel" (Acts 1:9-10).

"Then shall appear the sign of the Son of Man in Heaven: and then shall all the tribes of the earth mourn, and they shall see the Son of Man coming in the clouds of heaven with power and great glory" (Matthew 24:30).

Jesus says unto him, "Thou hast said: nevertheless, I say unto you, Hereafter shall ye see the Son of Man sitting on the right hand of power, and coming in the clouds of heaven" (Matthew 24:64).

"And then shall they see the Son of man coming in the clouds with great power and glory" (Mark 13:26).

Every eye shall see Christ's Second Coming worldwide through television, news channels, and internet website. When Christ returns, He will be visible to all, including those in Hell who persecuted Him and the saints. The world will have an emotional reaction to Christ's return because they did not believe in Him. The Jewish people, and those who persecuted the Lord, shall mourn because of their former disbelief.

"And I will pour upon the house of David, and upon the inhabitants of Jerusalem, the spirit of grace and supplications: and they shall look upon me whom they have pierced, and they shall mourn for him, as one mourneth for his only son, and shall be in bitterness for him, as one that is in bitterness for his firstborn," (Zechariah 12:10).

v.8 *"I am,"* Jesus said unless you believe "I am" (John 8:24), you will die with your sins. He said that before Abraham was "I am" (John 8:58), an intentional reference of Christ as the self-existent One of Exodus (Exodus 3:6-14) for which the Jews attempted to stone. When Jesus was approached by the band of soldiers in the garden of Gethsemane that came to apprehend Him, he spoke with the voice such command, "I am He." The men went backward and fell to the ground from the power of Jesus's voice (John 18:6).

The Word of God created the world. Men can make things with their hands and the knowledge to design. However, all created things were brought into existence by the Word of God.

"Alpha and Omega"- signifies God's eternity. The first and last letters (A-O) of the Greek alphabet. God has no beginning or end because He is the beginning of all things and will be the end of all things (cf. Revelation 1:11, 17, 18, Revelation 2:8, 22:13, and Isaiah 41:4, 44:6 48:12).

"Beginning and end," God is the Sovereign Creator. He has been a part of man history from the beginning of creation until the end of civilization. Everything that happens in human history did so under His dominion. He is the present Eternal One, "I am" (Rev 1:17).

Jesus is the Creator and Judge. He is the always one who could give revelation to His people.

For that which is (present), and which was (past), and which is to come (future), God is eternal.

"Before the mountains were brought forth, or ever thou hadst formed the earth and the world, even from everlasting to everlasting, thou art God" (Psalm 90:2).

The Glorified Christ, Judging His Church as High Priest (vv. 9-18) v. 9 John was exiled to the isle of Patmos as a prisoner for preaching the gospel. Many attempts were made on his life to silence him, but he was chosen by Christ to be a witness for Him and to testify on behalf of His earthly ministry and all the visions of Jesus' Revelation. John identified himself as a brother in the same tribulation [persecution] under Emperor Domitian. Emperor Nerva later released John after the death of Domitian, ca. 96 A.D.

The Persecution of the Early Church:

(1) **Nero Burns Rome**: History blames Emperor Nero for one of the greatest disasters to befall Rome. A great fire broke out the night of July 18, 64 A.D., utterly destroying the imperial city. Nero's intention was to bypass the Senate and rebuild Rome to his specification and to further his political agenda. In 67 A.D., the first persecution of the Church spread throughout the whole Roman Empire. Tradition says, "Paul the Apostle of the Gentile and Peter the Apostle of the Jews died under Nero's reign." Paul was beheaded, and Peter crucified upside down on a cross.

(2) **The Destruction of Jerusalem, 70 A.D.**: During the first war between the Roman and Jews, a decisive Roman victory

was made as they besieged and conquered Jerusalem. The city of Jerusalem and its Holy Temple was left in ruins, and three years later, the Masada fell by the hand Emperor Titus and his Generals. Jesus foretold of this event in Matthew 24:2.

(3) **Persecution of the Church: Under Emperor Domitian, 81 A.D.:** According to tradition, Domitian put out a decree to kill anyone in King David. Among the persecuted were Christian martyrs Simeon and the Bishop of Jerusalem, who was found crucified. Apostle John was boiled in oil and afterward banished to the Isle of Patmos.

v. 10 *"I was in the Spirit on the Lord's day…"* The Lord rose from the dead on a Sunday morning. John was in the Spirit or worshipping the Lord on Sunday and heard the Lord behind him. Alternatively, he could be referring to the voice of "I am."

"The Great Day of Judgment" The sound of blowing *"shophar"* is sharp and alert. It emphasizes the holiness and greatness of these days of remorse and the Day of Judgment as it approaches Yom Kippur.

"The coming of the Messiah," the horn will blow on when the Messiah arrives.

Blowing the *shophar* or trumpet on Rosh Hashanah symbolizes:

1) The origin of creation.
2) The mark of ten days that lead up to the day of repentance.
3) A token reminder that God gave the law at Mount Sinai.
4) A warning from the Prophets (Ezekiel 33:4-5).
5) A commemoration of the destruction of the Temple
6) The remembrance of the replacement ram for the sacrifice and binding of Isaac.
7) As a reminder of that, we should humble ourselves before God (Amos 3:8).
8) A reminder of the coming great Day of Judgment (Zephaniah 1:14-15).
9) Future worship of Israel on Mount Zion of Jerusalem, (Isaiah 27:13; Hebrews, 12:22).

10) The commemoration of the dead (Isaiah 18:3).
11) Crowning of the King (similar to blowing the horns at the inauguration of a King).

The Letters to the Seven Churches of Asia Minor (vv. 11-13)
Here Jesus introduced Himself as the eternal One ["I am"] He announced this phrase to Moses (Exodus 3:14). Jesus said, "before Abraham was born, I am" (John 8:58).

"Alpha and Omega" is also connected to the title as "the first and the last" found in Isaiah's writing. The sovereignty of Christ is eternal and self-existent.

> Isaiah 44:6 states, "Thus saith the LORD the King of Israel, and his redeemer the LORD of Host; I am the first, and I am the last; besides me, there is no God."

v. 13 *"And in the midst of the seven candlesticks one like unto the Son of man…"* The Menorah or the seven lampstands has always been God's idea to the world. It first appears in Exodus 25:31-37, as God instructs Moses how to make it. Menorah described in the book of Revelation as the seven-lamp (six branches) ancient Hebrew lampstand made of pure gold and used in the portable sanctuary set up by Levitical priests in the wilderness and later in the Temple in Jerusalem.

The massive Menorah would have been a powerful symbol of God's light and holiness in our dark and sinful world. It symbolizes God's glory, truth, and light into the world as prescribed in Isaiah 42:6. Jesus teaches in Matthew 5:14 that the Church is to be that light to the world.

"Clothed with a garment down to the foot" signifies the Divine Truth's proceeding Divine.
Christ's rights to govern and judge the churches. He wears the robe of the High Priest, reaching down to his feet was an oriental mark of dignity. Jesus is the only mediator between man and God. "For there is one God, and one mediator also between God and men, the man Christ Jesus" (1 Timothy 2:5; 1 John 2:1).

Descriptions of the Glorified Christ (vv. 14-16)
v. 14 John uses figures of speech in his description of the glorified Christ as High Priest and Judge. *"Hairs white like wools,"* symbolizes wisdom and dignity in the presence of God (Daniel 7:9). Signify his majesty, purity, and eternity.

Daniel gives a similar description of God, the "Ancient of days" in his vision. God uses this title because He existed before the heavens were created before time existed. Daniel depicts God judging the nation of Israel. John seems to describe Jesus in the same manner as Daniel in his vision. Specifically, His pre-existence, along with God the Father.

> "I beheld till the thrones were cast down, and the Ancient of days did sit, whose garment was white as snow, and the hair of his head like the pure wool: his throne was like the fiery flame, and his wheels as burning fire. A fiery stream issued and came forth from before him: thousand thousands ministered unto him, and ten thousand times ten thousand stood before him: the judgment was set, and the books were opened. I beheld then because of the voice of the great words which the horn spake: I beheld even till the beast was slain, and his body destroyed and given to the burning flame" (Daniel 7:9-11).

"His eyes were as a flame of fire," which described the ability to discern or penetrate all hearts and minds' secret thoughts. His judgement is in righteousness and holiness, (cf. Malachi 3:2,1 Corinthians 3:13, Hebrews 1:13, 4:13). Daniel describes the throne of God as fiery flames and burning fire (Daniel 7:9)

"His feet like unto fine brass," indicates the feet of judgment (Exodus 38:30, Numbers 21).

"His voice as the sound of many waters" We could imagine God's powerful voice sounding like Niagara Falls when He speaks (Daniel 10:6, Revelation 14:2, and 19:6). David also uses a metaphor to describe God's

voice as sounding like thunder (cf. Job 40:9, Psalm 29:3, 77:18, and 104:7). God's voice sounds like trumpets (Exodus 19:16, 19; Hebrews 12:19, Revelation 1:10, 4:1). God's words spoken through the mouth of His prophets and preachers. The sound of God's voice isn't heard, and they do believe (Zephaniah 3:2).

> Alludes to Ezekiel's visions: "When they went, I heard the noise of their wings, like the noise of many waters, like the voice of the Almighty, a tumult like the noise of an army; and when they stood still, they let down their wings" (Ezekiel 1:24).

> "And behold, the glory of the God of Israel came from the way of the east. His voice was like the sound of many waters; the earth shone with His glory" (Ezekiel 43:2).

"He had in His right hand seven stars," indicating His protection and righteousness; His control of the stars in His Almighty hand, (cf. Psalm 48:10,138:7, Isaiah, 41:10 and John 10:28).

"Out of His mouth went a sharp two-edged sword," The Word of God, (cf. Matthew 4:4-8, John 1:1,14, Hebrews 11:3)

"His countenance was as the sun shineth in his strength" Christ's glory is Light (Hebrews 1:3, 2 Corinthians 4:6). God's Light (Psalms 84:11, Ezekiel 10:4, Habakkuk 3:4). Christ inter-circle [James, Peter, and John] witness His Shekinah's glory of Light on the Mount of Transfiguration (Matthew 17:1-9). Paul has seen the countenance of the Lord on the road to Damascus and is blinded by Christ Glory (Acts 9:3-4). Moses' face shone after being in God's presence for forty days and nights on Mount Sinai (Exodus 34:29-35, 2 Corinthians 3:7-18).

> "This then is the message which we have heard of him, and declare unto you, that God is light, and in him is no darkness at all" (John 1:5)

The Glorified Christ (vv. 17-19)
The last time John saw Jesus was at His ascension on Mount Olive after several decades. When he asked in the presence of the glorified Christ, his physical body was unable to stand.

v. 18 *"I am he that liveth, and was dead; and, behold, I am alive for evermore, Amen; and have the keys of hell and of death."* Jesus will never again be under the control of men. He has authority over Hell (place of torment) and physical death. He has all power in His hand and decree who live or die (John 11:52,17:24 and 2 Corinthians 3:18).

v. 19 *"Write the things which thou hast seen, and the things which are, and the things which shall be hereafter;"*

1. **"The things which thou hast seen"**- Things mentioned in chapter one.
2. **"The things which are"**- Chapters two and three: the seven churches' present status in Asia Minor.
3. **"Things which shall be hereafter"** begins after chapter 4:1, whereas the Church is no longer mentioned throughout the pages of the Book of Revelation until after chapter 22.

The Explanation of the Seven Stars and Seven Lampstands (v. 20)
Paul and Christ's disciples planted many other churches besides the seven churches. Why did Christ choose these churches over the others? Perhaps these churches were selected because they possibly portrayed the history of the Church. In chapter one, the seven lamps are no longer located on earth but are now shown in chapter 4, in Heaven. Jesus explains the meaning of "the mystery of the seven stars." The lampstands indicate the bearer of the light [the gospel] to a world in darkness.

- *"Seven stars,"* angels or pastors
- *"Seven golden candlesticks,"* churches
- Each Church was in spiritual decline.

CHAPTER TWO

THE LETTERS TO THE SEVEN CHURCHES OF ASIA MINOR

PART II: WRITE THE THINGS WHICH ARE

The Letter to the Church in Ephesus (vv. 1-7)

v. 1 *"Unto the angel of the church of Ephesus write"* The word "angel" (Gk. *Aggelos*) probably refers to a "human messenger" or an angel. In this context, Angel supports the idea that the seven churches' angels could be human messengers: Matthew 11:10; Luke 7:25-27; James 2:25.

Furthermore, the messengers to the churches of Asia Minor could be the guardian angels of each church's elders: Matthew 18:10, Acts 12:15. The name Ephesus means "desired one." Ephesus is known as the "Queen of Asia," and Ephesus, the city was wealthy and beautiful.

The title angel here may refer to pastors or bishops (depending on the context in which its used) or elders of these seven churches (Acts 20:17). On Paul's second missionary journey (A.D. 52), he visited Ephesus after leaving Corinth and planted the church (Acts 18:19).

On Paul's third missionary journey (A.D. 54-56), Paul spent between two and three years teaching in the city. Paul's co-laborers Priscilla, Aquila, and Apollos nurtured this congregation (Acts 17, 18, 19:10-12 and 20:16-17).

Walvoord states that this is "a symbolic presentation of the fact that Christ holds the messengers of these churches in His right hand, a place of sovereign protection as well as the divine authority over them." [4]

vv. 2-3 Jesus says, *"I know your works,"* which indicates their moral behavior, labor, turmoil, and suffering for His name's sake. He commended Ephesus for their service under spiritual trials and persecution. The Ephesians maintained their Christian morals against the erosion doctrine errors. They didn't depart exclusively from their faith or stopped loving Jesus, but their enthusiasm and zeal began to gradually burn out over 40 years.

Jesus stated, *"Thou hast tried them which say there are apostles and are not"* false Apostles traveled from house to house and weren't vetted by the General Council of Jerusalem. As a result, they were able to propagate their false doctrines and erroneous teachings. These false teaching were contradictory to the gospel and misled the saints of God.

Jesus warned His disciples of *"false doctrine or leaven"* (cf. Matthew 16:3,6-12, 23:16-24; Acts 20:29-30). False teachings or false doctrine

---

4   Walvoord, John, Revelation, p.55.

had been a severe problem to God's people from Genesis to Revelation. False teachings plagued the church during the early church era and even the contemporary period of the 21st century.

The Epistles of the New Testament refutes Doctrines of Error:

1. Galatians-addresses the issues on legalism taught by the Judaizers.[5]
2. Colossians- addresses the problems of Antinomian Gnosticism.
3. 2 Thessalonians- addresses the issues of false teaching concerning the Tribulation period and the Rapture.
4. The Hebrews-encourages the Hebrews Christians who had become melancholy regarding Judaism and were ready to turn back. The author of Hebrews addresses the issues that Christ is fulfilling the Torah and is superior to all the patriarchs and angels.
5. The apostle Paul writes an epistle to Timothy addressing the "Doctrines of Devils" propagating amongst the church communities (1 Timothy 4:1).
6. The Apostle Peter warned that there were false prophets and teachers among the congregation who were propagating "damnable heresies", (2 Peter 2:1-2, 3:3,17).

vv. 4-5 The Lord gives three exhortations:

1. *"Remember"* from where you are fallen (go back to the point where you had changed and start your first works again).
2. *"Repent"* turn around and make a complete change in your heart desires.
3. *"Do your first work"* observed what you did when you were first born again through the blood of Christ and applied Christian values to your life that you might also bear fruits of the spirit.

---

5   Note: Judaizers is one who lived by the Jewish customs and laws. The Judaizers attempt to promote syncretism practices in the Gentile communities. The Apostle Paul and Barnabas refute this doctrine at the Jerusalem Council in Act 15.

Jesus warns Ephesus to go back to the time when they first established a relationship with Him. Ephesus was consumed with zeal and ready to reach the world with the gospel, that they might witness the great work of the Holy Spirit. They were exercising authority over evil and trusting the finished work of Christ. However, persecution and spiritual darkness slowed them down. Ephesus mind was clear from doctrine errors, and their hands were committed to God's work, but their heart was far from Jesus.

If Ephesus didn't return to their first love, their candlestick light would burn out and no longer be a competent witness. The church is a part of God's plan to help transform the world from darkness to light. When a church loses its glow, they lose their effectiveness in the community and become spiritually dead.

v. 6 There's much dispute about the application of the Nicolaitanes. According to Acts 6:5, Nicolas was a proselyte of Antioch. He wasn't a native Jew but had converted from paganism cult to Judaism. Later in his life, he was introduced to Christianity and turn from Judaism. He was one of the chosen seven deacons in Acts 6:5-7.

We know these facts about Nicolas of Antioch. According to tradition, Nicolas came from a paganism background and was deeply rooted in occult activities. He quickly embraces different occults and pagan practices. He later adopted the ideology of Judaism and was selected to serve the tables under the hands of Peter in the church. Such a double-minded man is unstable in all his ways (James 1:8). He was not afraid to embrace a new way of thinking or anything new.

The Nicolaitanes sect Doctrine was similar to that of Balaam, cast a stumbling block before the Children of Israel (Number 24:1-3).

The Nicolaitanes Doctrines:

- They practice orgies of idolatrous feasts in the church meeting.
- Encouraging eating meats and food sacrifice to the gods.
- They also embrace the teaching of Balaam.

v.7 *"To him that overcometh will I give to eat of the tree of life, which is in the midst of the Paradise of God."* This Letter closes with an invitation and the promise: (1) If you have an ear to hear, listen to what the Holy Spirit is saying and obey. (2) Jesus offers an invitation to all believing Christians that overcome the world entered into the Paradise of God in Heaven. This Paradise is not the same one mention in (Genesis 3 or Luke 16).

"Tree of Life" This tree stood in the Garden of Eden. The first family was not forbidden to eat from this tree, but they chose the tree of knowledge (Genesis 2:16, 3:22). Only after their sin does God forbid them to eat from it. If Adam and Eve had eaten from the tree of life, they would have removed death's curse and continued immortality as a sinner. God banished Adam and Eve from the Paradise Garden and never to return to it. The faithful saints, who already are immoral in God's Paradise in Heaven, will eat from this tree.

"Paradise" (Gk. *Paradeisos)* is also translated as Eden or garden (place of future happiness). In Luke 16:22, "Abraham's bosom" is used interchangeably with the term "paradise" located in Hades. Jesus promises the penitent thief: "Today you will be with me in paradise" (Luke 23:43). Paradise relocated in Heaven, and one day the saints will have eternal rest there with God.

The Letter to the Church in Smyrna (vv. 8-11)
Christ has no words of condemnation to utter, all encouragement, and promise. This city and church still exist today. The modern name of Smyrna and is "Izmir" located in Turkey. Many citizens of modern-day Izmir claim to know Christ as their Savior. Smyrna was known as a seaport city and wealthy. The gate of Ephesus was the main road that led to the Church of Smyrna.

Tradition holds that Smyrna's citizens were Jews, who disliked the church for their liberty in Christ. The citizen of Smyrna demands their local government brings impunity action against the Christians. Smyrna was rife with fragrances, especially the anointing oil known as Myrrh (Exodus30:23; Song of Solomon 3:6). The "Mixture of Myrrh and aloes" used in the anointing Jesus' body for burial (John 19:39-41).

The Christians of Smyrna were poor because they were singled out and living in a prejudiced community. The community disliked them because they believed in Christ. The fact that the Jews and Pagans would not give them work. Life was hard for them without any monetary support, but they were rich in spirit.

> The Apostle Paul wrote, "If we endure, we shall also reign with Him. If we deny Him, He will also deny us" (2 Timothy 2:12).

> "And you will be hated by all for my name's sake. But he who endures to the end will be saved" (Matthew 10:22).

The Jews in Smyrna were like the Jews in Jerusalem. They were not real Christian Jews because they rejected Christ. Jesus calls them "a synagogue of Satan" (cf. Acts 14:19, 17:5-8, v. 13). They were Satan's children, not Abraham's.

> Paul writes, "For he is not a Jew, who is one outwardly, nor is circumcision that which is outward in the flesh; but he is a Jew who is one inwardly; and circumcision is that of the heart, in the Spirit, not in the letter; whose praise is not from men but from God." (Romans 2:28-29).

v. 10 "Cast into prison for ten days," the meaning of this passage is unknown. Jesus was probably referring to "The ten days of persecution by the Roman Empire" [6]Under the reign of Nero, A.D. 67.

(1) Nero decreed the city of Rome to burn to the ground and murder innocent Christians.
(2) Emperor Domitian, A.D. 81, orders part of his officials to be killed.
(3) Under the reign of Trajan, A.D. 108.
(4) Under the reign of Marcus Aurelius Antonius, A.D. 16.
(5) Commencing with Severus, A.D. 19.

---

6   Thomas, Revelation 1-7. pp. 321-323.

(6) Under the reign of Maximus, A.D. 235.
(7) Under the reign of Decius, A.D. 249.
(8) Under the reign of Valerian, A.D. 257.
(9) Under the reign of Aurelian, A.D. 274.
(10) Under the reign of Diocletian, A.D. 303.

Satan made every attempt to destroy the early church. Satan used Jews leaders, and Roman Empire carries out great enmity toward Christ and Church communities (Genesis 3:15).

> James writes, "Blessed is the man that endureth temptation: for when he is tried, he shall receive the crown of life, which the Lord hath promised to them that love him" (James 1:12). The crown of life is imperishable and guarantees entrance to God's eternal rest.

> Paul writes, "Know ye not that they which run in a race run all, but one receiveth the prize? So run, that ye may obtain. And every man that striveth for the mastery is temperate in all things. Now they do it to obtain a corruptible crown, but we an incorruptible" (1 Corinthians 9:24-25).

The Letter to the Church in Pergamum (vv. 12-17)
v. 12 *"The Sharp Sword with Two Edges"* is mentioned (7) times in the Bible, (6) times in Revelation, and (1) time in Luke. Roman soldiers use their swords to cut, divide, and separate organs of the body.

The two-edged sword is the *"Word of God"* that flowed from the mouth of Jesus. His word goes forth in providing judgment and illumination. It is a light that pierces the depths of the hearts and minds of men. It has capable of pruning and purging so that all ungodliness of the flesh is cut off and cast into the fire.

"For the word of God is quick, powerful, and sharper than any two-edged sword." It pierces so deep even as to allow for the dividing asunder of

soul and spirit, joints and marrow, and discerns the heart's thoughts and intents. There isn't any creature that is not manifest in his sight, but all things are naked and opened unto God's eyes (cf. Hebrews 4:12-13; Revelation 1:16, Judges 3:16).

v. 13 Jesus says Pergamos is *"where Satan's seat is"* and where his influence dwells.

Satan's seat was likely referring to this altar of Zeus. The Pergamos community was known as "the City of the Serpent." The temple to Zeus, the chief of the Greek mythological gods and the sky's god, stood on the Acropolis overlooking Pergamos' city. Along with his two brothers, Hades and Poseidon, Zeus conspired against their parents, Gaia and Cronos, to seize power. Zeus was the strongest of the brothers and took dominion of the sky, giving Poseidon the sea and Hades the underworld. Due to his strength and sovereignty, he inherited the title of king of the gods."[7] The Temple of Zeus was erected about 2 B.C.

The City of Pergamos became the link between both ancient and modern worlds. The Papal system is similar to Babylon the Great. Jesus says the Pergamum community is where Satan's seat is, Pergamos was a city reputed to be sacred to gods and was one of the headquarters of idolatry.

"Wherein Antipas was my faithful martyr." The church is commended because of their loyalty and steadfastness during the persecution in which Antipas was a martyr. When this persecution occurred, we are not informed; and as to Antipas's identity. Some suppose him to have been the elder of the church.

vv. 14-15 *"hold the doctrines of Balaam and Nicolaitanes."*
The doctrine of Balaam (Intermarriage with heathen women
The Christian men seduced into intermarriage with the pagan women in Pergamum. Over time, these marriages slowly began to compromise the men's faith, and they adopted their wives' pagan practices. They

---

7   See. Merriam-Webster Dictionary: Zeus.

would attend feasts and commit sexual immortality until they become ineffective in the community as Christ's witness.

"Balaam Taught Balak to cast a stumbling," Balaam was once a prophet of God. "Which have forsaken the right way, and are gone astray, following the way of Balaam the son of Bosor, who loved the wages of unrighteousness" (2 Peter 2:15).

"King Balak summons Balaam to his palace to ask that he places a curse on Israel" (Numbers 22:6).

"However, each time Balaam issue a curse against the Israelites there came only a fresh flow of blessing upon them" (Numbers 24:10).

"For what God has blessed, no man can reverse" (Numbers 23:20).

In spite of this frustration, Balaam knew how to have God's blessings taken away from Israel and thus changed his strategy (cf. Numbers 25:1-9, and 31:15-16).

Balaam counseled Balak to send beautiful women into Israel's camp to seduce them during a special feast tribute to their gods. Balaam's evil scheme against the Israel men worked. They participated in orgies, and they drank wine and food offered to idols, and they bowed to their gods. The result of Balaam's counsel was 24,000 deaths in the camp. So, we see the process of compromise, little by little.

The Doctrine of the Nicolaitanes (moral departure)
The Nicolaitanes were those that nullified the law of God through the concept of grace. Jude 1:4 gives us a glimpse of this group using God's grace to promote lasciviousness or sexual freedom. They believed that the law didn't matter for God's grace covered them. Contrary to their belief, the verse calls them ungodly men.

The fourth-century showed the beginning of compromise, and their faith started to drift away. When Constantine converted to Christianity and made it the state religion, it was a 180-degree turnaround for Christians. Christians went from being persecuted and martyred for their faith to being received and respected by the state. Christians were now free to worship saints and the mother of Jesus.

v. 16 Balaam's life ended with a two-edged sword
The Lord introduces Himself to the Church of Pergamum as a two-edged sword, and later, He reprimands them for upholding Balaam's doctrine. In Numbers 22:31, the angel of the LORD stands with a sword drawn in his hand against the false prophet Balaam. The book of Joshua records Balaam dying "by the two-edged sword during a battle over the Reubenite occupation of the Moabite land" (Joshua 13:22; Numbers 31:8).

This church was now in the early stages of apostasy. The word of God (sword) exposes both the error of sexual immorality, spiritual superiority over others, and the error of spiritual pride.

v. 17 Threefold Promise by Christ:

1. *"Eat of the hidden manna,"* the Lord promises manna and a white stone with the new name "known but to God," these are offers of private intimacy within the temple. The manna is the food of angels (Psalms 78:25), which descended from Heaven because God commanded that it should. Thus, we live because of the words that have to come out of God's mouth to command living sustenance for man. (Deuteronomy 8:3).
   - Once the Children of Israel crossed over the river of Jordan, the manna stopped.
   - God had fed the nation for forty years.
   - The manna is, therefore "bread from heaven" (Exodus 16:4). Its location is within the Ark of the Covenant and therefore lies within the Holy of Holies' very inner recesses (Exodus 16:33). We will "know" our creator in greater intimacy

through exclusive access to this word/bread/manna from Heaven.

- When Christians crossover by death or Rapture to Heaven, the manna will stop because they're now in God's presence.
- In John 6, Jesus says, "I' am the bread that came down from Heaven." He is the "hidden manna." He is the food for the inner spirit and food that others aren't familiar with.

2. *"A white stone,"* used to gain admission to certain events in Roman times. That would imply that those who have received salvation, grace, overcome will be granted access to the Kingdom. The individual white stone given to each of those who come victorious, whereon is a new name written, which no man knoweth save he that receives it.
    - In ancient times, judges used stones to indicate a verdict. A white stone meant the accused was pronounced "not guilty."

3. *"A new name,"* that God will give to us at that time. The Lord will change many of the saints of old names. The Jews were forbidden to write or say His name. To know Christ's name is to know His character (Revelation 19:12).
    - Abram had his name changed to Abraham (Genesis 17:3 – 6). At the same time, his wife Sarai changed to Sarah (Genesis 17:15 – 16).
    - Jacob had his name changed to Israel (Genesis 32:26–30; 35:9 – 10).
    - Solomon called "Jedidiah" (beloved of the Lord) because God loved him. In (2 Samuel 12:24 – 25), it is not clear that God had his name changed, and he was always afterward called Solomon.

The Letter to the Church in Thyatira (vv. 18-29)
Thyatira was a colony of Macedonia. It was a Greek colony and greatly influenced by Hellenism. One of the significant parts of Hellenism is the worship of many gods, polytheism. This church was located in a small town, but very wealthy. Thyatira was known in ancient days for its unique purple dye made from madder roots.

Lydia was a very wealthy woman, and it's possible she was the one who planted the Church of Thyatira (Acts 16:14-15). The Church of Thyatira and Church of Laodicea received the worst reprimand by Jesus Christ. Thyatira was the most corrupt of the seven churches of Revelation.

Jesus was introduced as *"the Son of God,"* not as *"the Son of man"* here in the narrative. Jesus used this title when he was on Earth. After His ascension to Heaven, this is the first and only time in the Bible, Jesus introduced Himself as "The Son of God." Perhaps, Jesus used His deity title "the Son of God" to make Himself known to the Church of Thyatira.

Thyatira was much like the Pergamos community, where Zeus's throne resides and the worship of Asclepius, Apollo's son. Apollo is the son of Zeus, according to Greek Mythology. Apollo is known as the god of prophecy, music, medicine, and light.

"His eyes like unto a flame of fire" refers to the ability to illuminate man's soul and see through him (sins), discerning his every thought. Jesus sees man's genuine character and disguises.

"His feet are like fine brass," suggests His ability to trample sin and injustice underfoot along with authority to punish evil. The same description of Christ mentioned in Revelation 1:14-15.

v. 19 Jesus commended Thyatira's church first on their pastoral work and improving their ministry. This church is showed spiritual maturity more so now than they did when they first started and were found guilty of committing a terrible sin.

Thyatira good qualities commended by Jesus:

1. Love- Their love to God and each other; and followed Christ at all cost.
2. Service- commended for their services one another during hardship and persecution. We are serving God (Matthew 25:31-46, Galatians 5:13).

3. Faith- leads to perseverance that keeps you working for God and being patient. What Paul praises to the Thessalonians was similar to the Church of Thyatira's works; "Remembering without ceasing your work of faith, and labor of love, and patience of hope in our Lord Jesus Christ, in the sight of God and our Father" (1 Thessalonians 1:3).
4. Patience- Thyatira was steadfast under all circumstances.

vv. 20-23 *"False Prophetess Jezebel"* There was the presence of a woman who called herself a prophetess. She was guilty of teaching and seducing God's faithful servants to commit fornication and eating things sacrificed to idols. The church of Thyatira permitted this false prophetess to teach error and did not speak out against her. Idol worship is called spiritual fornication. Jesus condemned her in His rebuke.

This prophetess of Thyatira's real name wasn't Jezebel, but Jesus associates her practice with the wife of King Ahab, Queen Jezebel, found in the Old Testament (cf. 1 Kings 16:31, 21:25; 2 King 9:22). The original Jezebel worshipped Baal and ate with his prophets (Kings 18:19).

The church and the community adopted the doctrine of Jezebel and allowed her to influence the church. She soared above the pastor of the church and gave herself the title of a prophetess.

She was highly respected and became an icon of the church and community. She broke down the boundaries of moral separation [right and wrong]. The spirit of Jezebel, for thousands of years seduced God's servants. She gave them false assurances that God's grace is sufficient without repentance. The Bible states that "if we confess our sins, He is faithful and just to forgive us our sins and to cleanse us from all unrighteousness" (1 John 1:9).

"And I will kill her children with death" However, it is still imperative that we confess our sins. When we sin, we also need to repent to maintain an intimate relationship with God. The prophetess Jezebel will be cast into a bed of suffering or tribulation.

"Then hear thou in heaven, and do, and judge thy servants, condemning the wicked, to bring his way upon his head; and justifying the righteous, to give him according to his righteousness" (1 Kings 8:32).

"Say ye to the righteous, that it shall be well with him: for they shall eat the fruit of their doings. Woe unto the wicked! it shall be ill with him: for the reward of his hands shall be given him" (Isaiah 3:10-11).

"For the Son of man shall come in the glory of his Father with his angels; and then he shall reward every man according to his works" (Matthew 16:27).

"For the wages of sin is death, but the gift of God is eternal life in Christ Jesus our Lord" (Romans 6:23).

JEZEBEL OF THE OLD AND NEW TESTAMENT	
Jezebel, The Phoenician Queen 1 Kings 21:26	**Jezebel, The Prophetess of Thyatira Revelation 2**
She was the Queen of Northern Israel and grew up as a Priestess of Baal.	Jezebel sought to make herself a prophetess and was responsible for leading many Thyatira community and church members astray.
She was ruthless, conniving, thirst for power and control. Baal and idols. Serving the God of Israel at certain times and Baal at others.	She encourages Syncretism practice at Thyatira. Jezebel advocates both sexual immorality and idol worship to practice in the church.
Her followers were fleshy and ungodly.	Her followers were fleshly and undisciplined.
She manipulated her husband's through deception and used his authority, power, and kingship to carry out her plans.	Jezebel of Thyatira probably was married to the pastor and abused his authority, power, and pastoral position to mislead the church.

Her evil plot was to wipe out YAHWEH worship in Israel 1 King 18:4. Jezebel is responsible for killing off the prophets of the LORD.	She taught immorality and eating food sacrificed to idols was permissible (v. 20).
Perhaps Jezebel sees herself as an Ambassador of Israel. She unites the two lands and bring about cultural pluralism, peace to the region, and economic prosperity of land.	She sees herself as a prophetess of the church teaching her false doctrine that eases their mind through deception that "their past, present, and future sins forgiven for life?" Repentance wasn't necessary anymore.
Jezebel seduces her husband Ahab to build a sanctuary for Baal in the Northern Kingdom capital "Samaria."	Join unions: Combining Christianity belief w/ surrounding evil culture. Example: Santeria mixed with Catholicism.

Figure 1 Comparison of Jezebel of Thyatira and the Phoenician Queen Jezebel

vv. 24-25 *"The depth of Satan"* is the doctrine of errors. The art of Satan inculcating error and leading people astray. Religious syncretism isn't compatible with Christian theology's authentic core beliefs. Any alteration to biblical doctrines and tenets for the sake of a "better" religion is heresy. Jezebel doctrines were leading Christians into immorality and pagan worship. The Phoenician Queen Jezebel of the Old Testament led her husband, king Ahab, astray to serve Baal and Asheroth. The consequence of Ahab worshiping Baal led the Northern Kingdom of Israel into idolatry, and a terrible judgment fell upon both king Ahab and his wife. Ahab's death was a prophecy of Elijah (1 Kings 21:19). Jezebel's death was also prophesied (1 Kings 21:23).

The Queen was thrown from a tower and trampled on by horses and her body eaten by dogs. King Ahab was killed in the battle with the Assyrians (1 Kings 22:30-37).

The Syncretism ideologies are rapidly growing in many religious systems in the world today, such as Christian Science, the New Age movement, Hinduism, and Unitarianism. These religions are blends of multiple different belief systems and emerge as new religions or Philosophies.

The latest religion brought about by Syncretism is "Chrislam", which is the mixture of Christianity and Islam in practice.

vv. 26-27 The Messiah will rule over all nations of the world for 1,000 years. Jesus will share His reign with the Saints and the redeemed (Isaiah 9:6-9, 32:1, Revelation 20:4).

"*hold fast till I come*" meaning His second coming to earth destroyed the antichrist by the brightness of His glory, (2 Thessalonians 2:8).

"*The rod of iron*" translated from the (Heb. *shebet)* the shepherd's iron club; his weapon used to defend the sheep from vicious animals and anyone which to cause them harm.

The shepherd is one who cares for the sheep's well-being. The text should read: "He shall shepherd them with the shepherd's club." The "rod" instrument could be used for correction and punishment (Psalm 2:9).

Jeremiah speaks about the rod of iron as well (Jeremiah 19:10-11). The pastors prevent propaganda and distorted truths from spreading amongst his congregation and feed their sheep with the message of God's grace. In John 21:16, "Feed my sheep" (cf. Micah 7:14, 1 Peter 5:2 and Revelation 7:17).

v. 28 "*And I will give him the morning star*" Jesus describes Himself as the Bright and Morning Star in Revelation 22:16. Those who overcame in Thyatira and remained faithful till the end is giving the morning star. This passage applies to us today if we are faithful till the end of life. The phrase "morning star" is probably a speech figure referring to giving "great honor."

Williams Barclay, suggested several ideas, "He thought the expression could signify the coming resurrection of the righteous. Just as the "morning star" breaks forth from the darkness of night, the Lord's people will break out of the grave."

THE LETTERS TO THE SEVEN CHURCHES OF ASIA MINOR (CON'T)

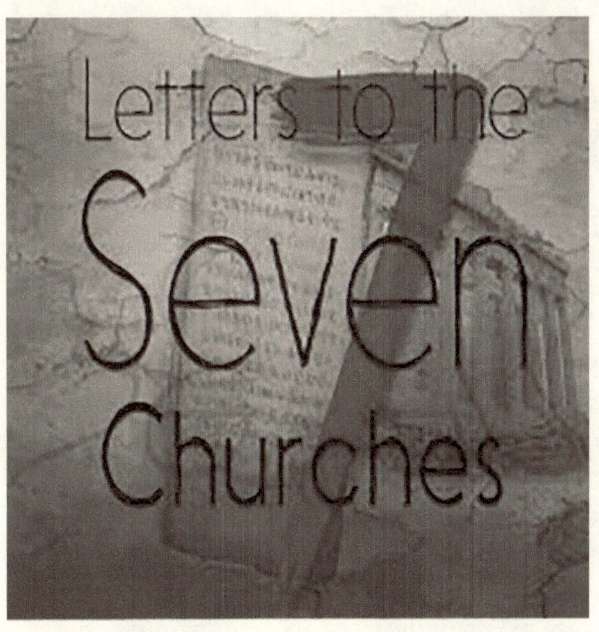

The Letter to the Church of Sardis (vv. 1-6)

Sardis was a city of failures, yet on the outside, the church looked prosperous. Jesus describes the church as being "dead", but in the community's eyes, she looked "alive." The Sardis Church lacked delegations and devotion to the Lord. The church wore the sign of Christianity, but in deeds and actions fell short. Jesus describes the Pharisees and the scribes in the following manner: "Woe unto you, Scribes and Pharisee, hypocrites! For ye are like unto whited sepulchers, which indeed appear beautiful outward, but are within full of dead men's bones and all uncleanliness "(Matthew 23:27).

The Church of Sardis was the oldest city among the seven churches addressed by Christ. It was known as the capital of Lydia's ancient kingdom and is associated with "the people of Lud," found in Ezekiel 27:10. Sardis was about fifty miles from the East of Smyrna and thirty miles southeast of Thyatira.

The Sardis Church didn't face much persecution, and the scriptures indicate the church was dead and in great need of a revival. Pagan worship was pervasive throughout the Roman Empire. Sardis surrounded by idolatry and idol worship. Evil was the habit of the people and even found itself in the practices of the church. The ancient city is known for its temple of the Mother goddess "Cybele," whose worship was similar to that of the Roman goddess "Diana" of Ephesus.

v. 1 To this church, Jesus introduces Himself as *"He that hath the seven Spirits of God, and the seven stars"* that is, He has control of the Holy Spirit's agency of the Godhead and his ministers of the seven churches (John 14:15-31). This expression, "seven Spirits" does not refer to seven different spirits. It could refer to the seven different ways the Spirit of God expresses Himself. The seven attributes of the Spirit of God (cf. Revelation 3:1, 4:5, 5:6). The seven-fold Spirit of God: as the Spirit of Wisdom, the Spirit of Understanding, the Spirit of Counsel, the Spirit of Knowledge, the Spirit of the Fear of the Lord, and the Spirit of Might (Isaiah 11:2).

"The seven stars" represent the seven angels or pastors of the seven churches of Asia Minor in Revelation 1:16,20. In Revelation chapters 1-3, "seven stars" are referenced four times (Revelation 1:16, 20,2:1 and 3:1).

v. 3 *"I will come on thee as a thief, and thou shalt not know what hour I will come upon thee"* The analogy of "a thief in the night" was common in the early period the church. A thief didn't rob and steal in the daylight hours since he is visible. During a time when the home was vacant, he could enter and steal without being detected. The return of Christ is likened to the coming of a thief in the night. In Matthew 24:43, Jesus speaks of His Second Coming at the end of the Tribulation.

Paul calls it "the day of the Lord" in 1 Thessalonians 5:4. Jesus says it will happen "after the tribulation of those days," Matthew 24:29.

v. 4 *"Garment not defiled,"* The words *"garment," "raiment"*, and "robe" indicate one character. Isaiah describes, "these garments as heavenly robes of the righteous and recipients of salvation" (Isaiah 61:10). The prophet Zechariah explains the defiled garment in Zechariah 3:1-4. Who have not defiled their garments, signifies, who are in truths, and have not defiled worship by evils practices? Only Christ's finish work on the cross can wash the sin stains or spots from defiled garments. If we are faithful to maintain our garments, He promises that we will walk with Him in white. When a man repents from sin and puts his trust in Christ, he is cloth with a new nature. (cf. Romans 13:14; 2 Corinthians 5:17; Galatians 3:37, 5:16).

"The white garments" contrast with their nakedness. Biblically, God uses it to symbolize righteousness (cf. Job 29:14; Ephesians 4:24; James 1:27; Revelation 7:9, 19:8). *"The wedding garment"* identifies the righteous, those who lived according to God's words.

> "And I said unto him, Sir, thou knowest. And he said to me, these are they which came out of great tribulation, and have washed their robes, and made them white in the blood of the Lamb" (Revelation 7:14).

v. 5 *"blot out his name out of the book of life."* The book of life is the names of the living citizens of Heaven and the living (Psalms 42:2; Mark 12:27; Luke 20:38)

All American citizens are issued a birth certificate, and their names are recorded in the U.S. Census. Upon death, their names are removed and given a death certificate. The citizen of Heaven's name will be listed forever unless God decides to erase it. Whether or not "the Book of

Life" is literal or a figure of speech is irrelevant. God keeps an accurate record of His people (Revelation 20:12-15).

"The Book of Life" lists the names of the righteous saints who received eternal life (cf. Exodus 32:32-33; Psalm 69:28; Isaiah 4:3; Daniel 12:1; Luke 10:20; Philippians 4:3; Hebrews 12:23; Revelation 13:8; 17:8; 20:12,15; 21:27).

The book of life is synonymous with others in the Bible.

(1) The Book of the living, Psalms 69:28.
(2) My Book, Exodus 32:32-33.
(3) The Lamb's Book of Life, Revelation 21:27.

GENRE BOOKS MENTIONED IN THE SCRIPTURES		
The Lamb's Book of Life	The names of the redeemed believers that are born again and trusting in the Lamb for their redemption	Revelation 21:27
Book of Remembrance	Record blessings, promises, and rewards for faithfulness.	Isaiah 65:6; Psalms 56:8, 139:16; Malachi 3:16
Book of Works	Good and evil deeds recorded both the believers and unbelievers' These deeds testify for you or against at the Judgment seat (BEMA) of Christ and Great White Throne Judgment.	Revelation 20:12-13; Daniel 7:9-13; Romans 3:19-24.
Book of Wars (lost)	A collection of songs, sung during wars to celebrate the triumph of God over Israel's enemies.	Numbers 21:14
The Book of Jasher (lost)	The early chronicle of the history of Israel	Joshua 10:13; 2 Samuel 1:18.

Figure 2 Other Genre Books

The Letter to the Church in Philadelphia (vv. 7-13)
Jesus highly commends the Church in Philadelphia to stay true to His Word and not deny His name during persecution. He opens doors of unlimited opportunity to spread the gospel to those who traveled on the main trade route to Sardis and abroad. "Alasehir" was one of the first cities with the name Philadelphia.[8] king Eumenes II of Pergamon discovered the city and named it after his love for his brother Attalus II.[9] Philadelphia was known as the City of God; however, the modern-day name is "Alasehir, which is located about 25 miles from the Church of Sardis. Philadelphia is written six times in the Bible as the city bearing the name "Brotherly Love."

Jesus introduced Himself to the Church of Philadelphia as:

- "He that is holy."
- "He that is the True."
- "He has the key of David" to open and closed all doors to the treasures of spiritual blessing and opportunities.

v. 7 The word *"keys"* is used allegorically as an authority, power, and dominion to open and closed. King Hezekiah of Judah witnessed the fulfillment of this revelation in Isaiah's era (Isaiah 22:15-25).

Types of keys cited in the Bible:
"The key of David" This key was given to David's servant Eliakim to open the door to King David's treasure room, and he closed the door so no one could open it again. When he opens it, no one else could shut it (cf. Isaiah 22:20-25, 36:3,22, 37:2; 2 Kings 18:18; Revelation 3:7). Jesus is the eternal fulfillment of Eliakim's purpose to open the doors of blessing and salvation (John 10:9).

"The Key of the house of David." This key implied that Jesus would have dominion over the house of David as a promise fulfilled by the Messiah.

---

8   See Wikipedia Encyclopedia: Alasehir
9   Ibid. Attalus II Philadelphus

Jesus would keep the Davidic covenant as ruler of New Jerusalem and Sovereign King and Lord of the Kingdom of Heaven (Isaiah 22:22).

"The Keys of the Kingdom of Heaven." The gospel's message is the key unlocked the Kingdom of God, and Jesus is the door that allows us passage to His Kingdom (Matthew 16:19, 1 Corinthians 15:1-8).

"The Keys of Hell and Death" Jesus holds the keys over Hade and death. The keys symbolize "authority and power." Jesus conquers death on the cross and goes to Paradise [Abraham's Bosom], in Sheol's realm (cf. Luke 16:19-31, John 11:25, Matthew 16:7, Romans 6:9, 14:9, and Revelation 1:18).

"The Key of the Bottomless Pit," The term "bottomless pit" is the Greek word *"abussos"* translated "abyss," which occurs several times in the Bible. The abyss is the holding place for the disobedient fallen angels that followed after Satan. The chasm exists in the realm of Sheol or Hell.

"The Key of Knowledge" Spiritual knowledge of God's Word, Proverbs 2:1-6). The expert (in the law) took away the key of knowledge by hindering others from the truth.

"Woe to you experts in the law, because you have taken away the key to knowledge. You yourselves have not entered, and you have hindered those who were entering" (Luke 11:52).

vv. 8-9 *"I had set before thee an open door"* The city of Philadelphia was the gateway (open door) to reach the world with the gospel. This church composed of Jewish Christians who kept their faith and did not deny Christ's name even when persecuted by the Judaizers that claimed to be Abraham's children. Jesus experienced the same problems in His earthly ministry and rebuked synagogue religious leaders (John 8:37-45).

> "But Woe unto you, scribes and Pharisees, hypocrites!
> For ye shut up the kingdom of Heaven against men: for
> ye neither go in yourselves, neither suffer ye them that
> are entering to go in." (Matthew 23:13).

Jesus said to Peter, "Upon this rock, I will build my church; and the gate of Hell shall not prevail against it" (Matthew 16:18). Since the gospel's door opened to the world, evil emperors and their empires have tried to shut that door, attempting to prevent the gospel from being heard.

Jesus used the terms *"Synagogue of Satan"* is a figure of speech referring not to a literal place, but as a community of people characterized as liars. Mention twice in 2:9 and 3:9, to the church in Smyrna. Christ called these antagonistic Jews "liars" because they claim to be true believers, while still rejecting Christ and his teachings.

Christ promised the Church of Smyrna and Philadelphia would triumph over the Synagogue of Satan. Today in Israel, there are still debates over ideology of the phrase "the Synagogue of Satan" referred to the Jewish people who rejected Christ. This estimation of the Jewish people is not scriptures supported. Because God will fulfill all covenants with their forefathers.

Today, Christians didn't replace God's chosen people, but instead, "engrafted onto Israel's olive tree" (Romans 11:16-24). The door is open to the Gentiles after the Jewish leaders' rejection of Jesus Christ as Messiah.[10] The church in Philadelphia's new Jewish converts given access to the Kingdom of God and treasures of spiritual blessing. Jesus is the legitimate heir of the Kingdom and holds the key to the doors.

vv. 10-11 The Lord promised to keep the church of Philadelphia from the Hour of Temptation. It will try those that are left behind during the Tribulation period. This references the last 3 ½ years of the Great Tribulation, (Revelation 19) it is mentioned in His Olivet Discourse, (Matthew 24-25). "The blesses hope, and the glorious appearing of the great God and our Savior Jesus Christ," (Titus 2:13).

---

10   Note: Rejection of the Cornerstone (cf. Psalms 118:22; Mark 12:10; John 6:60). Many disciples rejected Him (John 6:60-66). Rejection of His hometown (Matthew 13:54-58; Luke 4:16-30).

The expression "Hour of Trial" refers to future worldwide tests. The Great Tribulation God Wrath's will be poured on the unbelieving Gentiles and the Jews who rejected Christ. The scripture explicitly promises that those faithful saints of Jesus will be delivered from the hour of temptation (1 Thessalonians 5:1-11; Luke 21:34-36).

(1) The Day of the Lord (Jeremiah 30:7; Luke 21:35; Revelation 6:17)
(2) The Great Tribulation (Daniel 21:1; Matthew 24:15-21; Revelation 13:7-8

I come "quickly," (Gk. Tachu) indicates "without delay" or "by surprise."[11] These crowns reward to the overcomers and the church at the Judgment seat of Christ.

> James 1:12 says, "Blessed is the man that endureth temptation: for when he is tried, he shall receive the crown of life, which the Lord hath promised to them that love him."

vv. 12-13 "Him that overcometh will I make a pillar in the temple of my God, and he shall go no more out..." This verse speaks of how trials and tribulations will be no more. This spiritual temple is comprised of believers who live on throughout eternal ages with the Lord. The overcomers will be honored by the Lord in Heaven, as they honored Christ on Earth. Perhaps, a pillar will be erected in their honor. There are many pillars at the church of Philadelphia's remain standing at this present day.

"The name of the city of my God" is New Jerusalem. The Messianic name that belongs to Christ- "Jehovah Tsidkenu" translates as "Jehovah our righteousness.[12]"

---

11   Thayer's Greek Lexicon, 5035.
12   Hitchcock, Roswell D. *Entry for Jehovah-Tsidkenu*: "An Interpreting Dictionary of Scripture Proper Names". . New York, N.Y., 1869.

The Letter to the Church in Laodicea (vv. 14-22)
Jesus introduced Himself as "the Amen" which means "so be it or verily."[13] His predictions are accurate and guaranteed to come to pass. In Matthew 24:35, the Amen says, "Heaven and Earth shall pass away, but my word shall not pass away".

Jesus never described himself this way before, as the "beginning of God's creation "(v.14b). Jesus was unique in His birth as a man. Jesus became a man and was born. Although he was born as a man, Jesus Christ always existed as God.

While He was a man, he had a beginning, and as God, He is the beginning.

> John 1:1-3 says, "In the beginning was the Word, and the Word was with God, and the Word was God. The same was in the beginning with God. All things were made by Him; and without him was not anything made that was made." Jesus is the source of God's creation, old and new.

The Christian is a new creation in Christ (cf.2 Corinthians 5:17).

3:15 -16 *"Cold"* refers to the state of being spiritually naked and dead. "Hot" refers to the state of being spiritually on fire, carrying out the will of God. The Laodicea community was once on fire for the Lord, their enthusiasm spreading the truth of God's Word and allowing them to live a pure life before many.

"Lukewarm behavior" happens when the church or the Christian mixes the truth with worldly desires. Jesus used the community water supply as a metaphor in the context of the church's spiritual work. The community water supply would run down from Hierapolis (Pamukkale)

---

13 Strong's Greek Concordance, 281.

through an aqueduct as hot water, but midway the temperature would become lukewarm. At the bottom of the hill, the water became cold.

"I will spue thee out of my mouth," Laodicea was known for its hot springs and Roman baths.[14] The lukewarm water was unbearable to drink and created a feeling of nausea that caused one to regurgitate the water.

The Laodicean Church was self-satisfied. They went through the formality of church. They felt if they attended church once a week, they had done their duty as a Christian. Lukewarm worship is even worse than not being saved at all. God's displeased with those who would "ride the fence" on His Word and services.

vv. 16-20 There was no commendation. And say to Archippus, "Take heed to the ministry which thou hast received in the Lord, that thou fulfill it" (Colossians 4:17). Archippus may have been the Pastor of the church in Laodicea. Jesus addresses the root of the Laodicean problem with "lukewarm behavior." Their arrogant and lackadaisical attitude had left them spiritually bankrupt, blind, and naked.

The church thought of itself as wealthy, self-sufficient, and needing nothing from the Lord or anyone else. An earthquake destroyed Laodicea's city, and the Roman government said they would ship anything they needed. Yet still, the city's leadership told the Romans they did not require anything. Simply put, they said they would renovate their city without any aid or financial backing from the Roman government.

Laodicea may have indeed been wealthy and required little to, no help from anyone, but they are spiritually blind to the truth. As a result, they need white clothes to cover their nakedness before the Lord (cf. Revelation 3:4-5; 4:4; 6:11; 7:8). Laodicea's nakedness symbolizes their spiritual shame and inadequacy (cf. Ezekiel 16:35; 2 Corinthians 5:3).

---

14 Strong's Greek Concordance, 1692. "To Vomit"

Laodicea had shown lukewarm character by mixing worldliness with God's Word. Those that are stagnant in their faith will eventually go stale in their passion for God. Christ preferred we be spiritual maturity in the faith.

Applying these facts to illustrate the church's problems, Christ cited the arrogance of the Church of Laodicea: You say "I am rich, and have become wealthy, and need nothing." It's essential to notice that Christ isn't in the midst of them but on the outside knocking to come in. Why did Christ speak in parables? (read Matthew 13:10-17 and 34-35).

v. 21 *"My Throne"* Christ was raised from the dead and ascended through the heavens, sitting down at "the right hand" [figurative] of His Father in honor and victory on the cross until all His enemies are under His footstool (Psalms 110:1; Hebrews 1:3). Christ's "last enemy that shall be destroyed is death" (1 Corinthians 15:26). Jesus will rule as King of the nations during the Millennial Kingdom and sit on David's throne forever (cf. Ezekiel 37:24; Luke 1:32-33). The biblical allusions to God, i.e., "hand, mouth, eyes, backside," are *"anthropomorphic* descriptions of God in human terms (cf. Numbers 23:19, 1 Samuel 15:29, John 1:18)

"My Father's Throne" God is King of the Universe. "Heaven is my throne, and the earth is my footstool" (cf. 2 Chronicles 18:18, Psalms 11:4; Hebrews 8:1, 12:2; Revelation 1:4,3:21, 4:2). God's "throne" emphasizes God's transcendence, dignity, and sovereignty as ruler of the Universe.

THE LETTERS TO THE SEVEN CHURCHES OF ASIA MINOR						
The Seven Churches of Asia Minor	The Meaning of the Church Names	Jesus' Admonishment of the Churches	Personal Issues	Proposed: Period in Church History	Titles of Christ as Judge in Revelation	Rewards to Redeemed
Ephesus 2:1-7	"Desired One"	Need more commitment and not just doctrine	Neglected priorities "Lost their first love"	Apostolic Church	"He who holds the seven stars"	Eating from the Tree of Life in Paradise.

Smyrna 2:8-11	"Death or bitter myrrh" (Suffering)	Endure persecution and remain faithful.	Satanic oppositions No Issues	Persecuted Church	The first and the Last, which was dead and is alive. (Isaiah 41:4)	A crown of life and to not be hurt by 2nd death (James 1:12)
Pergamum 2:2-17	"Mixed Marriage"	Stand firm against the world-system and doctrine of errors.	Spiritual compromise: Practiced the doctrines of Balaam and Nicolaitanes	Compromise (The world and church mixed) Church	" He who has a sharp two-edged sword" (Ps. 149:1, Hebrews 4:12)	Manna, white stone, and a new name.
Thyatira 2:18-29	"Odor of Affliction"	Flee Pagan practices: eating things sacrificed to idols and sexual sins.	Flee Pagan practices: false prophetess Jezebel: Syncretism	Pagan of the Dark Ages Church	"The Son of God" (Daniel 10:5-6 Ezekiel 1:4)	Power of the nations
Sardis 3:1-6	"Spiritual Deadness"	Watchfulness, diligence	Reputation for being "alive" spiritually in the eyes of the community, but were really dead. Unsatisfactory work	Spiritually Dead Church	"He who has the seven Spirits of God and Seven Stars." (Number 24:17)	White remnant, and name not blotted out.
Philadelphia 3:7-22	"Brotherly Love."	Faithful Stewardship	No issues	Evangelistic Church	"He who is Holy and True; Hold the Key of David." Isaiah 9:7, Rev. 6:10	Pillar in temple, name of God, name of His city and new name, rapture up
Laodiceans 3:14-22	"Rule by the People"	Be zealous and repent.	"Lukewarm" Having a form of Godliness, but denying the power thereof God.	Apostate Church	"Amen, the Faithful and True Witness. The Beginnings of Creation of God" Matthew 24:45 Genesis 1:1	Jesus is on the outside knocking, Sitting with the Lord on His Throne

Figure 3 Jesus Assessment of the Seven Churches.

COMPARISON OF THE SEVEN CHURCHES, THE EPISTLES OF PAUL, AND THE NARRATIVE PARABLES OF MATTHEW'S GOSPEL			
Letter to the Seven Churches Revelation Chapter 2-3	**Epistles of Paul to the Churches**	**Seven Kingdom Parables of Matthew**	**Church era and Meaning of the Parables**
Ephesus 2:1-7	Ephesus	The Sower and The Seed 13:3-23	Explain 13:18-23
Smyrna 2:8-11	Philippians	The Tares & Wheat 13:24-30	Explain 13:36-43 Tare is evil kingdoms
Pergamum 2:2-17	1 & 2 Corinthians	Mustard Seed 13:31-32	No explanation given.
Thyatira 2:18-29	Galatians	The woman & leaven bread 13:33	No explanation given: Symbol of "sin and pride"
Sardis 3:1-6	Romans	The hidden treasure 13:44	No explanation given: The field is the world and buyer is Christ.
Philadelphia 3:7-22	1 & 2 Thessalonians	The pearl of great price, 13:45-46	No explanation given: Represent Jesus and Salvation He offers which can't be purchased with a price.
Laodicea 3:14-22	Colossians	The Dragnet, 13:47-50	Explained 13:47-50

Figure 4 The Seven Churches Compared to Matthew Parables

CHAPTER FOUR

THE THRONE ROOM SCENE

PART III: WRITE THE THING WHICH SHALL BE HEREAFTER

John Invitation to Heaven (v.1)
v. 1 *"After this I looked, and, behold, and the first voice which I heard was as it were of a trumpet talking with me; which said, Come up hither, and I will shew thee things which must be hereafter."*

"After this," After what John had seen and after what he was directed to writes in the previous chapters. The first voice John heard was that of "one like a Son of Man," The voice Jesus as He has detailed His as

Judge of the seven churches. He signified to John the next sequence of events to follow. He is the judge of the world.

"A door was opened in heaven" here in v. 2, John finds himself at God Almighty's throne room's heavenly realm. The scene wasn't the same as the glorious visions on Patmos indicated in 1:10. "The door" signifies the entranceway or portal to the third heaven. This reference is not earth atmosphere or the cosmos. The "Heaven of heavens) is mentioned in such passages as (Genesis 28:12; Deuteronomy 10:14 and 1 Kings 8:27) as a distinctly spiritual realm containing angels and God.

"Trumpet" (Gk. shofar) signifies an authoritative voice gives a command. A trumpet made from a ram's horn. The ancient instrument's a reminder to Jews that God is their King. The trumpet voice was sound he heard in 1:10.

The Shofar Horns:

- Uses to call attention or call to battle (cf. Ezekiel 1:1; Mark 1:10; John 1:51).
- Serves as a reminder of showing humility before God Almighty, (Amos 3:8)

"Come up hither" John heard a voice inviting him into the vision; He immediately became part of the oracles. Modern scholars argue this v. 1, as the church being rapture [caught] up to Heaven and saved from the final hour (the Tribulation period). Chapter four views the church being rapture and the beginning of the Book of Revelation's third divisions.

"And to wait for his Son from heaven, whom he raised from the dead, even Jesus, *which delivered us from the wrath to come*" (1 Thessalonians 1:10).

"John was translated into scenes of Heaven only temporarily. Though there is no authority for connecting the rapture with this expression, this sequence does seem to typify the order of events: that is, the church age first, then the rapture, then the church in heaven" (Walvoord).

"Hereafter," John was told to "Write things that shall be hereafter." After, John translated to Heaven in v. 1, and the chapters of Revelation unfold. The word "church" was the main focus in chapters 2-3, does not occur again until 22:16. The church is known as the wife or bribe of the Lamb (Revelation 19:7).

A Vision of God's Throne (vv. 2-3)

"I was in the spirit" may refer to the out-of-body experience of soul and spirit being transported into Heaven's dimension. John mentions being in the spirit twice in 1:10 and 4:2. Perhaps John was in a trance on the Lord's Day on earth and was told to "write the things which thou hast seen." v. 2 He was caught up immediately in the spirit and brought to heaven outside his body. John was told to "write all the things which shall be hereafter" (Revelation 4-22). Apostle Paul had experiences similar visions in 2 Corinthians 12:1-4.

"He hath said, which heard the words of God, which saw the vision of the Almighty, falling into a trance, but having his eyes open" (Numbers 24:4,16).

Religious ecstasy, "Ecstasy and Rapture: both suggest a state of trance or near immobility produced by an overpowering emotion. Religious ecstasy usually implies intense bliss or beatitude." [15]

In Ezekiel's vision of the LORD, it is described in the following points:

- "And the spirit entered into me when he spake unto me, and set me upon my feet, that I heard him that spake unto me" (Ezekiel 2:2).
- "The spirit lifted me up and took me away" (Ezekiel 3:14).
- "And he put forth the form of a hand, and took me by a lock of mine head; and the spirit lifted me up between the earth and the heaven, and brought me in the visions of God to Jerusalem, to the door of inner gate that looketh toward the north; where was

---

15   Merriam-Webster Dictionary. Entry ecstasy.

the seat of the image of jealousy, which provoketh to jealousy," (Ezekiel 8:3,11.1).

God's Wrath/Patterns	Revelation John's visions	Ezekiel's visions
The Throne-Vision	Chapter 4	Chapter 1
The Book	Chapter 5	Chapter 2-3
The Few- Plagues	Chapter 6:1-8	Chapter 5
The Slain under the Altar	Chapter 6:9-11	Chapter 6
The Wrath of God	Chapter 6:12-17	Chapter 7
The Seal on the Saint's Foreheads	Chapter 7	Chapter 9
The Coals from the Altar	Chapter 8	Chapter 10
No More Delay	Chapter 10:1-7	Chapter 12
The Eating of the Book	Chapter 10:8-11	Chapter 2
The Measuring of the Temple	Chapter 11:1-2	Chapter 40-43
Jerusalem and Sodom	Chapter 11:8	Chapter 16
The Cup of Wrath	Chapter 14	Chapter 23
The Vine of the Land	Chapter 14:18-20	Chapter 15
The Great Harlot	Chapter 17-18	Chapter 16, 23
The Lament over the City	Chapter 18	Chapter 27
The Scavengers' Feast	Chapter 19	Chapter 39
The First Resurrection	Chapter 20:4-6	Chapter 37
The Battle with Gog and Magog	Chapter 20:4-6	Chapter 38-39
The New Jerusalem	Chapter 21	Chapter 40-48

Figure 5 Comparison of John and Ezekiel visions

"Jasper stone and sardius stone" Jasper is the first stone, and sardius is the last stone on the High Priest's garment (Exodus 28:17-20). The sardius stone represents Reuben's tribe, the first son of Israel (Jacob) and the Jasper stone represents the last son, tribe of Benjamin. Each stone represented one of the twelve tribes.

"A rainbow round about the throne" John describes the radiant bow similar to that of an emerald gemstone in color, which is associated with Judah's name, and means "new life" (Exodus 28:13,20; Revelation

21:18). The rainbow in the sky, to Noah and family, constitutes the sure pledge of God's covenant promise not to destroy the earth with another deluge. The bow surrounding the throne is a symbol of God's covenant favor with his people eternally (Genesis 9:12-17).

The rainbow appears in the sky after a rainstorm, displaying its brilliant color through refraction. The halo rainbow is said to be a reflection of the visible appearance of the glory of God. The seven colors of a rainbow (1) red (2) orange (3) yellow (4) green (5) blue (6), subleindigo (7) violet.

The Twenty-Four Elders (v. 4)
The difference of opinion identity who the twenty-four elders are. Some scholars agreed that elders are glorified men and not angels.

Paul writes in Hebrews 1:14, "Are they not all ministering spirits, sent out to render service for the sake of those who will inherit salvation?" The elders and the living creature represent themselves as the host of people redeemed by the blood of every kindred, tongue, and nation (Revelation 5:9).

"Twenty-four seats," the word seats are rightly translated as thrones. The thrones may describe as an officiating judge's seat or dignitary status in heaven.

> Jesus said to them, "Verily I say unto you, that ye which have followed me, in the regeneration when the Son of Man shall sit in the throne of His glory, ye also shall sit upon the twelve thrones, judging the twelve tribes of Israel," (Matthew 19:28).

The elders wore the golden crowns also indicate these are men, not angels. Some suggest that these twenty-four elders are a counselor of the throne of God.

The Seven Spirits of God (v. 5)
"The seven lamps of fire burning before the throne" symbolize the Holy Spirit (cf. Exodus 25:31-40; Hebrews 8:1-5, 9:23). The seven symbols of

the Holy Spirit symbols: (1) The Dove, a Symbol of Peace, (2) A Cloud, (3) Oil, (4) The Holy Spirit in the Wind, (5) Water, (6) Fire, (7) Wine.

The Four Living Creatures (vv. 6-8)
Jesus calls Heaven "God's throne" (Isaiah 66:1, Matthew 5:34).

"Throne of God" emphasis God's transcendence or sovereign rule in heaven, and earth is His footstool.

"The crystal sea is like glass before God's throne." The Bible provides little information about this crystal sea and its meaning. Perhaps the sea of glass may be similar to the bronze laver, or basin that was located between the brazen altar and the holy place in the Tabernacle. It was used for cleansing oneself before serving God, Exodus 30:18. The Tabernacle of Moses was patterned after the Heavenly things in heaven (Exodus 25:40, 27:19; Hebrews 8:5, 9:23).

Ezekiel describes the living beasts, *"Around about the throne, were the four beasts full of eyes before and behind"* the word "beast" (Ezekiel 1:4-28, 10:6-22). These heavenly beasts are described similar in Isaiah 6:2 and Ezekiel 10:20 as cherubim.

"Full of eyes" represents the omnipresence of God. There were no wheels in John's vision.

The Four Living Creatures

1) *A Lion-* depicted the king of all beasts; omnipotence (all-powerful), and majesty.
2) *An Ox-* the most patient animal and an incessant laborer.
3) *A man-*the most intelligent and persuasive of all creatures on earth.
4) *An Eagle-* the greatest of all the birds' kingdom, dominion, and superiority.

The Four Traits of Jesus in the Gospels:

1. *Lion-* Matthew portrays Christ in his Gospel as the Lion of Judah's tribe.
2. *Ox (calf)* – Mark's portrays Christ as the conquering servant.
3. *A Man-* Luke represents Christ as the Son of man.
4. *Eagle-* John portrays Christ as the Son of God and His Divinity.

"His own standard" Heb. *"degel"* refers to a banner or flag. Each of the 12 tribes carried a particular standard with the tribe's name embroidered, probably in different colors, on the banner to identify their tribes or guiding flag pole.

The Tribes of Israel pitched their camp around the Tabernacle in the cardinal direction (Numbers 2:2).

1) *The Lion* represents the tribe of Judah (Eastside), Numbers 2:3-7.
2) *The Ox* represents the tribe of Ephraim (Westside), Numbers 2:18-24).
3) *Man represents* the tribe of Reuben (Southside), Numbers 2:10-16.
4) *The Eagle* represents the Tribe of Dan (Northside), Numbers 2:25-31.

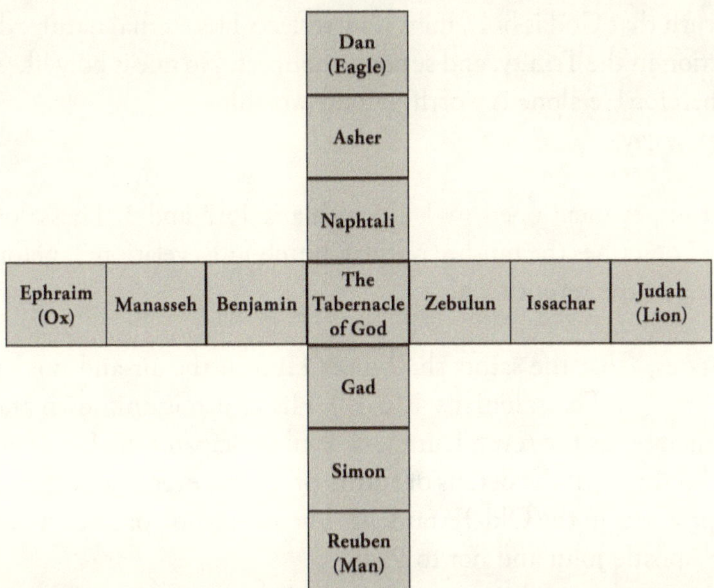

Figure 6 The Order of the Camp assemble in the Wilderness.

The Living Creatures and Elders Worship God (vv. 9-11)
"Holy, Holy, Holy" **c**ontribution to the Triune God. This refrain is the same as we find in Isaiah and thirty-four passages in the bible.

> "And one cried unto another, and said, Holy, Holy,
> Holy, is the Lord of Hosts: the whole Earth is full of
> His glory" (Isaiah 6:3)

In this hymn God is described as Holy in three different qualities: (1) Holy God (2) Holy Almighty (3) Holy Immortal

The truth that God is holy, holy, holy reflects His eternal nature, divine perfection in the Trinity, and supreme holiness. No one is holy like God, and therefor He alone is worthy of our worship.
-Philip Wijaya

The trumpet mentioned in 1 Corinthians 15:2 and 1 Thessalonians 4:16 -17 describes the rapture of the Church in Revelation 3, before the breaking of the seventh seal.

Paul states, "that the saints shall meet Him in the air and not on the earth here," (1 Thessalonians 4:16-17). His return is unknown and not as predictable as the seven trumpets. Paul anticipates the Lord's return in his lifetime. All the details of future prophetic events were concealed from prophets in the Old Testament. The Revelation of Jesus was given to the Apostle John and not to Paul.

Matthew writes, "no man knows the time or hour of Christ's return for the Church," (Matthew 24:26).

The Three Views on the Rapture of the Church and Seventh Trumpet:

Pretribulation Theory

The pretribulation view places the church rapture before any of the events of the seals, trumpets, and bowls judgments of Revelation. The entire seven years of Daniel's 70th week is the tribulation period, and the Great Tribulation begins the Wrath of God or the seventh trumpet and that the Christians will not be present:

1. "God hath not appointed us to wrath (1 Thessalonians 1:10, 5:9).
2. The church is no longer mention after (Revelation 4:1).
3. The word "church" does not appear again until chapter 19. whereas "rapture of the church" is a picture of Christ meeting His bride in the air.
4. The rapture is imminent, could occur at any time (Revelation 3:3. 16:15, Matthew 24:42-43) confirms that He could return at any time, and His bride must be ready.

Mid Tribulation Theory

The mid-tribulation view divides the seventh week into two divisions: The Great Tribulation and God's Wrath. This places the rapture after the sixth seal, but before the seventh trumpets and seventh bowls Judgment (Revelation 6:12-17)

1. "For the great day of his wrath is come; and who shall be able to stand?" (Revelation 6:17).
2. The "sealing" of the servants of God, and after a great multitude seen in heaven.
3. The mid-tribulation view looks to (2 Thessalonians 2:1-4), which says the rapture will not occur after "that man of sin [Antichrist] be revealed" (2 Thessalonians 2:3).
4. This event, which Jesus calls the abomination of desolation (Matthew 24:15), happens at the midpoint of Daniel's 70th week (Daniel 9:27).
5. The post-tribulation views say that the second coming of Christ will only occur once; the church is rapture at Christ's triumphant return.
6. The mid-tribulation suggests the Church and Israel will be mixed during the Tribulation period. This view places the rapture in Revelation 11.
7. Described the Church going through the first 3 ½ years of the Tribulation and be raptured before the last trumpet (1 Corinthians 15:2, Revelation 11:15 are synonymous).
8. Since 1 Corinthians references "the last trumpet," and Revelation also mentions, "the seventh angel sounded," they must be the same trumpets.

Post Tribulation Theory

The post-tribulation view, similar to mid-tribulation views, placing the rapture after the sixth seal. The differs in that it generally views the seals, trumpets, and bowls judgment as running simultaneously rather than concurrently. Placing the rapture after the sixth trumpet, and after the sixth bowl, and at the end of Daniel's seventy weeks.

The post-tribulations suggest that the rapture occurs at the end of the Great Tribulation period. The Church would be raptured and returned to Christ after the seven Bowl Judgments. The Church and Israel will go through the whole seven years of the Tribulation. Their supporting scriptures come from Matthew 23:21, 29; Revelation 13:7, 19-20, and 20:9. Post-Tribulation's points out that the first resurrection occurs after the seven-year tribulation period (Revelation 20:5). The resurrection associated with the rapture in 1 Thessalonians 4:16 will not happen until then.

Therefore, to says the church will not be rapture until after the Wrath of God is poured out on unbelievers and those with the beast's mark. This group view holds that the rapture and the second coming of Christ as one event.

This is a brief overview and comparison of the pretribulation, mid-tribulation, and post-tribulation views on last trumpet [rapture] views. Each view has keys points for their views on the rapture. The information is not trying to prove whose right or wrong but allows the readers to see each view.

Revelation 1	Revelation 4
1:10 - Heard a great voice as of a trumpet.	4:1 - The first voice as of a trumpet.
1:10 John was in the Spirit: Earth	4:2 - John was in the Spirit: Heaven
1:12-17 - Description of Christ.	4:2-3 - Description of Christ.
1:12 - Seven golden candlesticks.	4:5 - Seven lamps of fire
1:4 - From the seven Spirits which are before His throne.	4:5 - Before the throne, which are the seven Spirits of God
1:6 - Hath made us kings and priests unto God.	4:4; 5:9-10 - Hast made us to our God, kings and priests.
1:19 - Write the things which shall be hereafter.	4:1 - I will show thee things which must be hereafter
1:20 - An introduction to the seven churches.	5:1-5 - An introduction to the seven seals.

Figure 7 Comparison of Revelation 1 and 4

CHAPTER FIVE

THE SCROLL WITH SEVEN SEALS

The Scroll with Seven Seals (vv. 1-4)

The Scene in Heaven
v. 1 "I saw in the right hand of him" occurs about 167 times in scripture. The right hand signifies strength, a place of honor. Verse one, we see Jesus using His right hand throughout this book.

The right hand and right foot both symbolize sovereignty and authority. The right hand also symbolizes a special place of honor, rulership, and protection (cf. Exodus 15:12; Deuteronomy 33:2; Psalms 16:8,11, 89:13; Isaiah 41:13; Mark 12:36; Acts 7:55-56; Colossians 3:1).

"In *His right hand* he held seven stars, from His mouth came a sharp two-two edge sword, and his face was like the sun shining in full strength" (Revelation 1:16)

"On *the right hand* of Him who was seated on the throne a scroll from the hand of him who was seated on the throne" (Revelation 5:7)

"He held the scroll open in His hand. And He set *his right foot* on the sea" (Revelation 10:2).

v.2 *"Strong angel"* this was one of three strong introduce in this book, the second strong angel, 10:1 cloth with cloud and rainbow upon his head. The third strong angel appears in 18:21, announce the destruction of Babylon the Great. The second strong angel could be Michael in Daniel 10:21. The strong angel's names and identities are unknown.

"to open the book" The Greek word for *"book"* (Gk. *Biblion)* could mean a scroll, roll, or writing. Isaiah writes, "And the entire vision will be to you like the words sealed in a scroll. If it is handed to a reader, he will say, "I cannot read it, because it is sealed."

v. 3 *"And no man in heaven, nor in the earth, neither under the earth, was able to open the book, neither to look thereon."* Whoever was worthy of opening the scroll would be given power and authority over heaven and earth. The angels in heaven, twenty-four elders, no created beings of all times did not qualify for the job. Archangel Gabriel sent as a worthy messenger to Daniel to communication future events written on a scroll, but not found worthy to open the scroll.

The Lamb and Lion of the Tribe of Judah (vv. 5-10)
"Who is worthy to open the scroll" John wept because no one was found worthy to open the book and tell him the oracles. Until one of the elders comfort him, and the elder nominates "the Lion of Judah's tribe, the Root of David" to open and loose the seven seals' scroll.

"The Lamb of God" The blood offering ritual in the Old Testament serves as a temporary covering for sins. When he is called the "Lamb of God" in John 1:29, 36, it refers to Him as the perfect and final sacrifice for sin.

"And he shall take away all the fat thereof, as the fat of the lamb is taken away from the sacrifice of the peace offerings; and the priest shall burn them upon the altar, according to the offerings made by fire unto the LORD: and the priest shall make an atonement for his sin that he hath committed, and it shall be forgiven him" (Leviticus 4:35, Hebrews 9:22).

Romans 8:3 gives a summarizing why Jesus is called the Lamb of God. It states, "For what the law could not do, in that it was weak through the flesh, God sending his own Son in the likeness of sinful flesh, and for sin, condemned sin in the flesh."

"The Lion of the Tribe of Judah" the lion symbolizes strength, wisdom, dignity, high majesty, dominating, authority, leadership, and riches. The lion is the king in the animal kingdom. Throughout the book of Revelation, symbols are used to describes Jesus, even call him the "Lion of the tribe of Judah" In Luke 3:31-34 and Matthew 1:1-6, Jesus is a member of the tribe of Judah by lineage. The Lion Jacob called his son Judah a lion's cub (Genesis 49:9-12, Hosea 5:14). Jesus is the legitimate heir to the throne of David and the chosen One from the tribe of Judah (cf. Psalm 98:9, Psalm 72:4, 12-14; Isaiah 2:2-4, 11:9, 30:20-21, 32:5-6, 35:3-4; Jeremiah 16:19, 31:33-34).

After King Solomon's death, the United Kingdom of Israel was split into a southern kingdom (Judah); they used Judah's lion as their symbol or standard. The northern kingdom retains the name Israel which comprise of ten tribes.

"The Root of David" Jesus is "the branch, vine or stump "of David and Jesse (originator of the roots). The branches (Israel) broken off were replaced by wild olive shoots (Gentile) and engrafted into the roots' olive tree. The Gentile will become a part of God's redemptive plan, by faith dependent on the central source of life through the root (Jesus) of David (cf. Isaiah 11:1,10; Jeremiah 23:5, Romans 5:12, Revelation 22:16 and Matthew 1:1).

> "And in that day there shall be a root of Jesse, which shall stand for an ensign of the people; to it shall the Gentiles seek: and his rest shall be glorious, and there shall come forth a rod out of the stem of Jesse, and a Branch shall grow out of his roots" (Isaiah 11:1).

> "And again, Esaias saith, there shall be a root of Jesse, and he that shall rise to reign over the Gentiles; in him shall the Gentiles trust" (Romans 15:12).

> "That the Gentiles should be fellow-heirs, of the same body, and partakers of his promise in Christ by the Gospel" (Ephesians 3:6).

> "I am the vine; ye are the branches: He that abideth in me, and I in him, the same bringeth forth much fruit: for without me ye can do nothing," (John 15:5).

v. 6 *"A Lamb as it had been slain, having seven horns and seven eyes, which are the seven Spirits of God sent forth into all the earth."* The Lamb of God, who was slain from the foundation of the world, found worthy to receive the book from the right hand of God.

"The seven horns" represent His kingship, honor, and power, (cf. Daniel 7:13-14, 7:24, 1 Kings 22:11, Zechariah 1:18, Psalm 112:9 and Revelation 13).

"Seven eyes" refers to the omnipresent nature of the Spirit of God, are Christ's expression in God move for God's building. Seven eyes represent what Christ is to the believers.

> "And the spirit of the Lord shall rest upon him, the spirit of wisdom and understanding, the spirit of counsel and might, the spirit of knowledge and of the fear of the Lord" (Isaiah 11:2).

> "For who hath despised the day of small things? for they shall rejoice, and shall see the plummet in the hand of

Zerubbabel with those seven; they are the eyes of the
LORD, which run to and fro through the whole earth"
(Zechariah 4:10)

v. 10 *"And hast made us unto God kings and priest: and we shall reign on
the earth."*
Revelation 20:4-6 describes a millennial Kingdom, a 1,000 years literal
period on earth, proceed Christ's Second Coming to earth. Jesus will
reign from His throne in the New Jerusalem (cf. Daniel 7:27; Zechariah
14:9; 1 Corinthians 6:1-3; Galatians 3:29; 1 Thessalonians 4:17; 2
Timothy 2:12).

Worship of the Angelic being (vv. 11-12)
The second chorus of the song, all the angelic hosts join in with the
four beasts and twenty-four elders on one accord praising the Lamb of
God. The Lamb alone was worthy to open the sealed book and receive
authority over all the Earth and Heaven (Psalms 8:5; Hebrews 2:9).

The Doxology: "Worship of all Creation" (vv. 13-14)
The new song's final chorus gives praise and honor both to the Father
and the Son.

Daniel also saw Christ given sovereign power and honor, "I saw in
the night visions, and, behold, one like the Son of man came with the
clouds of heaven and came to the Ancient of days, and they brought him
near before him. And there was given him dominion, and glory, and a
kingdom, that all people, nations, and languages, should serve him: his
dominion is an everlasting dominion, which shall not pass away, and his
kingdom that which shall not be destroyed" (Daniel 7:13,14).

Paul writes, "Having made known unto us the mystery of his will,
according to his good pleasure which he hath purposed in himself"
(Ephesians 1:9-10).

CHAPTER SIX
THE FOUR HORSEMEN OF THE APOCALYPSE

"The Beginning of the End"

Opening of the Seven Seal Judgments (6:1-8:5)
The Scene on Earth

vv. 1-2 **Opening of the First Seal:** White Horseman, "The Antichrist" John says the first beast's thundering voice will say *"come"* to the first Horsemen and invite him to "see" the vision. John enters into the heavenly dimension and sees things that will happen upon the earth as never seen before.

"The noise of thunder" indicates something is about to happen attributed to one of the four beasts' commanding voice. The thunder has an

explicit meaning that draws our attention to the Old Testament writing. It often accompanies God's punishment and judgment of His enemies (1 Samuel 7:10). It is also associated with His power and glory (Psalms 29:3-9, 77:13). Thunder signifies God in all His Majesty (Job 37:4-14, Ezekiel 12:3-13)

It seems like each of the four beasts gave the command "*come*" to each of the four horsemen, and John was told to "see" or witness the events unfold in actions. The breaking or opening of the first four seals begins with the four riders of the apocalypse.

John's attention is direct to the horrific events that will happen upon the earth as the seven seals usher in the new world order under the leadership of the "man of sin." The seals' opening represents the end of God's Grace and the beginning of the Tribulation.

The Olivet Discourse of Christ explains these events in Matthew 24:4-31. The Tribulation period will last for seven years. The Antichrist will establish a new world order and become the first united world leader. The Jews will be at peace in their land because of the false treaty made with the Antichrist. The third Jewish temple will be in full operation.

The *"Abomination of Desolation"* will occur in the middle of the Tribulation period when the Man of Sin desecrates the Holy Temple in Jerusalem; the last 3 1/2 years is called the "Great Tribulation," the completion of the 70th weeks described in Daniel 9:27. The Tribulation period will focus on the Jews and Israel. During the time of "Jacob's trouble," their pain escalates (cf. Jeremiah 30:4-6).

God's judgment will serve as a refinery for the Jewish people to test their value in the same way as gold is purge through fire. The Gentile nations will be affected by the Wrath of God.

The purpose for the Tribulation: Deuteronomy 27:1-26, 28.

1. to finish the transgression.
2. to make an end of sins.

3. to make reconciliation for iniquity.
4. to bring in everlasting righteousness.
5. to seal up the vision and prophecy.
6. to anoint the most Holy (Daniel 9:24).
7. to bring Israel to saving faith and covenant relationship their Messiah.

The first beast commands the first horsemen to "come" and John to "see," the first seal judgment. The white horse is the first of the Apocalypse riders to come forth. This verse does not give the identity who rides this white horse. Who is this knight on the white horse? No, it isn't "Jesus" but the "Antichrist!" (Daniel 9:26-27, 1 Thessalonians 5:3). This rider represents a conquering power back by Satan himself, and no one can resist him (Matthew 24:3-6). This rider is not Christ in (Revelation 19:11-19). He is Satan's counterfeit of Jesus Christ.

The White Horse symbolizes domination and righteousness. However, it doesn't mean the rider is righteous, as can be seen in this context. The "man of sin" emulates the rider in Revelation 19, the *"Word of God"* Himself. The rider is *"the first beast"* in Revelation 13:4. He brings a false peace to the world (Daniels 9:26).

The rider has *"a bow and no arrows,"* indicating that he comes in a false peace and exercises his strength and authority through diplomacy. In the first half of the Antichrist tenure, he appears as a super intellectual that can solve all the world's problems. There's no need for weapons of war in the early period of his reign. He will use diplomacy and his superior military's backing to keep the peace. The breaking of the first four seals will be a chain reaction effect on the world. The conquer rider fits the "lawless one" depicted in (2 Thessalonians 2:3-10).

A *"stephanos crown"* will be given to the Antichrist because of his ability to resolve world issues as they occur. The world will have found their leader, and now he will establish himself as the world's most popular leader. The crowns Jesus wears in (Revelation 19:12) refer to *"diadems"* crown of royalty. The "man of sin" emulates the rider in Revelation 19, the "Word of God" Himself. The rider is "the first beast" in Revelation 13:4. He brings a false peace to the world (Daniels 9:26).

> Jesus said, "I am come in my Father's name, and ye receive me not: If another shall come in his own name, him ye will receive" (John 5:43).

vv.3-4 Opening of the Second Seal: The Red Horsemen "Wars"
When the Lamb of God broke the second, John the second living creature, "come" and another, a red horseman, went out, and the rider who sat on it was granted to take peace from the earth, and that men would slay one another; and a great sword was given to him.

The *"red horsemen"* symbolizes "bloodshed and wars." Today, wars happen more frequently in the Middle East and many other countries around the world. During the Tribulation period, wars will continue to intensify and bloodshed.

These wars may be used to adopt a peace treaty with Israel and falsify peace in the world during the first 3 ½ years of the seven years of Tribulation. This rider will break the peace treaty that the white horsemen made with Israel and cause war to break out throughout the Middle East, and most likely, it would be with Islamic nations and Israel allies nations. The war could spread around the world.

> Matthew 24:6-7 reads, "And ye shall hear of wars and rumors of wars: see that ye be not troubled: for all these things must come to pass, but the end is not yet. For nation shall rise against nation, and kingdom against kingdom: and there shall be famines, and pestilences, and earthquakes, in divers' places."

> (Matthew 24:6). These wars will eventually spread throughout the world. Once this occurs, the Antichrist's real identity will be known to the world; he will break the peace treaty with Israel and desecrate their Holy Temple. He decrees the world to worship him or die.

The world will be at war, and new sanctions strictly enforced—the stage set for the last two riders of the apocalypse.

"*A great sword*" is symbolic of authority to put combatant to death or "to slaughter or butcher (Romans 13:4).

"And I will call for a sword against him throughout all my mountains, saith the Lord God: every man's sword shall be against his brother" (Ezekiel 38:21).

vv. 5-6 Opening of the Third Seal: The Black Horsemen "Famine, and diseases"

The third horsemen of the apocalypse, who ride out early in the Tribulation, will take massive numbers of deaths and create sickness from wars. The Black Horse is the symbol of famine, disease and suffering. Dead carcasses spread over the battlefields of countries, and new pandemics will break out as a result. Another great depression and the economic recession will happen globally. The stock market will crash; the wars will bankrupt countries and generate a scarcity of food. The world will be in chaos, and nations will desperately need a leader to guide them out of havoc and spiritual dilemma. The man of sin will appear on the scene at the right time in history and become the hero and savior of the day. The Antichrist will establish a new world order and a new economic system of a cashless society. This system leads to a more secure way of buying and controlling the economy on the market. The new world order will mandate the "mark of the beast" to alleviate economic disorder.

"*Pair of balances in his hand*" symbolizes a global catastrophe and the resulting need for a conventional food system, rationing, and price regulation.

A measure of wheat and barley for a penny wheat is expensive food for the wealthier class, and barley is cheap food for the lower class. Regardless, whether one is rich or poor, the economic inflation will impact all, but the poor will suffer the most.

A "*denarius*" Latin origin means "pence, penny" and was what an ordinary worker paid for one day's labor in John's time (Matthew 20:1-16). Suppose we assume a day's wage at a minimum of $ 9.00-hour x 8 hour a day that would tally $72 a day. The cost to feed a family will be enormously high, and the money system will become cashless.

vv. 7-8 Opening the Fourth Seal: The Pale Horsemen "The Guardian of Death"
The bible is a fantastic book; the four horsemen are found in (Revelation 6:1-8). In Zechariah's vision: four chariots of horses were found in the same chapter and verses (Zechariah 6:1-8). The four-horse chariot of judgment in Zechariah's vision is differentiated in colors: red, black, white, and gray or dapples.

"*A Pale Horse*" The rider of this horse is Death. Maybe this refers to the Guardian and records keeper of death (physical death) and Hade (Spiritually death: the collector of disembodies spirits).

God buried Moses Himself in a valley in the land of Moab... (Deuteronomy 34:5-6). Archangel Michael contended with Satan over the body of Moses (Jude 9). Modern scholars suggest God buried Moses secretly and without a grave marker to prevent the grave from becoming a shrine or a place of worship. Others believe that Moses was translated in the manner of Enoch and Elijah.

Luke's narratives of Sheol after the death of unbelievers (Luke 16:19-31).

> "Therefore, hell hath enlarged herself, and opened her mouth without measure: and their glory, and their multitude, and their pomp, and he that rejoiceth shall descend into it," (Isaiah 5:14).

Matthew states in his account that "Moses and Elijah were present at the Mount of Transfiguration. The three disciples [James, Peter, and John] saw them with their own eyes and asked to set up three tabernacles (Matthew 17:1-8).

"*The beasts of the earth*" at creation, God places a distinctive fear into all animals' conscience, so that man will have dominion over all living things on earth (Genesis 1:26, 28; Psalms 8:6). The famines will have a significant impact on food supplies. The lack of food would cause the ferocious animals in the wild to turn on humanity for survival (Jeremiah 15:2-3, 29:17-18; Ezekiel 5:12).

The eagles and all other sorts of birds shall be gathered together to eat the flesh of men killed in the wars in the latter part of the Great Tribulation (cf. Luke 17:37, Matthew 24:28, Ezekiel 39:4, 17).

The Different Names of the Tribulation Period:

- The Day of the Lord, (Isaiah 2:12, 13:6-9; Ezekiel 13:5).
- The Indignation of the Lord (Isaiah 34:2).
- The Day of visitation (Isaiah 10:3).
- Time of Jacob's trouble (Jeremiah 30:7).
- The Great Day, (Jeremiah 30:7, Zephaniah 1:14).
- Daniel Seventy Weeks (Daniel 9).
- The Day of Jehovah (Zephaniah 1:7).
- That Day (Zephaniah 1:15).
- The Day of Judgment (Matthew 10:15, 2 Peter 3:7).
- The Great Day of His Wrath (Revelation 6:17).
- The Hour of His Judgment (Revelation 14:7).

These plagues come to discipline humanity for destroying the earth and rejecting His plan of salvation. These four horsemen were given authority by God to carry out His judgment of righteousness upon the earth. Prophets, preachers, believers warn humanity of the pending Wrath of God. The first six seals will claim the lives of one–fourth of the earth's population; an educated estimate of over a billion people will die. The first four seals judgment would claim 1/4 of the populace lives. Humanity will become vulnerable to the animal kingdom he once had dominion over.

While it is true that God's pattern was used to discipline Israel in the past: the sword, famine, and pestilence (Jeremiah 24:10, Ezekiel 12:16). There no future prophesies against Israel but Jerusalem only.

> "For thus saith the Lord GOD; How much more when I send my four sore judgments upon Jerusalem, the sword, and the famine, and the noisome beast, and the pestilence, to cut off from its man and beast?" (Ezekiel 14:21).

vv. 9-11 **Opening the Fifth Seal:** Martyrdom of the Saints
The Scene Shifts to Heaven

John writes, *"I saw under the altar the souls of them that were slain for the word of God, and the testimony which they held"* (Revelation 6:9). The saint's blood that has been shed throughout the church ages and will continue through the Tribulation period (Matthew 10:32-34; Romans 12:2).

"I saw under the altar" means a place of sacrifice (cf. Matthew 5:23,24; Romans 11:3; Hebrews 7:13; James 2:2). The martyrs' disembodied spirits are seen at the altar crying for their bloodshed vindication and refusing to take the Mark of the Beasts (666) and paid the ultimate price to stay true to Jesus.

Two altars in Heaven:

(1) The altar of those who had been slain because of God's word (Revelation 6:9).
(2) The golden censer altar for the prayer of the saints (Revelation 5:8, 8:3).

> Paul addresses the Thessalonian community by stating, "seeing it is a righteous thing with God to recompense tribulation to them that trouble you; and to you who are troubled rest with us, when the Lord Jesus shall revealed from heaven with his mighty angels, In flaming fire

taking vengeance on them that know not God, and
that obey not the gospel of our Lord Jesus Christ,"
(2 Thessalonians 1:6-8).

v. 11 *white robes* the Tribulation saints will be given white robes of righteousness.
These saints have not yet received a glorified body. Therefore, how could they be clothed? Maybe their spirit and soul need spiritual garments in heaven. The angels in heaven are clothed and other living creatures (cf. Revelation 7:13).

Adam gave up his nakedness in the Garden of Eden when he sinned and sought to clothe himself.

God provided clothing for both Adam and Eve. Jesus was clothed with humanity to bring man back into fellowship with God. We are clothed in Christ's forgiveness and righteousness. Jesus will forever be cloaked in human form as an infinite sign of God's love for us (John 3:16).

"Nakedness" is a (Heb."ervah") idiom that indicates something "sinful, shameful, and indecent." God asks Adam, "Where are thou" Genesis 3:9-11. Adam was naked physically but also spiritually exposed by an omniscient God. There are no hidden sins for our Creator; the world stands exposed and naked before Him.

Whom we must give an account to for our sin, (cf. 1 Corinthians 4:5; 2 Corinthians 5:1-4; Hebrews 4:13). Humanity to stand before our Holy Creator, their nakedness must be clothed and exchanged for a garment of righteousness through Jesus Christ, our Lord, and Savior. There is no other way to God, but through Jesus Christ and Him alone, (cf. John 3:16, 8:24, 14:6; Acts 4:12; 2 Corinthians 5:19; Romans 1:4)

The martyrs will be given these *"white robes"* to show they have overcome the world and washed their garments in the Lamb's blood. The cleansing application of fire will test the purity of their commitment to Christ.

vv. 12-17 **Opening the Sixth Seal:** The Wrath of God has come
The Scene Shifts Back to Earth

John tells of an earthquake so enormous that "every mountain and island fled away." Possibly, John was referring to a huge tsunami or tidal wave that toppled island and mountain. John saw "the sun become black as a sackcloth of hair, and the moon became like blood." This supernatural phenomenon could be explained by a volcanic eruption which has often turned the sky black from its smoke and ash scattered in the atmosphere.

"The Great Earthquake" The first four seals described judgments that humanity inflicted on themselves because of their thirst for power and control of the world. The sixth seal describes a judgment that is clearly supernatural. All life forms on earth depends on cosmic lights for daily basis.

"The sun and the moon" stabilize our planet's rotation, i.e. waves, gravity and provide plants to grow for human consumption. Humanity would have no knowledge of how to live under these new conditions on earth. A dark sun and blood moon would have a psychological and physiological effect on all life forms on earth.

The astronomists and media worldwide observed four total lunar eclipses that occurred consecutively within one year and a half from April 2014 through September 2017. The moon appeared red-orange during each lunar eclipse; which took place on the Jewish Holidays.

According to John Hagee, "The blood moon prophecy corresponds on two major Jewish holidays and is a sign of the end times." This event is mentioned in (Joel 2:30-31, Acts 2:20 and Revelation 6:12).

Great commotion occurs in heaven. "And there shall be signs in the sun, and in the moon, and in the stars; and upon the earth distress of nations, with perplexity; the sea and the waves roaring, Men's hearts failing for fear, and looking after those things which are coming on the earth: for the powers of heaven shall be shaken, and then shall they see the Son of man coming in a cloud with power and great glory" (Luke 21:25-27).

It is undetermined whether or not there is any relevance to these apocalypse prophecies concerning the "blood moon" with the natural phenomenon that occurred in 2014 and 2015 on the Jewish Holidays of Sukkot [Feast of the Tabernacle] and Passover. One thing we know for sure is that these signs and prophecies will come to pass in God's own time.

The sixth seal brings natural catastrophes of various kinds, (Matthew 24:7, 29). The earth and the heavenly bodies will go into convulsions. This terrible earthquake was foretold in Isaiah's writing, "And they shall go into holes of rocks, and into the caves of the earth, for fear of the Lord and for the glory of his majesty, when he ariseth to shake the earth terribly" (Isaiah 2:19).

In Ezekiel 32:7-8, we read about the darkness of the sun, moon, and stars. In Matthew 24:29, describes of this same thing in the heavens. "Immediately after the tribulation of those days shall the sun be darkened, and the moon shall not give her light, and the stars shall fall from heaven, and the powers of the heavens shall be shaken."

Thousands of meteors and asteroids will impact the earth's surface and its bodies of water. One can only imagine the damage it will cause: earthquakes, tsunamis, tidal waves on major cities across the globe.

The Old and New Testament both speak of the earth's annihilation. These major earthquakes shall shake earth's foundation at a magnitude not found on the Richter scales (Isaiah 7, 13,17).

"Let no man deceive you by any means: for that day shall not come, except there comes a falling away first, and that man of sin be revealed, the son of perdition," (2 Thessalonians 2:3).

We read in Isaiah, a similar passage, "And all the host of heaven shall be dissolved, and the heavens shall be rolled together as a scroll: and all their host shall fall down, as the leaf falleth off from the vine, and as a falling fig from the fig tree." (Isaiah 34:4).

The wealthy, dignitaries, and even those with presidential status will not be exempt from God's righteous judgment. Men will wish to die and try to commit suicide, but death will only allow them to live and face God's wrath, (Revelation 9:6). The most horrific "Day of the Lord" will humble men through God's judgment.

"I also will laugh at your calamity; I will mock when your fear cometh; When your fear cometh as desolation, and your destruction cometh as a whirlwind; when distress and anguish cometh upon you. Then shall they call upon me, but I will not answer; they shall seek me early, but they shall not find me" (Proverbs 1:26-28). John's horrific vision seems like a nightmare; they are things he sees that will come upon humanity. His visions are not in any particular sequence or order.

v. 17 The sixth seal's opening, God's judgment upon his saints' persecutors, symbolized in natural calamities, earthquake, darkness, bloodshed. Stars are falling, the sky receding as a scroll, mountains, and islands removed. These are horrific pictures of destruction on earth. This verse is the beginning of the last half of the Great Tribulation. God's divine clock has finally arrived to deal with the sins of the wicked. The Day of LORD will impact the world, and His wrath will punish the ungodly. Men will seek death, but death will flee from them and force them to face God's wrath. The dispensation of grace ends, and the day of wrath falls on the earth's inhabitants (Zephaniah 1:1-7; Joel 1:15; 2:1,11,31; Matthew 24:21-22).

THE SIGNS BEFORE "THE DAY OF LORD" WRATH			
Revelation 6	**Matthew 24**	**Mark 13**	**Luke 21**
White Horseman: War (vv. 1-2)	Rumors of Wars (v. 6)	Rumors of Wars (v. 7)	Wars and commotions (v. 9)
Red Horseman: worldwide discord and bloodshed (vv. 3-4)	Rise of nations and Kingdoms against one another (v. 7)	Rise of nations and Kingdoms against one another (v. 8)	Rise of nations and Kingdoms against one another (v. 10)
Black Horseman: Famine (vv. 5-6)	Famines (v. 7)	Famines (v. 8)	Famines (v.11)
Pale Horseman: Pandemic diseases (vv. 7-8)	Pestilences (v. 7)	other catastrophes, events to follow (v. 8) Sorrow	Pestilences (v. 11)
Persecution and martyrdom (vv. 9-11)	Persecutions and martyrdom (vv. 9-13)	Persecutions and martyrdom (v. 9-13)	Persecution and martyrdom (vv. 12-19)
Great earthquake; De-creation (vv. 12-17)	earthquakes in divers' places (v.7) De-creation: Great Tribulation (vv. 15-31)	earthquakes in divers' places (v. 8) "De-creation" (vv. 14-27)	Great earthquakes in divers' places (v. 11) De-creation (vv. 20-27)

Figure 8 A Comparison of The Sixth Seal Judgment and the Olivet Discourse.

---

16 Note: In de-creation, sin triumphs over evil and that is the cause of the shortening life span.

CHAPTER SEVEN

AN INTERLUDE: THE SEALING OF THE 144,000 JEWISH SERVANTS

First "Parenthetical Period[17]"

God Wrath on Hold (vv.1-3)
The Scene on Earth

"After these things," This phase indicates a significant transition from opening the first six seals to the seventh. The first vision in v.1 includes four angels being commanded to hold back the four winds on earth.

---

17 Note: The first parenthesis comes between the sixth and seventh trumpet judgments: (1) The ministry of the 144,000 servants of God in 7:1-8. The Great multitude who comes to faith during the Tribulation period in 7:9-17.

Symbolically, this refers to God suspending His judgment for a short time and resumes His wrath after the sealing of God's 144,000 servants.

There is a gap or a brief interlude between the sixth and seventh seal Judgment, which is called the Parenthetical periods. These events occur seven times throughout the book of Revelation.

"the four winds" phase is used to describes the whole earth. Jeremiah describe the judgment of God by referring to wind, "And upon Elam will I bring the four winds from the four quarters of heaven, and will scatter them toward all those winds; and there shall be no nation whither the outcasts of Elam shall not come" (Jeremiah 49:36).

"Then said he unto me, Prophesy unto the wind, prophesy, son of man, and say to the wind, Thus saith the Lord God; Come from the four winds, O breath, and breathe upon these slain, that they may live" (Ezekiel 37:9).

"Daniel spake and said, I saw in my vision by night, and, behold, the four winds of the heaven strove upon the great sea" Daniel 7:2, 8:8, 11:4).

"The number four" derives from the Genesis creation, "the fourth day of the week." God brought into existence the firmament of the Heavens: the moon, sun, and all the stars; this showed God's absolute control over the world (Genesis 1:14-19).

v. 2 *"And I saw another angel ascending from the east, having the seal of the living God"* John proceeded to record his vision. There were four angels posted in the four cardinal directions on the earth, holding back the wind, while the angel from the east sealed the servants of God to minister to the world. We are not told what God's seal is, but it would be placed in the recipient's forehead. The four angels are told not to hurt the earth, sea, and trees until God servants are sealed. These events occur after the sixth seal and before the seventh seal begins.

The Church seal of promise
The Apostle Paul writes that "the Holy Spirit seals all believers the moment they trust Christ as Savior" The Holy Spirit indwells our hearts. The church is promised that their seal of salvation is secure both now and forever (cf. 1 Corinthians 3:16, 2 Corinthians 1:22,1 Peter 2:5).

"In whom ye also trusted, after that, ye heard the word of truth, the gospel of your salvation: in whom also after that ye believed, ye were sealed with that holy Spirit of promise, which is the earnest of our inheritance until the redemption of the purchased possession, unto the praise of his glory" (Ephesians 1:13. 4:38).

v. 3 *"till we have sealed the servants of our God in their foreheads."*
The purpose of God delay is sealed the chosen servants and protect them from Satan and evil forces on earth.

God's protection during ancient time

- God protected Noah and his family by placing them in an Ark (cf. Genesis 6:1-10, Hebrews 11:6-7).
- He protected Rehab, the prostitute, and her family and marked her house with a scarlet rope outside her window (cf. Joshua 2:8-13.6:17-25).
- He protected Lot, his wife, and his two daughters. Who were all swiftly moved outside Sodom's city to a safe place by an Angel (cf. Genesis 19:16-26)?
- Israel's children were protected from Pharaoh and his armies in the Red Sea by dividing it with a pillar of cloud or strong east wind (cf. Exodus 14:15-29, 15:8-19).

John Piper explains the seal of the church age that "God sends the Holy Spirit as a preserving seal to lock in our faith, as an authenticating seal to validate our sonship and also as protection to keep out destructive forces." "When you believed, you were marked in Him with a seal, the promised Holy Spirit, who is a deposit guaranteeing our inheritance until the redemption of those who are God's possession."

The Sealing of the 144,000: Jewish's Servants (vv. 4-8)
The Bible does not tell what the seal is or whether it is a visible mark on their forehead. The 144,000 Jewish Israelites are sealed from the outpouring of God's wrath. They will go through the Tribulation without any impediment by evil forces, or deception from the Antichrist (Matthew 24:14), to preach the eternal gospel worldwide.

Judah is Jacob's fourth son, and 12,000 from Judah's Tribe will be marked first out of the twelve tribes. Jesus is from the tribe of Judah. God promised that David's throne would rule forever (cf. Ezekiel 46:2,16; Luke 1:32-33).

Some commons theories on why Dan excluded:

- Dan is the tribe responsible for leading Israel into idolatry, (cf. Deuteronomy 18:20-21; Judges 18:14-20; 30-31; 1 Kings 15:34, 22:52-53).
- Dan is the tribe that makes an excellent candidate for the Antichrist to arise from (Genesis 49:17).
- Dan's tribe is first to receive portions of the land during Christ's 1,000 years reign (Ezekiel 48:2).

Walvoord argued, "In this list, Manasseh is mentioned, but Ephraim is not, and in place of Ephraim, Joseph's name is given in Revelation 7:8. No explanation is made concerning this substitution."

Ephraim is not a tribe of Israel but the son of Joseph. Possibly Ephraim was sealed under the tribe of Joseph. However, the tribes of Ephraim and Dan were the first to lead Israel into idolatry (Hosea 7:8, 8:11-12).

Joseph's sons receive a double portion. Jacob adopted Joseph's two sons, Manasseh and Ephraim, share in Jacob's inheritance equally with Jacob's twelve sons (Genesis 48:1-15). Jacob also blessed Joseph for what he had done for the family while in Egypt. Joseph and his brother Benjamin were the only children of Rachel, whom Jacob loved so dearly, but lost her in Benjamin's birth (Genesis 35:20,48:17).

Levite tribe did not receive land in Israel because God was their portion. The Levitical priesthood provides ritual service for their communities and the Temple in Jerusalem. The Roman destroyed the second Temple in 70 A.D. The Jewish in Israel will rebuild the third and final Temple on Mount Moriah before or during the Tribulation. However, the Antichrist will enter the Temple and desecrate it setting up an image of himself and forcing many to worship it (Revelation 13:14).

The Great Multitude Gather at the Throne to Worship (vv. 9-10)
"After this, I beheld, and, lo, a great multitude" as a result of their ministry, innumerable multitudes will come to know Christ. The Holy Spirit will empower the 144,000 Remnants with all the gifts they need to achieve God's purpose (Joel 2:28). Jewish and Gentile nations will come to salvation during the Tribulation period but at high cost and persecution.

The gospel will reach the furthest parts of the earth (Isaiah 55:11, Matthew 24:14, 28:19-29). Heaven's Kingdom was postponed for over 2,000 years because the Jewish leaders and people rejected Christ as Messiah. The Kingdom of Heaven is a physical and visible place that Jesus will occupy with the saints on earth (Daniel 7: 13-14, Revelation 20:4,1 Corinthians 6:2).

"Nation" in the scriptures always references other Gentile nations and not the Jewish nations (i.e., Israel, Judah).

"clothed with white robes" The signification of white symbolizes truth and purity. These saints will receive the robe of righteousness because they will be: (1) worthy, (Revelation 3:4); (2) the overcomer, (Revelation 3:5); (3) martyrs of the gospel, (Revelation 6:11).

"I will greatly rejoice in the LORD, my soul shall be joyful in my God; for he hath clothed me with the garments of salvation, he hath covers me with the robe of righteousness, as a bridegroom decketh with ornaments, and as a bride adorneth with her jewels" (Isaiah 61:10).

"Palms in their hands," the great multitude are clothed with white robes and carry palm branches in their hands is emblems of victory and tokens of a triumph. The imagery of the Feast of Tabernacles: just as the seating reminded us of the protecting sign of the lintels of the houses of Israel in Egypt, so do these palm branches and songs of joy recall the ceremonies of later feast (Exodus 23:16, Leviticus 23:43, Nehemiah 8:14-17).

The Angelic Hosts join in Worships (vv. 11-14)
All the angels, twenty-four elders, the four living beasts, and the great multitude of saints collectively prostrate themselves in worship before God Almighty, as in chapter 5. One of the twenty-four elders says to John these are Great Tribulation saints that wash their robes in the Lamb's blood. God cleanses our sinful life with the blood of Christ.

The purpose of the Tribulation period is to prepare Israel for her conversion and acknowledgment of Jesus Christ as her Messiah (cf. Deuteronomy 4:29-30; Jeremiah 30:3-11; Zechariah 12:10,13:7-10, Isaiah 26:9, Hosea 5:14, Daniel 12:7). The Tribulation period is also known as the "time of Jacob's trouble." A great Tribulation is a future event in which God will enact divine judgment against those who reject Him, and the only provision for salvation is "Jesus Christ" (Daniel 12:1; Jeremiah 30:7; Matthew 24:21). This completes His plan of salvation for Israel (Daniel 9:24-27).

The Scene shifts back to Heaven (vv. 15-17)
The expression of "serve Him day and night" means without ceasing or continually. There is no day or night in Heaven because God is the light. John could be talking about the millennial Temple on earth. Jesus told the Laodicean Church, "to him that overcometh will I grant to sit with me in my throne, even as I also overcame, and am set down with my Father in His throne" (Revelation 3:21).

These martyred saints will be slaughtered between the 5th and 6th seal judgment. The Tribulation saints will be killed and reside in Heaven during the Parenthesis period of silence between the 6th and 7th seal (Revelation 8:1, 3-5). The martyred saints will rest in Heaven around God's throne, and God will meet all of their spiritual needs.

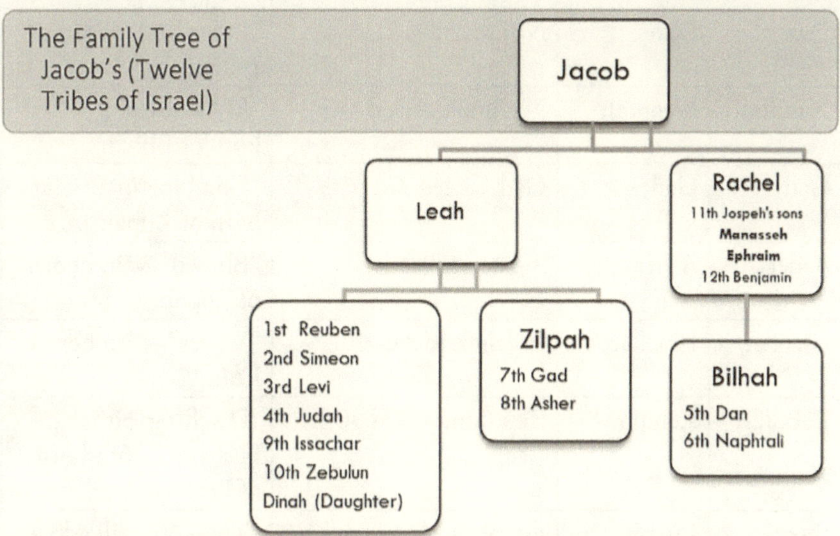

Figure 9 The Family Tree of Jacob's sons (12 Tribes of Israel)18

Genesis 29-30	Numbers 1	Revelation 7 "The Marking Order"	Meaning of Names
Reuben	Reuben	Reuben, sealed 2nd	"Behold a son -1st born of Leah
Simeon	Simeon	Simeon, sealed 7th	"God hears" – 2nd born of Leah.
Levi	Not mentioned	Levi, sealed 8th	"Joined"- 3rd born of Leah
Judah	Judah	Judah, sealed 1st	"Let him [God] be Praised" – 4th born of Leah.

---

18   Note: Jacob had two wives, Rachel and Leah (who are sisters and first-cousins of Jacob, two concubines name Bilhah and Zilpah (Genesis 30-3-9). Bilhah is Rachel's maid, and she conceived and bared Jacob's two sons: Dan and Naphtali (Genesis 30:3-6). Zilpah Leah's maid conceived, and bare Jacob's two sons: Gad and Asher (Genesis 30:9).

Dan	Dan	Not sealed	"Judge" – 1st born of Bilhah
Naphtali	Naphtali	Naphtali, sealed 5th	"My wrestling" – 2nd born of Bilhah
Gad	Gad	Gad, sealed 3rd	"Good fortune" - 1st born of Zilpah
Asher	Asher	Asher, sealed 4th	"Blessed" – 2nd born of Zilpah
Issachar	Issachar	Issachar, sealed 9th	"Wages" – 5th born of Leah
Zebulun	Zebulun	Zebulun, sealed 10th	"Dwelling with husband" - 6th born of Leah
Joseph	Joseph	Joseph, sealed 11th	"The Lord will add a son" – 1st born of Rachel
Not listed	Ephraim	Not mentioned	"Fruitful"- 2nd son of Joseph.
Not listed	Manasseh	Manasseh, sealed 6th	"Making to forget1st born of Joseph.
Benjamin	Benjamin	Benjamin, sealed 12th	"Son of the right hand" - 2nd born of Rachel

Figure 10 The Marking order of the 144,000 Jewish's Servant

CHAPTER EIGHT

THE SEVENTH SEAL/SILENCE IN HEAVEN/SEVEN TRUMPETS JUDGMENT (1-4)

Silence in Heaven (vv. 1-5)

v. 1 *"there was silence in heaven about the space of half an hour,"* In fact, such an interpretation of silence would be literal and not symbolic. The eschatological wrath of God is about to finally happens. It, so dramatic is God's wrath that all the heavenly activates cease for thirty minutes- Usually, there is no moment in Heaven in which silence occurs because God is worshiped incessantly. Just before the climax of the seventh seal unfolds, catastrophic events on earth begin to intensify.

v. 2" *And I saw the seven angels which stood before God; and to them were given seven trumpets*" The ancient apocryphal book of Tobit suggests that there are five of seven archangels: Phanuel, Uriel, Raphael, Sarakiel, and Raguel. In the canonical Bible, two archangels mentioned: Gabriel and Michael.

However, these seven angels are not the seven Spirits of God, but high-ranking angels God selected for this occasion.

Tim LaHaye, suggests "the seven seals take place in the first quarter, and the seventh seal begins the seven-trumpet judgment which began the next 21 months or second quarter of the Tribulation."[19] John identified these angels as those who stand before God. All angels stand before God one time or another for instructions, but these angels remain standing. These angels are assigned to inaugurate the "Wrath of God," known as "The Day of the LORD" that occurs in the middle of the Tribulation period.

The Purpose for the Shofar Horns in the Old Testament

- An instrument of music, (1 Chronicles 13:8).
- The Day of Atonement (Leviticus 25:9).
- Rams' horns, (Joshua 6:4, 20).
- The sacrifices on the feast day (Numbers 10:10, Psalms 81:3).
- All religious processions and ceremonies, (1 Chronicles 13:8, 1Chronicles 15:24-28, 2 Chronicles 5:13-14).
- Assembling the people to war (Judges 3:27, Jeremiah 4:19, 42:14).
- Assembling the people for instructions and movement (Numbers 10:1-36).
- Proclaiming Kings, (2 Kings 9:13, 11:14).
- Giving alarm in cases of danger (Ezekiel 33:2-6).

---

19   Tim LaHaye, Left Behind: A Novel of the Earth's Last days, (Tyndale House Publishers, Inc, 1995).

- The priests to blow the Ram's shofar is one of the earliest musical instruments. To usher in Israel's biblical festivals (Numbers 10:8; 2 Chronicles 5:12, 7:6).
- The return of the Ark of Covenant (2 Samuel 6:15).

vv. 3-5 **The Pattern of Heavenly Things**

"Altar Incense" is connected to worship and prayers. The Holy place of the tabernacle was a symbol of Christ as the mediator between man and God (Hebrews 7:25; 9:24). God considers the saints' prayers as a sweet-smelling aroma (Psalms 141:2, 2 Corinthians 2:15, James 5:16). The altar incense was to be kept burning at all times. The altar was located before the veil and the throne of God.

The Tabernacle of Moses was designed and given by God while on Mount Sinai, and it is based upon the Tabernacle in Heaven (Exodus 25:40, Hebrews 8:5). The Earthly tabernacle was to prophetically point the way to God the Father through Jesus Christ.

No error was allowed in its construction.

> "Who serve unto the example and shadow of heavenly things, as Moses was admonished of God when he was about to make the tabernacle: for, See, saith he, that thou make all things according to the pattern shewed to thee in the mount" (Hebrews 8:5).

The angel fills the censer with fire from the altar and casts it upon the golden altar
Both the smoke of the incense the prayer of the saints ascends to God.

"there were voices, thunderings, and lightning, and an earthquake" describes God's wrath is about to fall on the earth. There were voices, akin to thundering' and lightning, followed by an earthquake. After God speaks to Heaven's heavenly hosts, an earthquake initiates the beginning of God's wrath on the earth.

The First Trumpet: "the third of earth inhabitable surface burnt up" (vv. 6-7)
The Scene on Earth, 8:6-9:21

"*The first angel sounds his trumpet,* " followed by a horrific thunderstorm of hail and fire mingled with human blood on earth. It unleashes horrific plagues parallel to one in ancient Egyptian before the exodus (exodus 9:13-35). The first trumpet plagues burnt up the inhabitable part of the earth's surface has been reduced by one-third. Hailstones weighing about a talent [129 lbs.]. Which is parallel to the method of destruction for the ancient cities Sodom and Gomorrah, (Genesis 19:1-29). The trumpet and bowl judgments parallel ten plagues in Egypt.

These judgments intensify causing havoc on the earth. The people will know that these judgments are of God, and will still refuse to repent. So, the climax of God's wrath continues.

The Second Trumpet: "A Burning Mountain Ruins a Third of the Sea"(vv.8-9)
"*great mountain burning with fire*" the removal of mountains suggests the overthrow of governments and kingdoms (Isaiah 64:1-3, Jeremiah 51:24-25, Micah 1:2-4, Nahum 1:5-6). The "sea" is comparable to the beast rise out of the sea and out of the earth in (Revelation 13:1, 11). The sea symbolizes a water body, "people, multitudes, nations, and tongues" (Revelation 17:15). The sea will also be affected by an enormous surge of gases from the asteroid that will alter the earth's atmosphere, water bodies, and climate globally.

"The sea is smaller than oceans and is usually located where the land and ocean meet. Typically, seas enclosed by land."[20] The earth comprises seven major oceans in the world. According to earth science, "About

---

20   U.S. Department of the Interior | U.S. Geological Survey: Retrieve on 1 June 2017. http://water.usgs.gov/edu/earthhowmuch.html

71 percent of the earth's surface is water-covered, and the oceans hold about 96.5 percent of all earth's water."[21]

If one examines this through John's perspective, he was probably referring to the Mediterranean Sea as opposed to the surrounding land is comprised of three continents: (1) Europe, (2) Asia, and (3) Northern horns of Africa. One-third of 47.4 million square miles will be affected by this plague, killing the sea life and poisoning the saltwater. The gigantic asteroid's impact will cause natural disasters such as tidal waves, tsunamis, hurricanes, and earthquakes destroying all in their paths.

The Third Trumpet: "A Star Poison the Freshwater" (vv. 10-11)
"The third angel sounds his trumpet" this judgment targets fresh waters system: rivers, lakes, stream, and spring reservoirs. The populaces on earth could only survive a few days without water and food. Humanity resources for survival have been target by the first three judgments. One-third of land burnt up, one-third of the seas and oceans saltwater and marine life poison. The wormwood has contaminated one-third of the freshwater reservoirs; the death rates are soaring. God gave man dominion over the earth, and now these plagues have diminished man's authority.

The phrase *"Wormwood"* is only mentioned one time in the New Testament and cited eight times in the Old Testament. The wormwood in verse 11 is not a plant but an unknown star in the Universe. Its effect is similar to the plant with the same outcome death, poison, and bitterness taste (cf. Deuteronomy 29:18; Jeremiah 9:15, 23:15; Lamentation 3:15,19).

Our Creator has always supplied all of humanity's needs, and now man must provide for themselves. The world will come to realize that El-Elyon is Sovereign and God of the Highest over the entire Universe. God is our El-Shaddai because He supplies all our needs. Humanity

---

21 Matt Williams, *Earth Science*. Universe Today.

chooses not to worship the Creator, but instead himself and other created beings (Romans 1:24-26).

> "Thus saith the Lord, In this thou shalt know that I am the Lord: behold, I will smite with the rod that is in mine hand upon the waters which are in the river, and they shall be turned to blood. And the fish that is in the river shall die, and the river shall stink; and the Egyptians shall lothe to drink of the water of the river" (Exodus 7:17-18).

The Fourth Trumpet: Third of Celestial Smitten with Darkness" (vv.12-13)
"The fourth angel sounds his trumpet," smiting a third of the celestial bodies' lights and forcing them to darken—the translation for (Gk. *smitten*) means to strike or of uncertain derivation.

The first four trumpets focus on natural objects and the celestial bodies: land, sea, freshwater, the sun, the moon, and the stars. The havoc that these trumpets will unleash on our civilization will be as never seen in humanity's history. Man will know that they are experiencing God's wrath and Judgment, yet they will not repent.

These plagues are unfolding before the eyes of man. Target not only nature but the celestial bodies as well. If the sun were smitten completely, all inhabitants would die, and our civilization would become extinct. The sun is the primary energy source that supports life on earth, and all forms of life depend on the sun for survivability.

The two minor prophets, Amos and Joel, predict the pending Doom Day's judgment of humanity and planet earth (Amos 8:9; Joel 2:10). After the church is rapture, humanity introduces God's absence, much suffering, and pain because of sin and its rebellious nature.

"*Woe, woe, woe*" (Gk. Ouai) means to utter grief or denounce calamity. The number three denotes Divine completion and perfection. Each "*woe*" is parallel with the last three trumpet judgments. The expression "*woe*" is mentioned several times in other passages in the Bible as a single word "woe." However, it is written three times, meaning that God's wrath is not complete until the last trumpet's blast.

v. 13 "*an angel flying* through the midst of heaven" Many modern scholars argue that "an angel flying" is a mistranslation and should read "an eagle flying" (Job 39:27-30, Hosea 8:1, Habakkuk 1:6-8, Revelation 12:14).

THE WOE, WOE, WOE SERIES OUTLINE:

First woeful series: the fifth trumpet (9:1-12)

- Star fall and the opening of the bottomless pit, vv1-6.
- The release of the locust demons and their king Apollyon to torment men for five months, vv. 7-11.
- The 1ˢᵗ woe passes, v. 9:12.

Second Woeful Series: The Sixth Trumpet (9:13-11:14)

- The sound of the sixth trumpet v. 9:13.
- Release of four angels and two hundred million demonic armies, vv. 9:13-16.
- The death of a third of humankind: killed by fire, smoke and brimstone, vv. 17-19.
- The rest of the men who refuse to repent, vv. 9:20-21.
- The seven thunders utter, vv. 10:1-4
- The two witness's ministry, vv. 11:1-6.
- The death of the witnesses, vv. 11:7-10.
- The resurrection of the two witnesses, followed by an earthquake, vv. 11:11-13.
- The 2ⁿᵈ woe passes, vv. 11:14.

Third Woeful Series: The Seventh Trumpet (11:15-16:17).

- The seventh trumpet: herald a new King: "The kingdom of the world is now the Kingdom of our Lord," v. 11:15

- The final woe is the seven "Bowls" Judgment integrated within the seven Trumpet Judgment, 16:1-21.
- John never says, "when the third woe has passed" in the way he clearly announces the last two woes, "woe is past."
- The last woe is officially over when the mystery of God fulfilled. In (Revelation 10:7) suggests the third woe marks the finale of God's wrath on sin and continues until chapter 19, the Lord Jesus establishes His Kingdom on earth for a thousand years.

The Judgment in Revelation	The Plagues Judgment in Exodus
First Trumpet: "hail and fire" Revelation 8:7	Seventh plagues: "Thunderstorm of hail and fire" Exodus 9:13-35
Second Trumpet: "Turn the sea into blood" Revelation 8:8-9 Third vial "river and fountain water turn into blood" Revelation 16:4-7.	First plague: "water turn into blood" Exodus 7:17-21. Drinking water from the river, turn into blood, Exodus 7:14-25
Third Trumpet: "Water made bitter" Revelation 8:10-11	Not listed, but found in Exodus 15:23-25
Fourth Trumpet: "Darkness for three days" 8:12-13	The Ninth plague: "Darkness for third days" Exodus 10:21-29
First vial: "Sores outbreak" Revelation 16:4-7	Sixth Plague: "Boil outbreak" Exodus 9:8-12
Seventh vial: "Thunder, lightning, great earthquake, great hail" Revelation 16:17-21	Seventh Plagues: "Thunder, Hail, and fire" Exodus 9:22-26

Figure 11 The Trumpets and Bowls Judgment: Foreshadow the ten Plagues of Egypt

CHAPTER NINE

THE FIFTH & SIXTH TRUMPETS JUDGMENT (5-6)

Fifth Trumpet: "Demonic Locusts from the Bottomless Pit" (vv. 1-12) vv. 1-2 *"I saw a star fallen from Heaven"* As John's vision continues, he sees a star fall from heaven, to the earth. This fallen star is an intelligent being and a mighty fallen angel, compare to the prince of the bottomless pit, Abaddon, and other incarcerated devils. The fallen star is none other Satan himself; whose name is "Lucifer" (Heb. *Heylel)* refers to light-bearer, shining one or morning star. In the vision, he is given the key to release all of his subordinates. The "key" symbolizes "authority" given by the one who is the key custodian (Revelation 1:18).

The Bible mentions twice that Lucifer cast out of Heaven: (1) before the creation, (cf. Isaiah 14:12-15, Ezekiel 28:6-10, Luke 10:18) (2) Michael and his angels fought against the Dragon and cast his angels out of Heaven to the earth (cf. Jude 6; Revelation 20:14).

"Bottomless" (Gk. *Abussos*) refers to the abyss, unfathomable depth. The fallen angels that had sinned with the daughters of men in Genesis narrative of giants cast down to "hell" (Gk. "*Tartarus*") Peter uses the word in referring to the place of judgment for evil angels, (2 Peter 2:4).

vv. 3-5 **The Locusts Given Authority**

John describes a great army emerging from the bottomless pit. The fallen star opened the bottomless pit, and demon locusts swarmed into the atmosphere like smoke billowing out of an erupted volcano. The sun and sky darkened because the locusts that came from the pit were like smoke in the sky. Their mission was to invade the earth and torment men for five months. They are commanded not to harm the vegetation, crops, or any green land. The life span of a locust is five months, and here in the context, they are given five months to torment men. A third of the earth's inhabitable surface burnt up under the first Trumpet Judgment in Chapter 8:6-7. The 144,000 remnants seal and are protected in 7:4-8.

The Hebrews knew them as countless and innumerable like the sea sands. They are the most destructive force of the grasshopper family. These insects usually swarm together and were the instruments of God's wrath upon Ancient Egypt. (cf. Deuteronomy 28:38–42; 2 Chronicles 7:13; Joel 1:4; Psalm 78:46). These locust-like creatures were given one mission to torments the unbelievers for five months with fears, agony, and pain. God can raise any sources of His creation as an instrument to accomplish His purposes in future events.

v. 6 "And in those days shall men seek death, and shall not find it; and shall desire to die, and death shall flee from them (Revelation 9:6). As

Ryrie put it, "bodies will not sink and drown; poisons and pills will not affect lives, and somehow even bullets and knives will not do their intended job."[22] The wicked unbelievers will seek death, look for the same fate they inflict on martyrs but they will not find it. They will desire for death, but death will flee from them to face their righteous judgment.

v. 7 John describes these demon locusts as an ancient military horseman (cavalry) prepared for battle. We have limited knowledge concerning the demonic realm and its transformative capabilities. Their appearance looks like a scene from a horror movie or like an extra-terrestrial from another Planet. Although locusts usually have no king (Proverbs 30:27), these demonic locusts do. There is a hierarchy of power among the demons, fallen angels, and Satan.

> "For we wrestle not against flesh and blood, but against principalities, against powers, against the rulers of the darkness of this world, against spiritual wickedness in high places" (Ephesians 6:12).

"Horses" in the Bible are connected to warlike operations (Job 39:19-25; Isaiah 28:28; Joel 2:4-5). The demonic locusts are not in battle, but a preparatory phase of the battle. If the order is given, they are ready to carry out God's orders. The leader of all the demonic like locusts is (Gr. Abaddon or Apollyon). Joel also compared the horse with the locust (Job 39:19-20).

"Their faces were as men's faces" meant they look like a human, but not necessarily a man. Faces of men suggested the intellectual capability and authority of men and not locusts.

v.8 *"Long hair like a woman"* is a representation of strength and vitality. Samson wore long hair and seven braids (Judges 16:13,19). It was the

---

22   Charles C. Ryrie, Revelation, Moody Press, Chicago, 1968, p. 62.

source of his power. Absalom was also a warrior who wore long hair (2 Samuel 14:25-26).

"Their teeth were as the teeth of lions" strong as those of ferocious lions.

v. 9 *"Breastplates of iron"* symbolizes their invulnerability. The breastplate's primary purpose was to protect the heart, lungs, intestines, and other vital organs. These creatures are invulnerable.

"Their wings" sound like chariots of charging horses rushing off to battle. The locusts' noise is very intimidating and will put fear into the heart and mind of the listener.

v. 10 *"there were stings in their tails: and their power was to hurt men five months."*

The King over the Demons (vv. 11-12)
v.11 "Whose name in the Hebrew tongue is Abaddon, but in the Greek tongue hath his name Apollyon." The Hebrew word "Abaddon" (Heb. *abaddwn*) means "destruction or destroyer and is the name of the angel that is the Prince of the Infernal Regions, the Lord of Death, and the author of havoc on the earth." "Apollyon (Gk. *Apolluwn*) means destroyer, or the angel of the bottomless Pit, (cf. Joel 26:6, 28:22; Matthew 7:13; John 17:12). The angel Apollyon will lead his armies of demons to invade one-third of the earth for five months, and men will seek to destroy the army of demon locusts with modern technology and sophisticated armaments. However, all attempts will fail.

v. 12 *"One woe is past; and, behold, there come two woes more hereafter."*

Sixth Trumpet: "Two Hundred Million Army" vv. 13-21
v. 14 *"The Euphrates river"* is first mentioned in Genesis during Adam and Eve's time. It was one of the four rivers named in Paradise, Genesis 2:14. Moses says, "On the same day the Lord made a covenant with Abraham, saying, unto thy seed have I given this land, from the river of Egypt unto the great river, the river Euphrates" (Genesis 15:18).

The ancient city of Babylon refers to the operations of Satan and will again emerge in the future. Babylon's location is near the Euphrates river, where the four angels are bound. The Ancient Roman Empire also saw it that way. The region just to the west of the Euphrates called the Far East or Asia. The region to the east of the Euphrates is called Asia Minor or the Near East.

The second woe is worse than the first. An army of 200 million horsemen (demons) leads by four angels bound in the Euphrates River[23]. It is suggested that each angel would have 50 million horsemen of demons, and their campaign would be global from the four cardinal directions.

v.13 *"And the sixth angel sounded,"* and commencement of the second woe begins.
The forces of evil will sweep through the land, brings havoc on the unbelievers. Demonic possession will be more prevalent than ever before. The prayers of the saints are about to be answered. "The souls of the martyrs cry out to God, how long must they wait to be vindicated of the truth and their blood they had shed," (cf. Revelation 6:9-11, 17:6, 18:24).

The Golden Altar is where the Levite priests were commanded by God to burn incense every morning and evening; simultaneously, the daily burnt offering was made, Exodus 30:34-38. The incense served as a sweet aroma to the Lord. The incense's odor is symbolic of the prayer of the saints (Psalms 141:2; Isaiah 56:7; Revelation 8:3-4).

The Army of Two Hundred Million Horsemen: A Third of Humanity Dies **(vv. 15-19)**
v. 14 "Loose the four angels bound in the great river Euphrates" These four anonymous wicked angels are bound in the Euphrates river near Baghdad, Iraq. They are held there until God's chosen time of release. They are the four commanders of the *"two hundred thousand thousands"*

---

23   Note: The Euphrates River will dry up under the Sixth Vial in Revelation 16:12-14. In the war of Armageddon invasion against Israel by an enormous army from the king of the East.

[two hundred million] supernatural armies that will carry out their invasion on humanity. The context gives clues that these angels are bound in the Euphrates river and indicates they are fallen angels and not God's sons. Some argue that the two hundred million horsemen refer to the Red China Army of the East and other armies of the world combined.

v. 15 *"And the four angels were loosed, which were prepared for an hour, and a day, and a month, and a year, for to slay the third part of men,"* These angels will lay dormant for 391 days and 60 minutes to invade earth by the executive order of God. An estimated 2.3 billion people will perish under the second woe judgment.

v.18 *"By these three was the third part of men killed, by the fire, and by the smoke, and by the brimstone, which issued out of their mouths"*

The Earth's Populace Diminish: "The Wrath of God"

- Fourth Seal Judgment: fourth of the earth's populace dies, (Revelation 6:7-8).
- Third Trumpet Judgment: Many men will die because of a lack of water supplies (Revelation 8:10-11).
- Sixth Trumpet / second woe Judgment: third of the earth's populace dies, (Revelation 9:13-21).
- Seven Bowl/vial Judgment: Many dies because of the Great earthquake (Revelation 16:1-21).
- "Upon the wicked he shall rain snares, fire and brimstone, and a horrible tempest, this shall be the portion of their cup" (Psalm 11:6).

The Defiant Heart of the Wicked (vv.20 -21)
The second woe sixth trumpet judgment claims the life of one-third of the earth's populace by "fire," "smoke," and "brimstone." These elements of natural disaster are used in God's divine judgment.

"The rest of the men" that survive the seals and trumpets judgment. Even with disasters that humanity on the earth experienced, they still refuse

to acknowledge God and prefer to die than repent. They continued worshiping images of the Antichrist, idolatry, they continued to murder, engage in sexual sins and looting.

> Jesus says, "except that the Lord had shortened those days, no flesh should be saved: but for the elect's sake, whom he hath chosen, he hath shortened the days" (Mark 13:20).

The future and past judgments seem to be a pattern: "fire," "smoke," and "brimstone."

- "Then the LORD rained upon Sodom and Gomorrah brimstone and fire from the LORD out of heaven" (Genesis 19:24).
- "Moses stretched out his staff toward the sky, and the LORD sent thunder and hail, fire ran down to the earth, and the LORD rained hail on Egypt's land" (Exodus 9:23).
- "Upon the wicked, He will rain snares; Fire and brimstone and burning wind will be the portion of their cup" (Psalm 11:6)
- "From the brightness before Him passed His thick clouds, hailstones, and coals of fire" (Psalm 18:12).
- "For the LORD will execute judgment by fire and by His sword on all flesh, and those slain by the LORD will be many" (Isaiah 66:16).
- "A clamor has come to the end of the earth; because the LORD has a controversy with the nations, He is entering into judgment with all flesh; as for the wicked, He has given them to the sword, declares the LORD" (Jeremiah 25:31).

CHAPTER TEN
THE MIGHTY ANGEL AND THE LITTLE SCROLL

The Second "Parenthesis Period"[24]

The Mighty Angel with the Little Book (vv. 1-7)
The Scene on Earth vv. 1-4

The four mysteries of God:

- Who is this mighty Angel? v.1
- What did the seven thunders utter? v. 4
- What is the mystery of God? v.7
- What are the contents of the little book? vv. 8-11

---

24 The second parenthesis coming between the sixth seal and seventh trumpet
Judgment: (1) The small scroll (Revelation 10:1-11, (2) The two Witnesses (11:1-14).

The First Mystery: Who is this mighty Angel?
John sees another angel that was different from all the previous angels. This mighty angel has Godlike attributes "clothed with a cloud," "crowned with a rainbow," "his face was as it were the sun," and "his feet as pillars of fire."

v.1. "Another mighty Angel" had a similar description of Jesus' title in the Old Testament as the "Angel of the Lord." The theophanies of Jesus Christ in the Old Testament:

1. He appears to Jacob (Genesis 31:11).
2. He appears to Abraham (Genesis 16:7-14).
3. He appears to Moses in the burning bush (Exodus 3:2-4).
4. Appears to Balaam (Numbers 22:22-38).

"Another" (Gk. *Allos*), translated as another of similar type or the same kind, means that this Angel is not like the angels of the seals and trumpet judgments, but instead a higher-ranking angel. He is an intelligent being and mighty in power but still limited in power compared to God and Christ.

"Clothed with a cloud" describes the manifestation of God's Shekinah Glory and hidden in greatness. The cloud also conceals God's Glory (cf. Exodus 13:21-22, 1 Kings 8:12, Job 38:9 Psalms 97:2, 18:11). The Mighty Angel is robed in a cloud similar to God. Jesus' ascension to heaven was in a cloud (Acts 1:9).

A rainbow was upon his head, bring to mind the rainbow that encircles the throne of God (Ezekiel 1, Revelation 4:3). The Angel has a rainbow crowned on his head. John sees him standing on the sea and earth, but not on a throne.

His face was as it were the sun, indicating God's deity, a divine, righteous being constant in the Creator's presence (cf. Exodus 34:35, Daniel 12:3, Matthew 7:2). The mighty Angel has similar attributes of God and Christ. The face of Christ is like the sun (Matthew 17:2-5, Revelation 1:16). God is light (Ezekiel 1:28,8:2, 1 John 1:5).

His feet as pillars of fire, symbolizes of judgment (Revelation 1:15).

If John had not specifically called him "another mighty angel." Jesus would not come into mind. In other words, the mighty Angel has a rainbow aura and attributes of deity about him and could easily be mistaken as God or the Lamb.

Many scholars would interpret this mighty Angel as "Jesus Christ" because of Godlike appearance. The New Testament canon never introduces Christ as an angel. However, He was known as the Angel of the Lord or the Captain of Hosts in the Old Testament.

This suggests that the mighty Angel fits the description of the Archangel Michael. He is known as the protector of Israel and associated with the Book of Daniel (cf. Daniel 10:13, 21, 12:1; Jude 1; Revelation 12:7-9).

Archangel means "Chief of the Angels." He is the commander of the Lord's army of angels in heaven. He is also the personal protector of Israel (Daniel 12:1).

The name "Michael" (Heb. *Mikael*) means "Who is like God?" He is the only Archangel who is named in the Bible. Gabriel's name is mention in both the Old and New Testament. The Archangel Michael's appearance could be easily mistaken for God. God created him expressly to reflect many of His attributes visibly. However, the mighty Angel mentioned here could be any other powerful angel in the highest ranks of the Seraphim not known to man.

The mighty Angel stands astride with his left foot on the land and his right foot on the sea as one who is sovereign over both land and sea. God's Wrath is a connection with the first two trumpet judgments. Michael is acting on behalf of God and the Lamb with a scroll-like a book in his hand already opened and prepared to read the little book's contents. The little book seems small compared to the stature of the mighty Angel astride over both land and sea. The scroll book with the seven seals was opened by the Lamb of God (Revelation 5:2). The little book is in the context that was introduce by a mighty Angel, and contents are undisclosed.

The Second Mystery: What the Seven Thunders Uttered?
John understood those things that the seven thunders uttered, for he was about to write them down. However, before he could, "a voice" (singular) says to John" writes them not." This suggests that the mighty Angel that spoke like a lion and the seven thunders that uttered new revelation were subordinate to the voice that told John to seal up those things uttered and write them not.

The voice that spoke to John was God or Christ. Another mighty angel was identified as high-ranking angels, and the seven thunder voices are plural *"their voices."* The voices of the seven thunders are anonymous. The Bible does not disclose what the seven thunders uttered. His wisdom has withheld them from our understanding; has not revealed to us what they are.

> Isaiah was told, "the entire vision will be to you like the words of a sealed book" (Isaiah 29:11).

> Daniel was also told "to conceal these words and seal up the book" (Daniel 12:4).

> Daniel was also told, "Son of man, understand that the vision pertains to the time of the end, (Daniel 8:17)

> This time, the voice told John, "do not seal up the words of prophecy in this book..." (Revelation 22:10).

The Third Mystery vv. 5-7_
The mighty Angel swore by God Almighty indicates that he is not a deity but an angel. Time has run out for humanity to receive the mystery of God. The time of the end is rapidly approaching. When the seventh trumpet has sounded, the world will move toward fulfilling all the Bible prophecies without any delay. The mystery of God's that Jesus will fulfill the Old Testament prophecies about His second coming and

the establishment of His Kingdom on earth; put an end to Satan and his activities. God's King over the whole universe, Heaven and the earth, but He never reigned on earth as King to present.

Jesus is King over the whole universe but never reigned on earth as King at present.

From generation to generation, millenniums have passed. The world is waiting for Christ's second return. Nevertheless, He has not come yet.

> "Surely the Lord God will do nothing, but he revealeth his secret unto his servants the prophets" (Amos 3:7).

> "And the Lord shall be king over all the earth: in that day shall there be one Lord, and his name one" (Zechariah 14:9)

> "For he hath put all things under his feet. But when he saith all things are put under him, it is manifest that he is excepted, which did put all things under him. And when all things shall be subdued unto him, then shall the Son also himself be subject unto him that put all things under him, that God may be all in all" (1 Corinthians 15:27-28).

> "Now to him that is of power to establish you according to my gospel, and the preaching of Jesus Christ, according to the revelation of the mystery, which was kept secret since the world began, But now is made manifest, and by the scriptures of the prophets, according to the commandment of the everlast God, made known to all nations for the obedience of faith," (Romans 16:25-26).

God designated the right time that Jesus Christ will unite all things in heaven and on earth under His sovereignty (cf. Colossians 2:2-3, Ephesians 1:9-10, 1 Corinthians 2:7, Revelation 2:7).

One of God's mysteries is that the Gentiles will also hear the gospel of Jesus Christ and accept salvation (Ephesians 3:5-6).

"Even the mystery which hath been hid from ages and generations, but now is made manifest to his saints; to whom God would made known what is the riches of the glory of this mystery among the Gentiles; which Christ in you, the hope of glory: Whom we preach, warning every man, and teaching every man in all wisdom; that we may present every man perfect in Christ Jesus," (Colossians 1:26-28).

The Fourth Mystery: What are the contents in the little book? (vv.8-11) The third time we have been reminded of the Angel standing on the sea and land. John was commanded to take the little book from the hand of the mighty Angel. Here is another reason why this mighty Angel is not God or Jesus in chapter 5:6-9; it states, "who is worthy to take the scroll from the hand of God, only the Lamb was worthy."

John eats the little book as directed by the angel. This prophecy had been told and read by many peoples, nations, and provided in different tongues worldwide. Prophecies fulfilled in the gift of the Book of Revelation. By eating the small book, God is saying to John, "the knowledge in little book contents will be told to people, nations, and kings at God-appointed time."

The little book is God's divine revelation given to John to tells all that will hear. It was sweet to John's soul but will be bitter to those who disobey God's words and reject it. Both Ezekiel and Jeremiah shared a similar experience of eating a book's content and being told the information within (cf. Ezekiel 2:9-10, 3:1-4, 3:14, Jeremiah 15:11-18, Psalms 19:10-11).

CHAPTER ELEVEN

THE TWO WITNESSES AND THE LAST TRUMPET

Interlude: The Scene Continues on Earth **vv.** 1-14

Measuring the Temple of God (vv. 1-2)
The parenthetic between the sixth and seventh trumpets continues,
two more visions are seen. John is given a reed and told to measure

the Temple of God, the altar, and those worshipping there. He was instructed not to measure the court outside the, for it has been given to the Gentiles who will tread underfoot the holy city of Jerusalem will undergo great persecution during the Jewish war, which lasted about 42 months.

v. 1 "A reed is like unto a rod" "reed" (Gk. *Kalamos*) translates as a measuring rod. A reed is about nine feet in length (six cubits) (Ezekiel 40:5). The rod is an instrument, like a reed used for measuring length. It was a tool used to measure the Temple, the furniture, the altar, and those worshiped therein. Also, a rod signified an act of judgment and was used to measure those who enter into God's holiest place.

"Rise, and measure the temple of God," the third Temple erected at the end of the church age or the beginning of the Tribulation (cf. Ezekiel 40-48; Daniel 9:26-27,12:11; Matthew 24:1-2,5; 2 Thessalonians 2:1-4).

The destruction of the two Temples in Jerusalem:

- The first Temple, destroyed by the Babylonians in 587 B.C.
- The second Temple, destroyed by the Romans in 70 A.D.
- For over 2000 years, Jews have prayed for the rebuilding of the third Temple.

The Gentiles received the outer courtyard outside of the Temple because they did not measure up to God's standard. They were intentionally omitted from the measurement of the holy things within the Temple wall and left out because of their role during the Tribulation period.

Jesus explained the Gentiles' role in (Luke 21:24) "And they shall fall by the edge of the sword and shall be led away captive into all nations: and Jerusalem shall be trodden down by the Gentiles until the times of the Gentiles be fulfilled."

John used the idiom "tread down" (Gk. *Pateo*), meaning to trample, crush with the feet, or desecrate the holy city by devastation and outrage. They will sacrilege the third Temple and the Holy City of Jerusalem.

The city left in ruins; sacred artifacts trample and destroyed the house of God.

Daniel's prophecy states, "Then I heard one saint speaking, and another saint said unto that certain saint which spake, how long shall be the vision concerning the daily sacrifice, and the transgression of desolation, to give both the sanctuary and the host to be trodden under foot?" (Daniel 8:13).

These Gentiles nations are a part of the Antichrist and the new world order. They will be given 42 months to do as they please. God will use them as an instrument to bring Israel to repentance and accept their Messiah. God patterns of ancient past using the Gentiles nations to discipline His people: (1) Assyrians, (2) Babylonians, (3) Persian, (4) Grecians, (5) Romans, and others.

"Altar" refers to the brazen altar in the court where others could come to make their sacrifices.

The Two Witnesses (vv. 3 -6)
"I will give power unto My two witnesses," John never mentions the identity of two witnesses in his writing, but there a few views to consider:

1. Enoch and Elijah, the only two men in history who ascend to heaven without dying in their natural bodies (cf. Genesis 5:23-24; 2 Kings 2:11; Hebrews 11:5).
   - "And as it is appointed unto men once to die, but after this the judgment" (Hebrews 9:27).
   - Two witnesses experience death (Revelation 1:7-12).

2. Elijah and Moses are a pattern of Old Testament judgment.
   - Elijah calls fire down from heaven, (Revelation 11:5-6).
   - Moses turns the Niles river into blood and similar plagues on Egypt.
   - Moses dies on Mount Nebo, and God buries him privately (Deuteronomy 34:1-6).

- Elijah and Moses are seen at the Mount of Transfiguration with Christ (Matthew 17:2; Mark 9:2-3).
- Elijah will come again at the latter end of the Tribulation period (Malachi 4:5-6).
- The contextual evidence of God's abilities to raise the dead to life again is compelling (cf.1 Kings 17:2, 17-22; 2 Kings 4:32-35; Matthew 27:50-53; Luke 7:11-15, 8:41:49; John 11:44; Acts 9:36-41, 20:9-10).
- The Malachi prophecy would be fulfilled here in verses 3-6 on his return.
- John the Baptist was thought to be Elijah because he came in Elijah's spirit and power (Luke 1:17 and Matthew 11:14).
- A dispute between Archangel Michael and Satan over Moses's whereabouts (Jude 1:9).

3. If not Elijah, Enoch or Moses, then who might the two witnesses be? Can a conclusion be reached that is based on substantial Biblical evidence rather than on comparisons and assumptions?

Moses would most likely be the best candidate as the second witness. Moses was the last of all the tribesmen to die and was buried in a valley in Moab's land.

v. 3 *"they shall prophesy a thousand two hundred and threescore days"* refers to (1) 1260 days (2) 42 months (3) 3 ½ years.

- The Jewish calendar has 29.5 –30 days per month, depending upon the month of the year.
- A Prophetic year is "composed of 360 days. "They shall prophesy a thousand two hundred and threescore days, clothed in sackcloth" (Revelation 11:3).
- "The woman [Israel] fled into the wilderness… a thousand two hundred and threescore days" (Revelation 12:6).
- "Power was given unto him [Antichrist] to continue forty and two months" (Revelation 13:5).

- "Change times and law: they shall be given into his hand until a time [1 year] and times [2 years] and the dividing of time [1 divide by ½ = ½ year]," (Daniel 7:25).
- "Swear by him that liveth forever that it shall be for a time, times, and a half, and when he shall have accomplished to scatter the power of the holy people, all these things shall be finished, (Daniel 12:14, Revelation 12:14).
- Hebrew calendar: one month is equivalent to 30 days.

Clothed in sackcloth, "Sackcloth is a coarse, black cloth made from goat's hair that was worn together with the burnt ashes of wood as a sign of mourning for personal and national disaster, it was also worn as a sign of repentance and at times of prayer for deliverance." The two witnesses will deliver a strong message of repentance to the world leaders and a final warning.

v. 4 "The two olive trees and two candlesticks standing before God."

The two olive trees in the Old Testament:

(1) Zerubbabel, the appointed Governor of Judah.
(2) Joshua, the High Priest (Zechariah 4:3,9-11).

Olive trees provide oil and light to the candlesticks in a dark world. The Holy Spirit's central role in providing the two lamps of Israel with the power and strength needed to accomplish all tasks.

The two witnesses whom God elect will be Jesus representative for 1260 days at the beginning of the Tribulation period. Moses represents the Law, and Elijah represents the Prophets in the Spirit of Christ teaching and preaching on earth. The Holy Spirit's work will be demonstrated through the two witnesses without measure. The Holy Spirit symbolizes the oil energy for the two lampstands of Israel.

Elijah	Moses	Revelation 11 (The Two Witnesses)
Perform recorded 16 miracles.	Ten plagues of Egypt (Ex. 7-12)	To smite the earth with all plagues, as often as they will.
Power over Jordan river (2 Kings 2:8)	First Plague: Turn the Nile river into blood (Ex.7:14-25)	Power over waters to turn them to blood
Control the weather (1 Kings 18:41)	Seventh Plague: Hailstorm (Ex. 9:13-35)	Rain not in the days of their prophecy
Drought (1 Kings 17:1, James 5:17)	Eighth Plague: Locust invasion (Ex.10:1-20)	Power to shut heaven
Sacrifice consumed by fire (1 Kings 18:38)	Ninth Plague: Darkness (Ex. 10:21-29)	Fire proceeded out of their mouths.
Directed at the false prophets, priests of Baal and the god Baal (1 Kings 18:41-45)	Tenth Plague: Directed at the gods of Egypt; Pharaoh and all the first males born of Egypt (Ex. 11:1-12:36)	Directed at the Antichrist, False Prophet, Satan, and unbelievers.

Figure 12 Moses and Elijah's Work Correlated with The Judgment in Revelation 11.

The Beast out of the Bottomless Pit (vv. 7-10)
v.7 The beast out of the bottomless pit- Satan himself. The idiom "Beast" is referenced 36 times in the Book Revelation. The unholy trinity: Satan (Beast from the Pit), Antichrist, Beast from the sea, (Revelation 13:1), False Prophet or the religious leader, Beast from the Earth, (Revelation 13:11).

The Two Witnesses are Killed (vv. 8-10)
At the ending of the three and a half years, the scene changes. The beast who comes up from the bottomless pit kills the two witnesses of God. Their ravaged bodies are left in the streets of Jerusalem for all to see. The slaughter takes place at the hand of the beast. Jerusalem,

"the Holy city," then turns into a city of sinful decadence, tyranny, and selfishness for three days and a half. Also, the Antichrist, the beast, and the world celebrated the two prophets' death by exchanging gifts. The two prophet's death will be televised on all networks around the world.

On May 6th, 2011, when the notorious terrorist "Osama Bin Laden" was slain by the American Navy Seals. People around the world celebrated and rejoiced over his death. The President of the United States of America said, "We got our man."

v. 8 Jerusalem is called the spiritual city of "*Sodom and Egypt*" because both Sodom and Egypt were a part of Israel's history. The "great city" here in v. 8 is not to be mistaken as the Great Harlot in (Revelation 17:18), which refers to Babylon as "the great city." Sodom was a great city destroyed for her wickedness and homosexuality (Genesis 18-19). Egypt was not a city in ancient days, but an empire.

(1) Sodom was a city of "*sexual immorality*" (Genesis 18:20). Sodom may also be a symbol of warning and an example of God's people fleeing the coming wrath at His second coming (Luke 17:29-32; Matthew 24:15-18).

(2) Egypt was "a *materialistic empire* "of antiquity. The Egyptians held Israel in captivity and oppression for over four hundred years as slaves (Exodus 1-15). The name Egypt refers to a place of idolatry and many gods.

The Resurrection of the Two Witnesses (vv. 11-12)
The Spirit of Life entered into their nostrils, and the two will stand up on their feet as if they had never died. The world will stand in awe, and trepidation will grasp their hearts and minds. In that same hour, a great voice from heaven will say, "come up hither" A cloud will cover them as they ascend to heaven. The two witnesses will levitate out of sight of their adversaries.

Parallel to Christ's ascension, "And when he had spoken these things, while they beheld, he was taken up; and a cloud received him out of their sight. And while they looked steadfastly toward heaven as he went up, behold, two men stood by them in white apparel" (Acts 1:9-10).

The world will be in a panic, and their hearts will beat with fear! Their resurrection confirms them as men of the true God, and then silence will come, followed by a great earthquake. It will be the first time in modern history that the voice of God will be heard worldwide. Over 70,000 citizens will be present in the city of Jerusalem when this event occurs. Within the same hour that second woe passes, there will be a great earthquake.

A great earthquake rumbles the city, slaying a tenth of the city's residents. His splendid work broadcasts on live networks, social media, and the internet to send a strong message to the unbelievers.

v.13 *"gave glory to the God of Heaven"* He receives the glory, and fears fell on all who observed the acts of God. However, the condition of the heart will not result in repentance. The *"God of Heaven"* is mentioned twenty-one times in the Old Testament, and two times in (Revelation 11:13, 16:1).

v. 14 *"The second woe is past; and, behold, the third woe cometh quickly."* The Tribulation period is coming to an end, and the stage of the reign of Christ comes quickly.

The Seventh Trumpet and the Third Woe (vv. 15-19)
The Scene in Heaven

v. 15 *"And the seventh angel sounded; and there were great voices in heaven, saying, The kingdoms of this world are become the kingdoms of our Lord, and of his Christ, and he shall reign forever and ever."*

Jesus taught his disciples to pray, "After this manner therefore pray ye: Our Father which art in heaven, Hallowed be thy name. *"Thy kingdom come,"* thy will be done on earth, as it is in heaven" (Matthew 6:9-10).

"The kingdoms of the world become the Kingdom of Christ" The kingdoms of the world are currently under siege by Satan and have always been since Adam's fall. However, the time nears that all of Christ's enemies will be underneath His footstool.

The heavenly hosts prostrate and worship God, chanting, "He shall reign forever and ever, amen."

David writes, "The LORD said unto my Lord, sit thou at my right hand until I make Thine enemies thy footstool" (Psalms 110:1).

"The LORD said unto my Lord, sit thou on my right hand, till I make thine enemies thy footstool" (Matthew 23:44).

According to 1 Samuel 8:11-19, Israel's demands for a king to rule over them. Israel rejected Samuel and went against God. The LORD warns them of the danger of asking for a king without His approval.

In the context, verse 8 illustrates that the demand for a king could lead to idolatry because their spirit is the same as when they left Egypt. Therefore, the time is near that Jesus Christ will soon rule as King over Israel with a rod of iron.

The Worship of the Twenty-Four Elders (vv. 16-17)
The Twenty-four elders prostrate before God's throne and give Him thanks for answering the saints' prayer of all ages, along with God's judgment against sin.

"Thou shalt break them with a rod of iron; thou shalt dash them in pieces like a potter's vessel" (Psalm 2:9). The Messianic prophecy fulfilled in (v. 17) Jesus Christ, the anointed King of the House of David who will reign over all the earth.

"Which art, and wast, and art to come," indicates that God is the Eternal One. Hebrews 13:8 explains this idiom as: "Jesus is the same yesterday, and today, and forever."

The Beginning of God's Wrath v. 18

"*And the nation were angry, and thy wrath* is come - the unbelieving nations which have been enraged because of God's judgments and the resurrection of the two witnesses who were pronouncing those plagues seek retaliation on God people. The Antichrist compels them to make war against Israel (Revelation 16:14-16, 17:14, 19:19). Their failure to acquiesce to God results in their destruction.

Psalm 2:1-2 speaks of an angry response from the nations when God enthrones His Son as King of the nations. The reason the nations are enraged is that Jesus' lordship demands submission and recognition of His sovereignty which the nations reject (Revelation 16:9).

"*Your wrath has come*" God's wrath is expressed in the bowl judgments, (Revelation 15:1). God's judgment involves the righteous dead only. A necessary event before Jesus second coming and Armageddon war. The bowl judgments constitute the beginning of Christ's eternal reign on earth, and the destruction of Satan's temporary reign.

"*Destroying those who destroy the earth*" The word "*destroy*" has a wide-ranging meaning: (1) those who corrupt (2) most claim a figurative meaning here. The sense is those who morally ruin the earth. God will physically destroy those who have corrupted the people. The bowl judgments constitute the beginning of Christ's reign on earth, the destruction of Antichrist supremacy.

Three classifications of "the righteous" during the Tribulation period:

1. Two Jewish prophets (Revelation 10:7).
2. The ordinary believers or "saints" trigger the sequence of seven trumpets (Revelation 5:8; 8:3-4).
3. The unbelievers will learn discipline during the Tribulation period and the sequence of God's judgments. They will come to know that God is the Creator of the Universe and Supreme Ruler over all things (Revelation11:11-13).

As these events begin to unfold, judgment fall on the Babylon systems: the great city and the fall of the ecclesiastical and commercial systems (Revelation 14:8-11, 16-18).

v. 19 *"The temple of God"* at Jerusalem was the Temple's pattern in Heaven (Hebrews 8:1-5). John, possibly, looked into the abode of heaven saw the Glory of God as a vision of the real Temple opened in heaven.

"The ark of his testament," the original ark of his testament observed in heaven, indicates "the righteousness of God." Moreover, the copy of the heavenly pattern was given to Moses while in the wilderness (Exodus 25:10-22).

The Lost Ark of the Covenant
Moses and Aaron were commanded by the LORD to "preserve Manna, and the two tablets of stone containing the written laws" (Exodus 16:34, 25:21; 1Kings 8:9; Hebrews 9:2-5).

The last time the Ark of the Covenant spoke was about circa 586 B.C. It seems that it disappeared sometime before the Babylonian Captivity in the 6th century B.C. Often, we ask when the Ark of the Covenant disappears, and why did God allow it? The Bible does not say why God allowed the Ark of the Covenant to vanish. God's will is mysterious and generally only known to Him.
In Jeremiah 3:12-16, God told Jeremiah His Prophetic Plan for Israel's nation once they returned to their land. He tells him that the Ark of the Covenant will not be available to them.

"there were lightnings, and voices, and thunderings, and an earthquake, and great hail" The similarity of the last trumpet chapter 11:19 and last seventh seal chapter 8:5.

Both judgments followed by (1) lightning, (2) voices, (3) thunders, and (4) an earthquake, which symbolize the divine Majesty of God's presence (Exodus 20:19-20).

CHAPTER TWELVE

THE WOMAN AND THE DRAGON IN HEAVEN

The Third "Parenthesis Period"[25]

---

25 The third Parenthesis comes between the seventh trumpet and the vial judgments, reveals seven personalities in Chapter 12: (1) The Sun Clothed woman (2) The Dragon (3) The Man Child (4) The Archangel (5) The Jewish Remnant; Chapter 13 (6) The Beast out of the Sea (7) The Beast out of the earth.

The Woman and The Dragon (vv. 1-6)

A Great Wonder: The Woman
v. 1 *"The first Great wonder,"* the term a great *"wonder"* (Gk. *Semeion)* means a sign, miracle, or token. The context describes the sign as a *"maga semeion"* in Greek because of its greatness compared to signs he had witnessed beforehand. According to James Strong, a great wonder "authenticates the Lord and His eternal purpose, especially doing what man cannot replicate to take credit for." The word is frequently translated as miracle, (cf. Luke 23:8; John 4:54; Revelation 12:3; 13:14; 15:1; 16:14-16; 19:20).

Double Reference Prophecy
The great wonder has already taken place at Christ's birth and will occur again on earth as a sign of "Jacob's trouble" or "birth pangs," indicating that the world is approaching the Tribulation period. The climax will intensify, like a woman in labor pains. The woman is a picture of Israel persecuted during the Tribulation. Israel constitutes the ancestral seed of Jacob as God's chosen nation.

"Surely the Lord GOD will do nothing, but he revealeth his secret unto his servants the prophets" (Amos 3:7).

"A woman clothed with the sun" This woman is associated with many different figures in the Bible, namely Eve, the mother of humanity who gives birth to the offspring that will overthrow the serpent and now serpent is on the trail trying to kill her offspring before he born.

> In Genesis 3:15, "And I will put enmity between thee and the woman, and between thy seed and her seed [offspring]; it shall bruise thy head [serpent], and thou shalt bruise his heel.

The woman has traits of Mary, who give birth to the Messiah. The incident in Matthew's nativity narrative (2:16-18), Herod, the king of Judea, orders a death decree of all male children two years old.

The woman could represent the old Israel of the covenant and the child as the church portraited as the new covenant and the Roman empire as the dragon seeking to destroy the church. The woman could be portrait as the church and the Christians as the child, whom Satan seeks to devour.

The woman here in verse one symbolizes the nation of Israel. Throughout the Old Testament, Israel refers to a woman (Isaiah 26:18, 54:1-6 Jeremiah 4:31, 31:32, Ezekiel 16:32, Hosea 2:16). John's reference to the sun, moon, and stars in the woman's description is similar Joseph dream in (Genesis 37:9-11).

"the moon under her feet, and upon her head a crown of twelve stars" Joseph explained his vision "And he (Joseph) dreamed yet another dream, and told it to his brethren, and said, Behold, I have dreamed a dream more; and, behold, the sun and the moon and the eleven stars made obeisance to me. And he told it to his father, and to his brethren: and his father rebuked him, and said unto him, what is this dream that thou hast dreamed? Shall I and thy mother and thy brethren indeed come to bow down ourselves to thee to the earth?" (Genesis 37:9-10).

- The sun reflects the brilliant glory of God, showing Israel as His chosen nation.
- The sun represents Joseph's father, Jacob.
- The moon shows his mother Rachel as the mother of Joseph, the dreamer.
- She wears a "crown" (*Gk. Stephanos*) with honor and glory, representing triumph over her enemies.
- The eleven stars represent his brothers, the tribes of Israel.
- The woman can be identified in association with the fulfillment of the Abrahamic covenant and it will be fulfilled during the millennial reign.
- Israel is the source in which the blessing of God comes (Romans 3:2).

v.2 *"And she being with child cried, travailing in birth, and pained to be delivered."* The pain described refers to travail of Israel at the time of

Christ's birth under Roman occupation and oppression by Herod the Great (Matthew 2:13-23).

Another Wonder: The Red Dragon
v.3 "And there appeared another wonder in heaven" there appeared another wonder" in heaven, not more significant than the first in verse one.

"Behold a great red dragon" The dragon is Satan's invisible form, and the beast is his visible form. The dragon makes up the worldly Empires and represents Satanic power (Revelation 9, 20:2). The color "Red" could refer to shedding the blood of humanity, or murder. The first shedding of innocent blood was introduced by Lucifer, in the biblical narrative of Cain slaying Abel, (cf. Genesis 4:1-16, 9:6; Deuteronomy 19:10, Psalm 79:10; Proverbs 6:17-19; Isaiah 59:7-8, John 8:84).

Three Beasts that Match this Description:

1.   The Red Dragon, which is Satan (Revelation 12:3).
2.   The Beast from the sea, which is the Antichrist (Revelation 13).
3.   The harlot is riding on the scarlet beast (Revelation 17).

"Having seven heads" A Great Red Dragon is depicted as having "seven heads": the mountains of government, kingdoms or empires (Revelation 13; 17).

The "ten horns" symbolize the governmental power of the beast over the ten kings.

The *"seven crowns"* (Gk. Diadema) which describes them as "kingly crowns," are the type of crowns worn by the seven kings in the Great Tribulation period.

The Great Red Dragon represents the nation or government, which Satan has used to persecute God's people (cf. Daniel 7:7, Revelation 13:1,17:3,7-10). The beast with seven heads and ten horns has always referenced Satan and his evil influence (Revelation 13:1).

The Legendary Sea Dragon: Leviathan
The Leviathan (Hebrew *"Livyathan"*) of the book of Job was a legendary beast that God created to rule the sea, and the behemoth was a massive beast to rule the land. God was the only thing to control them (Job 40-41). The Leviathan of the Middle Ages was used as an image of Satan, endangering God's creatures in the sea by attempting to eat them and threatening the harmony in the water.

The Leviathan, a mythical sea creature, occurs six times in the Bible as a metaphor to a dragon, serpent, and a powerful sea monster (Job 3:8, 41:1; Psalm 74:14, 104:26, Isaiah 27:1).

> "In that day the Lord with his sore and great and strong sword shall punish leviathan the piercing serpent, even leviathan that crooked serpent; and he shall slay the dragon that is in the sea" (Isaiah 27:1).

The Leviathan creature roamed the sea, breathing fire and spewing smoke from his nostrils." Yahweh then created the universe, day and night, and the four seasons. Scriptural references to the end of time say that the flesh of Leviathan will be part of a feast served on the Day of Judgment." [26]

> "Thou brakest the heads of leviathan in pieces, and gavest him to be meat to the people inhabiting the wilderness" (Psalm 74:14).

> "So is this great and wide sea, wherein are things creeping innumerable, both small and great beasts. There go the ships: there is that leviathan, whom thou hast made to play therein. These wait all upon thee; that thou mayest give them their meat in due season" (Psalm 104:25-27).

---

26 Leviathan Myths Encyclopedia forum.

Third Part of the Stars: Fallen angels
v. 4 *"And his tail drew the third part of the stars of heaven"* Isaiah describes the Dragon as Lucifer, "How are thou fallen from heaven, O Lucifer, son of the morning! How art thou cut down to the ground, which didst weakens the nations! For thou hast said in thine heart, I will ascend into heaven; I will exalt my throne above the stars of God: I will also sit upon the mount of the congregation on the side of the north: I will ascend above the heights of the clouds; I will be like the most high" (Isaiah 14:12-14).

Summary of the fall of Lucifer (Satan):

- The Prophets, Ezekiel, and Isaiah give Lucifer's narrative of leading one-third of the morning stars into rebellion (cf. Job 38:7; Isaiah 14, Ezekiel 28).
- Jesus confirms the fall of Lucifer (Luke 10:18).
- John describes the fall of Lucifer as a shooting star to earth (Revelation 9:1).
- Sometime before man's creation, many other angels rebelled, losing their light status and becoming fallen angels (Jeremiah 4:23-28).

The beast here is Satan, who seeks to devour and destroy Christ at His birth. He influences Rome's Pagans to slaughter all the children, two years of age and under (Matthew 2:16). Later, Satan influence the Jewish religious leaders and others to kill Jesus (Mark 15:6-15). Our Lord dies on the cross and rose again on the third day (Romans 8:34, 1 Corinthians 15:3-8). He was seen for forty days and ascended His Father in Heaven (John 20:17, Mark 16:19, Acts 1:3).

> "I will put enmity between thee and woman and between thy seed and her, and her seed; it shall bruise thy head, and thou shalt bruise his heel." (Genesis 3:15).

> "Thou didst divide the sea by thy strength: thou breakest the head of the dragons in the waters. Thou brakest the heads of Leviathan in pieces and gavest him to be meat to the people inhabiting the wilderness" (Psalms 74:13-14).

The Man Child: Jesus Christ

v. 5 *"Who [Christ]was to rule all nations with a rod of iron"* (cf. Psalm 2:9, Revelation 19:15). Isaiah 7:14 reads, "Therefore the Lord Himself will give you a sign: Behold; the virgin shall conceive and bear a Son, and shall call His name Immanuel," and this prophecy fulfilled in Matthew 1:22-23.

Jesus rules all the nations of the earth during the Millennial kingdom and serves as "King of kings and Lord of Lords" for 1,000 years. king David serves as His co-regent (1 Chronicles 22:9-10; 1 Kings 9:5; Psalm 22:28; Daniel 2:21; Matthew 28:18; Acts 17:26 and Ephesians 1:22).

Jesus' Millennium kingdom consists of both mortal and immortal human beings. The mortal is those who survive the Tribulation period. The immortals are the saints who return with Christ and the angels at the Second Coming (Revelation 19:20). The Antichrist and the beast of the earth cast alive in the Lake of fire. The coming King Jesus destroyed the world's armies. Satan banishes to the pit in chains for a short season. The new Jerusalem comes down to earth and hovers over the old Jerusalem ruins. Then Jesus will establish His theocratic government and separate the nations. Summers said, "Some scholars of the continuous-historical school deny this, viewing the woman as the Church, and the Man-child as the sons and daughters born of the church's travail." [27]

L.S. White writes, "The child is a symbol of faithful Christians, and the woman is the church of the Living God."[28]

"Her was caught up unto God, and to his throne" the Man-Child was slain and resurrected. He was seen among the living for forty days and was *"caught up"* unto God, and seated on His right side (cf. John 13:1-3, 14:2-4, 16:28, 17:4-5; Acts 1:8-11).

---

27 Ray Summers, op. cit., p.171.

28 L.S. White, Sermons on Revelation (Cincinnati, Ohio: F. L. Rowe, Publisher, 1917), p.185.

v. 6 *"And the woman fled into the wilderness"* An Old Testament passage. It tells how the Israelites fled from Egypt, and the Pharaoh pursued them into the Red Sea (Exodus 14:5, Joshua 24:6). It foreshadows Israel's fleeing from the Antichrist; this could refer to the 144,000 sealed Jewish servants protected by God.

Jesus tells Jewish believers to flee to the mountains before the end time, just as Lot was told to flee the destruction of Sodom and Gomorrah. He also gives them two signs: (1) Jerusalem amasses armies (Luke 21:20-23). (2) The Abomination of Desolation arrives, spoken of by Daniel the Prophet, (Mark 13:14-21; Daniel 11:31, 12:11).

The Battle between Archangel Michael and the Dragon (vv. 7-9)

v. 7 *"And there was war in heaven: Michael"* The archangel Michael is a warrior angel and mighty in power, battle against the forces of darkness. In the book of Daniel, archangel Michael is described as "the great prince which standeth for the children of thy people: and there shall be a time of trouble, such as never was since there was a nation even to that same time: and at that time thy people shall be delivered, every one that shall be found written in the book" (Daniel 12:1). Michael is assigned to watch over Israel's children (Daniel 10:13, 21, Jude 1:9).

The archangel Michael will play a significant role during the last phase of the Great Tribulation of Israel. Daniel shows him contending against the Dragon and his angels (Revelation 12:7, 17).

"his angels fought against the dragon; and the dragon fought and his angels" Satan cast out of heaven twice.

1. Cast out as his role as anointed cherub: Satan was originally one of God's holy angels, but he rebelled against God and cast out of Heaven (Luke 10:18). That was only the first stage of his judgment. Satan's kingdom vanquished at the cross (John 12:31-32).

"Now there was a day when the sons of God came to present themselves before the LORD, and Satan also came among them. The LORD said to Satan, from where do you come? Then Satan answered the LORD and said, "From roaming about on the earth and walking around on it. The LORD said to Satan, "Have you considered My servant Job? For there is no one like him on the earth, a blameless and upright man, fearing God and turning away from evil" (Job 1:6-8).

2. Later, he will be bound in the abyss for one thousand years (Revelation 20:1-3) and then cast into the Lake of Fire for eternity (Revelation 20:10).

"Old serpent, called the Devil, and Satan, which deceived the whole world" *(1)* old serpent identified as the serpent who tempted Eve in the Garden of Eden, (2) the Devil is known as the false accuser of the brethren or slanderer one, (3) Satan the Hebrew word denotes "the adversary." He is a mighty fallen angel and the prince of darkness.

A Jubilant Announcement in Heaven (vv. 10-12)
v.10 Before Satan cast out heaven, he would accusation against the saints. His removal from heaven once and all. This event brings rejoicing in heaven. In contrast, Satan has no more access to God's throne and for the accuser of the saints. Now is come Salvation, strength, and power of Christ [the Anoint One or Messiah].

Satan is the accuser of the brethren; he reminds us of our sinful state and to God, gives a reminder of every mistake, every sin the brethren make (Zechariah 3:1-2, Job 2:1-6, 2 Corinthians 2:11). Trusting in the blood of Christ is our only defense against Satan.

v. 11 "And they overcame him [Satan] by the blood of the Lamb and by word of their testimony, and they loved not their lives unto the death."

> "But if we walk in the light, as he is in the light, we have fellowship one with another, and the blood of Jesus Christ, his Son, cleanses us from all sin" (1 John 1:7).

> "He made Him who knew no sin on our behalf so that we might become the righteousness of God in Him" (2 Corinthians 5:21).

Romans 3:22 states, "…even the righteousness of God through faith in Jesus Christ for all those who believe; for there is no distinction."

The world at this time is under the demonic influence by the master of deception, Satan himself.

There is no comparison to Christ's authority, nor His Kingdom to that of Satan's. Satan has no salvation to offer, but instead, death. The saints are redeemed and ransomed from Satan's hands by Jesus Christ. The faithful are victorious in Jesus through His finished work.

Michael and the heavenly armies destroy the hierarchy of Satan's kingdom. The dragon has a well-organized structure to execute his evil schemes on the inhabitants of the earth. The apostle Paul describes how Satan's kingdom as systematically aligned. He writes, "For we wrestle not against flesh and blood, but against principalities, against powers, against the rulers of darkness of this world, against spiritual wickedness in high places" (Ephesians 6:12). Paul tells us of Lucifer's powers and authority since his fall in ancient times.

John writes in John 12:13, "now is the judgment of this world: now shall the prince of this world be cast out."

"He was cast out into the earth, and his angels were cast out with him" All level powers of Satan dominion cast out on the earth and the sea. The inhabitants on earth are under the controlled and evil influences of the spirits of darkness. Satan always wanted to be a god and have his kingdom with all of his glory of darkness. The earth dwellers who received the mark of the beast and names not written in the book of Life is at Satan commands and authority. The Dragon gives this power to the first beast who recovered from the wound.

"Great wrath" (Gk. *thymos*) "expressed passion" - fierceness or indignation. Satan is cast down to the earth and has a short time during the Tribulation period to cause the earth dwellers revolt against God Almighty.

Satan is unleashing his indignation on the inhabitants of the earth. He is angry because he no longer has access to heaven to accuse the saints. He was conquered and cast out of Heaven, ultimately being denied worship from his desired kingdom as God of this world. He knows he has but a short time before Christ assumes power over all the world. The redeemed saints rejoice over the triumph of God and the appointed time of God's Wrath. The Doom's day clock is running out, and Satan is angry.

The Dragon Attack the Woman: God provide Protection (vv. 13-17)
The Scene on Earth

v. 13 *"He persecuted the woman which brought forth the man child"* Satan's plan fails in trying to destroy the man-child. Now he plans to take vengeance on the seed of the woman "Israel." He martyrs millions of Jews in human history, and he is on the prowl to seek and annihilated Israel.

v.14 *"And to the woman were given two wings of a great eagle"* The wings of a great eagle represent a swift escape from persecution. The wings of an eagle are a metaphor describing God's swiftness of protection and His providence (cf. Exodus 19:4; Deuteronomy 32:11, Psalm 55:6).

But they that wait upon the LORD shall renew their strength; they shall mount up with wings as eagles (Isaiah 40:31).

"she might fly into the wilderness, into her place" suggests that during this time, God protects Israel from the invading army of the Northern kingdom and gives them refuge in the wilderness (cf. Isaiah 33:13-16; Daniel 9:25-27,12:11; Micah 2:12-13).

Where she is nourished for a time, and times, and half a time - Israel had always been sought after by evil men of this world for centuries to annihilate God's chosen people. God will nourish His people at an exclusive place for the last three and a half years from the dragon and his evil villains. The God of Israel has always preserved them from their adversaries.

> "Then shall the Lord go forth, and fight against
> those nations, as when he fought in the day of battle"
> (Zechariah 14:3).

The context indicates "the serpent will be cast out of his mouth like "water as a flood" after the woman…" The "flood" is metaphorically speaking of the overwhelming aggression of Satan's army pursuing Israel. However, God intervenes with earthquakes, and the earth opens up and swallows the invading army.

"Remnant" (Gk. *Loipos*) means "to be left behind, the remainder, the rest, the others." The remnant possibly refers to either (1) Throughout Israel History, Satan sought to destroy the woman seed, but God is faithful to keep His word (2) the Gentile believers who are the seed of Abraham through Christ or (3) the loyal 144,000 Jewish evangelists who refuse to worship the beast and Satan.

The woman was to find refuge in the wilderness. Many commentators suggest that Petra is an ideal place. Petra is a fortified, hidden city located in the desert of Jordan, south of the Death Sea.

There, God will care for the fleeing Israelis for 3 ½ years. Satan is angry with the woman and attacks the rest of the small group that survives the war. The 144,000 Jews are under God's sealed protection and are included with the remnants that escape the invading armies.

CHAPTER THIRTEEN

THE TWO DREADFUL AND TERRIBLE BEASTS

The Beast Rises Out of the Sea: The Political and Commercial System (vv. 1-10)
The Scene on Earth

v. 1 The Beast Described: *"A Beast climbing out of the sea,"* John sees a dreadful beast rising from the Sea having seven heads and ten horns, and upon his horns ten diadem crowns, and upon his heads the name of blasphemy. This sea could be a reference to the Mediterranean Sea near Israel border. This beast from the sea is not an angel or a mortal man. Seiss states, "one who hails from that place must either be a dead man brought up again from the dead, or some evil spirit which takes possession of a living man. In either case, the beast as a person is an extraordinary and supernatural being." He will be cast alive into the Lake of Fire at the Second Coming of Christ. The Bible does not tell us of the beast history or his origin, other than he is called "the son of perdition" (2 Thessalonians 2:3).

The *"Beast of the sea"* in verse 1 resembled the "little horn" in Daniel's vision. "I considered the horns, and, behold, there came up among them another little horn, before whom there were three of the first horns plucked up by the roots: and, behold, in this horn were eyes like the eyes of man, and a mouth speaking great things," (Daniel 7:8). "The Beast" (Gk. *Therion*) referred to "a wild beast, hence: any animal; met: a brute."

Both Daniel and John saw the beast as a political system and a leader of Gentile lineage. John did not call the beast a Gentile because it looks like a brutal or savage man coming up out of the Sea.

The *"sea"* represents chaos, a corrupt system, and violent power. In the prophecy sea always symbolizes extreme conditions among people, nations, or countries. This beast from the Sea is known as the Antichrist and the white horse's rider in Revelation 6:2. He is the Tyrant over the ten rulers of the world, who will oppose God and a servant of the Dragon.

"But the wicked are like the trouble *sea,* when it cannot rest, whose waters cast up mire and dirt" (Isaiah 57: 20).

Three Beasts in Revelation fit this description:

- The Dragon Out Of The Pit (Revelation 11:7).
- The Scarlet Beast And The Harlot Rider (Revelation 13).
- The Sea Beast (Revelation 17:7-18).
- All Three Beasts Seem To Be The Same Beast.

"Seven Heads" refers to the seven Empires or kingdoms: (1) Egypt; (2) Assyria; (3) Babylon; (4) Persia; (5) Greece; (6) Rome; (7) Final world government and future empire, (Daniel 7:8).

"Ten Horns" refers to the ten kings and suggests the Roman empire's restoration (Daniel 7). Daniel wrote that he saw the rise and fall of four

Gentile nations: Babylon, Medo-Persia, Greece, and Rome. Daniel and Revelation described the beast coming from the sea of nations.

Satan says, in Isaiah 14:14, "I will be like the most high...." He will establish his counterfeit unholy trinity. Their roles will be (Satan) Father, (the Antichrist) Jesus Christ (the false prophet), The Holy Spirit.

The *"Ten crowns"* (*Gk. Diadema*) are considered "properly, a royal crown." According to the trench, the crown is a reference to "kingly ornament for the head."

"Upon their heads the name Blasphemy" (*Gk. Blasphemia*) means "abusive or scurrilous language." The "translation for "blasphemy is a railing or slander. This king or leader brags, exalt himself, and praises himself and thinks he is better than God and desires to worship as a god. (cf. Daniel 3:29, 7:25,11:36; Romans 2:24). He speaks horrendous things against Almighty God as other pagan kings.

v.2 The three beasts that John described in Revelation 13 is similar to three of the four beasts described in Daniel 7:3-8, except in the reverse order (Lion, Bear, Leopard, and the Great Iron Claws). In Daniel's vision, the Leopard represents the Greek Empire; the Bear is Medo-Persia; the Lion is Babylon, and the Great Iron Claws represent the Roman Empire, (Daniel 7:7, 23).

Here in Revelation 13:2, the beasts' arrangements are in reverse order in Daniel's writing: Leopard, Bear, and Lion. The beast from the Sea and the scarlet-colored beast in Revelation 17 have full blasphemy names, seven heads, and ten horns.

"The beast appearances like a leopard" The Leopard depicts Greece. This animal mobilizes with swift speed to attack it prey. *"Mouth of a lion,"* communicates his arrogance through its roar and ferocious body mass that strikes fear to all that hear and see it. When a lion roars, the sound disrupts all activities in his environment, or within hearing distance. Suddenly, fear of the kingly beast affects all creatures nearby (Amos 1:2,

3:8). *"mouth"* disseminates false teachings, deceptive ideology, and evil discourse to the world.

"The dragon gave him his power" This excerpt speaks of how Satan gives the Antichrist the ability to wreak havoc on the earth. Satan empowers the beast to destroy humanity. Satan attempts to counterfeit the Godhead with his inverted trinity. God is Christ's Father, and the Dragon is the father of the Beast [Antichrist] (Isaiah 14:14; John 8:44; 2 Thessalonians 2:8-10). *"And his seat and great authority"* (Gk. *exousia*) means the power to influence the minds of people, specifically their moral authority. This beast is the political and social leader is the end times figure known as the Antichrist.

Names and titles of the Antichrist:[29]

1. The King of Babylon, (Isaiah 10,11,13,14:4; Jeremiah 49:51; Zechariah 5; Revelation 18).
2. The Wicked one (Psalms 10:2; Jeremiah 30:7).
3. The Mighty Man (Psalms 52:1-7).
4. The enemy (Psalms 52:21, 55:3).
5. The spoiler (Psalms. 69:4; Isaiah 16:4-5; Jeremiah 6:26).
6. The Adversary (Psalms 74:8-10; Isaiah 59:19; Lamentations 4:11-12; Amos 3:11).
7. The Head Over Many Countries (Psalms 110:6).
8. The Violent Man (Psalms 140:1-11).
9. The Assyrian (Isaiah 10:5,12; 30:33).
10. The Profane and Wicked Prince of Israel (Ezekiel 21:25-27)
11. The Little Horn (Daniel 7:8-11, 21-26; 8:9-12).
12. The Prince that shall come (Daniel 9:26).
13. The Vile Person (Daniel 11:21).
14. The Willful King (Daniel 11:36).
15. The Lawless One (Daniel 11:36; Galatians 4:4; 2 Thessalonians 2:8; Hebrews 10:9).
16. The Idol Shepherd (Zechariah 11:16, 17).

---

29 Note, the term "antichrist" only occurs in 1 John 2:18-22,4:3; and 2 John 1:7.

17. The Antichrist (1 John 2:22).
18. The Beast (Genesis 1:2, Hebrews 7:26, Revelation 11:7).
19. The bloody and deceitful man (Psalms 5:6, 55:20, 83:4, Daniel 9:27, Revelation 6:10).
20. The man of the earth (cf. Psalms 10:18, Zechariah 14:7, Revelation 13:2).

v.3 The fatal wounded Beast, John said *"one"* of his heads was wounded, suggesting one of the nations will be revived or one of the kings could be raised to life again after being slain. Another possibility is that the beast himself died and then experience resurrection by the Dragon.

The Antichrist is a counterfeit of Jesus Christ. Jesus died on the cross and was resurrected by God. Satan sought after Moses's body and desired to use his corpse as idolatry against Israel. However, God buried Moses Himself, and no-one knows where his burial site (Deuteronomy 34:6, Matthew 17:2-4, Jude 1:9).

The word "wondered" means they admired or marveled after this person's miraculous recovery. He had a fatal blow to his head and died. Satan uses his body to carry out his evil plan against humanity. Many scholars believe this beast was the emperor Nero or Judas Iscariot or an evil tyrant like Stalin or Hilter. No-one knows for sure who the beast is, but once he comes on the scene of history, the world will be astonished by his presence.

v. 4 *"They also worshipped the first beast"* The Antichrist empires worshipped the Dragon for reviving the wounded. They praise and worshipped the beast for his dominion over the entire world or for providing safety under his leadership as their god. Who can make war with him? *"The first beast"* is a genius, a great military tactician with mystical powers given to him by Satan. He has sophisticated, smart weaponry and a tremendous military force, and powerful (Daniel 7:8; Revelation 6:2).

The Blasphemy of the Beast (vv.5-6)

v. 5 *"A mouth speaking great things and blasphemies"* blasphemy means to slander, speak evil or rail. There was given to the first beast a mouth speaking arrogant words and blasphemies allusion to (Daniel 7:8), where the little horn is given a mouth so that it can speak and say wicked things against God. Power and authority are given to the wounded beast by the Dragon to continue his campaign another forty-two months. The Antichrist first arrives on the scene as the white horsemen as a conquer in Revelation 6: 1-2 and resurrected from the dead to finish work against the saints of God. The beast blasphemy against God's name, worship place of God, and God's throne in heaven.

Later, he claims to have the godlike power of calling down fire from Heaven. He demands worshippers from the world's nations and identifies himself as God (Daniel 7:25, 11:20, 25, 36). The Antichrist will address the world through radio, internet, television, and satellite, speaking great things.

Jesus Christ's ministry lasts about forty-two months, and the Antichrist will rule for 3 ½ years or 42 months. Satan is a master counterfeiter, and he gives power to the two Beasts (Daniel 9; Revelation 19).

Antichrist Wage War on the Saints (vv. 7-8)

The Antichrist will wage war on the saints (cf. Daniel 7:25, 9:27, 12:10). God allows Antichrist time, plus times and a half of time to rule. Satan will be given a short time before God's judgment falls on the two Beasts and the wicked Empires.

There will be four kinds of people during the Tribulation:

1. Jews who hold to their ancient beliefs.
2. Jews and Gentiles (believers), saved during the Tribulation period.
3. 144,000 Jews sealed by God.
4. The unbelievers with the mark of the beast and names are not written in the book of life.

The book of life records the living spirits' names and elect citizens for the new heaven and earth. Their names are listed before the world came into existence. The Lamb's Book of Life and the Book of Life are synonymous (Revelation 3:5; 20:12; Philippians 4:3). The Book of Life's name changed after Christ's resurrection and ascension.

John Piper argues, "having our name written in the book of life from the foundation seems to mean that God will keep you from falling and grant you persevere in allegiance to God. Being in the book means you will not apostatize (Can the regenerate be erased from the book of life?"

"According as he hath chosen us in him before the foundation of the world, that we should be holy and without blame before him in love" (Ephesians 1:4).

Jeremiah writes, "Before I formed thee in the belly I knew thee; and before thou camest forth out of the womb I sanctified thee, and I ordained thee a prophet unto the nations." Jeremiah 1:5).

Exhortation to the Hearers: A sword to the deceivers (vv. 9-10)
John encourages the believers and reassures them to stand firm against the devil's wiles that will try their faith. He advises them not to give up but to be strong.

The two Beasts and the Dragon's victory is only temporary. The Apostle Paul writes to the Galatia Church, "Be not deceived; God is not mocked: for whatsoever a man soweth, that shall he also reap. For he that soweth to his flesh shall reap corruption; but he that soweth to the Spirit shall of the Spirit reap life everlasting," (Galatians 6:7-8). John's first epistles and the Book Revelation encourage the believers by promising eleven times of the reward they would receive for "overcoming" the wicked one.

"Understand, ye brutish among the people: and, ye fools, when will ye be wise? He that planted the ear, shall he not hear? He that formed the eye, shall he not see? He that chastiseth the heathen, shall not he correct? He that teacheth man knowledge shall not he know? The Lord knoweth the thoughts of man, which they are vanity," (Psalms 94:9).

The ways Satan weakens the saints: (1) ear gate; (2) mouth gate; (3) sight gate; (4) touch or feeling gate; (5) smell gate. The five senses are the primary sources for discerning right from wrong. One should not be ignorant of their adversary's devices, for all have been given many examples of how Satan operates. From Eve's narrative to the Antichrist's work, there are many written accounts of Satan's deception. The eyes of man are the windows to his soul, and his mind is considered the battlefield of decisions. The entity who controls the mind of men has lordship over his body and spirit (cf. Leviticus 24:12; Romans 7:25, 8:27, 11:34; 2 Corinthians 4:4; Ephesians 2:5).

What is the purpose of the Tribulation? To prepare the Jews in receiving their Messiah and bring about the conversion of the Jewish people (Deuteronomy 4:30; Jeremiah 30:7).

The Beast from the Earth: Ecclesiastical System (vv.11-15)
v.11 The description of the land Beast: John now sees the second beast, with the same essence of the first beast, coming up out the earth. Suggests that the second beast is coming up from Israel's territory and the second beast from the Mediterranean Sea.

This beast had two horns like a lamb, a counterfeit of the same offices of Christ as both Prophet and Priest. Some scholars suggest that the second beast is the Antichrist, and others believes he is the false prophet.

"He has two horns like a lamb" could potentially be a symbol of a false religious figure's powers. A goat looks like a lamb, but its character is different. The lamb and goat seem similar to each other at first glance but are not the same in looks and behavior.

A sheep is a social animal. They stay together in flocks and will gather in a circle to protect one another if needed. A goat is more independent and curious. The scriptures do not speak too well of goats because they symbolize wickedness like lambs symbolize innocence and righteousness.

"Beware of false prophets, which come to you in sheep's clothing, but inwardly they are ravening wolves," (Matthew 7:15).

"And no marvel; for Satan himself is transformed into an angel of light," (2 Corinthians 11:14).

"He speaks like a Dragon" The second beast is the forerunner or herald of the first beast. The Dragon empowers both beasts to speaks the oracles and performs miracles to match the ministry of the two witnesses of God. The False Prophet gains fame through his charismatic speeches and performing miracles throughout the world. John the Baptist was the forerunner of Jesus Christ.

He does Great Wonder: "Call fire down from heaven" (vv. 13-14) John emphasizes the second beast's ability to make fire come down from Heaven. The False Prophet answers back to the two witnesses by challenging them to a contest. The false prophet displays his great wonder of calling fire from the heavens to validate his office and teachings as God's dedicated representative. The second beast's ability to compete with God's two witnesses brings credit to himself and will deceive millions upon the earth.

The Jewish people are expecting Elijah to return before the Messiah comes (Malachi 4:5). John the Baptist came to Israel in Elijah's spirit and power (Luke 1:14-17). The second beast will imitate the miracles of Elijah by calling fire from Heaven.

Elijah proposes a contest between the God of Israel and Baal, a match between himself and Baal's 450 prophets. Elijah miraculous call fire from heaven results in the death of the priests of Baal (cf. 1 Kings 16:29, 17:1, 18:1-46). Elijah prays, and God answers with consuming fire. God was seeking to turn the hearts of His people back to Himself.

The world celebrates the beast's killing the two witnesses and will believe he is God (Revelation 13:3-4). In this contest, Satan will be winning in the first half of the Tribulation period. God provides doubt of Satan's victory by raising His two witnesses from the dead before the world.

In the last days and during the Tribulation period, people will be interested to see visible signs and miracles. God will allow the Beasts permission to perform signs and wonders before the world increasingly. These Satanic activities were predicted by Christ, who says, "For there shall arise False Christs, and False Prophets, and shall shew great signs and wonders; insomuch that, if it were possible, they shall deceive the very elect," (Matthew 24:24).

"Even him, whose coming is after the working of Satan with all power and sings and lying wonders," (2 Thessalonians 2:9).

"For the Jews require a sign, and the Greeks seek wisdom," (1 Corinthians 1:22).

The Image of the Beast (vv. 15-16)
"And he had power to give life unto the image of the beast, that the image of the beast should both speak, and cause that as many as would not worship the image of the beast should be killed."

> Daniel says, "Nebuchadnezzar the King made an image of gold, whose height was threescore cubit, and the breadth thereof six cubits: he set it up in the plain of Dura, in the province of Babylon. And whoso falleth not down, and worshippeth shall the same hour be cast into the midst of a burning fiery furnace" (Daniel 3:1, 6).

The second beast will erect a statue of the Antichrist and demand worship. The statue of the beast will come alive by demonic magic performed by the False Prophet. Satan mimics the power of God by giving the image of the beast a "spirit" or "breath," (Genesis 2:7). This will probably be done by demonic possession or a Holographic illusion. The idolatrous image of the beast will perform, unlike any statue ever erected in human history. The statue will be able to speak and think on its own as if it were alive. The talking statue propagates his laws to the people, and the death sentence will be enforced on those who do not submit to its image and its laws.

The false trinity mocks God and responds to the scriptures: "The idols of the heathen are silver and gold, the work of men's hands. They have mouths, but they speak not, Eyes have they, but they see not, neither is there any breath in their mouths," (Cf. Psalm 115:5, 135:15-17; Isaiah 46:7; Jeremiah 10:5; Habakkuk 2:18-19).

The False Prophet will display his demonic power to the world and deceive them by making the statue appear to be alive.

"Let no man deceive you by any means: for that day shall not come, except there come a falling away first, and that man of sin be revealed, the son of perdition; Who opposeth and exalteth himself above all that is called God, or that is worshipped; so that he as God sitteth in the temple of God, shewing himself that he is God," (2 Thessalonians 2:3-4).

The beast's image will influence many to receive the Mark of the Beast or face execution by beheading. The Antichrist writes into law a detestable edict, demanding that all people worship him and his image. The Antichrist's image worshipping is a shadowy reflection of the image that King Nebuchadnezzar had set up (Daniel 3:1-7).

The Mark of the Beast: 666 (vv. 16-18)
Restrictions are imposed on the world economic system by the Antichrist. The second beast performed and making the first beast image speak and come alive.

The second beast threatened the world with death if they did not worship the first beast image. Every human being on earth is ordered to takes the beast mark on their right hand. This made it impossible for anyone who did not have this mark to buy or sell for their daily needs.

The "Mark" (Gk. *charagma*), comes from the same one as a scratch, etching, or stamp." It will be seen as a badge of servitude. It will be a stamp, an imprinted mark on the forehead or right hand, as a badge of the followers of the Antichrist.

The Church will have already been removed from the earth (Revelation 4). God marks the believers with the seal of the Holy Spirit (2 Corinthians 1:22). A seal shows ownership, and the owner knows his mark. The Holy Spirit resides within our hearts as a deposit or guarantee of purchase.

God's elect 144 000 Jews of the tribes of Israel receive his seal on their foreheads (Revelation 7:1-8). God provides a seal of protection and equips His servant is to minister in the power of the Holy Spirit (Ezekiel 9:4). Satan will counterfeit God's seal with similar markings on the forehead or the right hand. The Antichrist's marks also illustrate the ownership and purchase of those who will be damned to Hell for eternity. The Antichrist's seal marks each unbeliever as a rebel against God in Lucifer's same tradition, causing one-third of the angels to rebel against God.

What is the Mark of his Name? Unknown
The Bible yields very little information on what the Mark of the Beast is. Some scholars believe that the mark is a literal marking upon the forehead or right hand. Modern technology has already invented the microchip that could be surgically implanted under the skin. Since scripture deals with buying and selling, the mark is probably a physical identification similar to the stamp barcode or a microchip, using biometrics identification. The Mark of the Beast consists of three things: (1) a mark, (2) the beast's name, and (3) the number of his name. Perhaps it could be a numeric system that calculates ancient Hebrew and Greek languages into a modern name's value.

The microchip is already here; the question is, when will our government make the implanted chip mandatory for its citizens. The world has already promoted a cashless society. Consumers can conveniently shop online from the comfort of their home using a credit card with a chip. The use of smartphones and apps can be used to accommodate every individual's needs.

The young generation is in a trance from their smart gadgets and not aware of their surroundings. A chip will be developed to make the world safe and promote an efficient economy. The chip contains personal data, social security numbers, and one's bank account information. It is a system that allows one to scan your hand to access your account. This chip can track one's location anywhere in the world. Finally, the world revolves around a smart cell phone and the use of apps capable of performing virtually any functions or tasks imaginable in our daily lives. Smart gadgets may also be a useful tool for the 666 system.

Number 666
The number "six" in the Bible correlated to man and the day of his creation. (1) The first six are also associated with the first false religion of man influenced by Satan. Number "seven" is the perfect number, and "three" often correlates to the Trinity of God. 666 falls short of the perfection of 7 and contains three iterations of the number six to mock the Holy Trinity. Satan's unholy trinity is 666. (2) The second six symbolizes the corrupt governments of humanity. (3) The third six symbolizes the false trinity and imperfect economy. (4) God created man on the sixth day (Genesis 1:26-28); six is the number of imperfect men. (5) The Mark of the Beast is 666, and the height of the statue in Daniel 3:1 is 66 cubits. (6) Goliath's height was six cubits, he had six armor pieces, and his spear weighed 600 shekels of iron (1 Samuel 17:4-7). (7) There are six passages in the scriptures that speak about the Mark of the Beast: Revelation 13:16-18, 14:9-11,15:2, 16:1-2, 19:20, and 20:4.

CHAPTER FOURTEEN

THE FINAL HOURS TO A NEW BEGINNING

The Fourth "Parenthesis Period"[30]

The Lamb on Mount Zion (vv. 1-5)
The Scene in Heaven

We are still at the middle point of the Tribulation period, and God's wrath is climaxing. God is about to command His Angels to started

---

30   The fourth Parenthesis Period comes between the seventh trumpet and the seventh vial judgment, revealing events on earth. (1) The Lamb on Mount Zion (2) The three Angels (3) The Blessed Dead, and (4) The Harvest and Vintage, Chapter 14:1-20.

the doom-day clock on the earth dwellers. The saints that were martyrs in Revelation 6:10 "cried with a loud voice, saying, how long, O Lord, holy and true, dost thou not judge and avenge our blood on them that dwell on the earth?"

John sees the Lamb of God standing on the mount Sion with the 144,000 Jewish saints sealed with His Father's name written on the elects' forehead in chapter seven. Mount Sion is the ancient mount in Jerusalem surrounded by serial of mounts like mount Moriah and mount Olives. Mount Zion metaphorically refers to the heavenly Jerusalem, God's eternal city in Heaven (cf. Galatians 4:26, Hebrews 11:10, 16, 13:14). There are two mount Zion locations in the Bible (1) a copy in Jerusalem on earth and (2) the origin mount Sion in the third Heaven. Most expositors argument on the location of *"Mount Sion"* in this context, were John referring to Heaven or earth? (cf. Hebrews 12:22) is debatable. The term "Zion" occurs 160 times in the Bible and is related to Jerusalem.

John does not always write in chronological order and does not give all the details of his visions. Suggests that John was referring to the heavenly Mount Sion.

"But ye are come unto mount Sion, and unto the city of the living God, the heavenly Jerusalem, and to an innumerable company of angels, To the general assembly and church of the firstborn, which are written in heaven, and to God the Judge of all, and to the spirits of just men made perfect" (Hebrews 12: 22-23)

Christ second coming- The place of His departure will be the place of His return. Just as Zechariah predicted the first coming of the Messiah, who appeared on the Mount Olives, the prophet foresaw the Second Coming of Christ whose "feet will stand on the mount of Olives" (Zechariah 14:1-4, 9).

Perhaps, the Lamb stands and presides over all the sacred mounts, including mount Zion as King of kings during the Millennial Kingdom on earth. The mount Olives will be splits according to Zechariah

14:9. In John's vision, Jesus in His Second returns accompanied by the Church, heavenly hosts, the martyred saints.

"Yet have I set my king upon my holy hill of Zion. I will declare the decree: the Lord hath said unto me, Thou art my Son; this day have I begotten thee. Ask of me, and I shall give thee the heathen for thine inheritance, and the uttermost parts of the earth for thy possession. Thou shalt break them with a rod of iron; thou shalt dash them in pieces like a potter's vessel" (Psalms 2:6-9).

"For the Lord hath chosen Zion; hath desired it for his habitation. This is my rest forever: here will I dwell; for I have desired it" (Psalms 132:13-14).

"And it shall come to pass in the last days, that the mountain of the LORD's house shall be established in the top of the mountains, and shall be exalted above he hills; and all nations shall flow unto it" (Isaiah 2:2).

v. 2 *"And I heard a voice from heaven, as the voice of many waters, and as the voice of a great thunder"* The voice of God associated with the elements in a storm: thunder, lightning, rain, and earthquakes. The great, thunderous voice of God is a manifestation of His divine power, (Exodus 19:16, 20:18; Job 18:13,40:9, 18:13; 2 Samuel 22:14; Revelation 10:3-4).

Job describes God as voice "roareth, he thundereth with the voice of his excellency; and he will not stay them when his voice is heard. God thundereth marvellously with his voice; great things doeth he, which we cannot comprehend" (Job 37:4-5).

Ezekiel 44:2 "And, behold, the glory of the God of Israel came from the way of the east: and his voice was like a noise of many waters: and the earth shined with his glory."

v. 3 *"New song"* redeemed saints are singing the song of redemption as a mass choir before the throne of God. They will sing a new song which no one can learn except the 144,000 sealed with the Father name. John describes singing, playing musical instruments, and the celebration of God's triumphant victory over the two beasts. The 144,000 will sing about their triumphant victory over evil and how God keeps them safe through that period.

Moses and Miriam taught the Children of Israel a new song after Egypt's exodus and triumphant victory over Pharaoh and his armies in the Red Sea (Deuteronomy 31:19, Exodus 15:1).

The new song gives witness to what God has done, and the new song adds to the praise that is already in session.

"O sing unto the Lord a new song: sing unto the Lord, all the earth," (Psalm 96:1).

No one can learn a new song unless they experience the lyrics in the music themselves; the lyrics tell how God protected them and won the victory over the power of darkness on the earth.

The word *"redeem"* (Gk. *Agorazo*) is not redeeming in the sense of "buying back" but rather focuses on how the believers now belong to the Lord as His unique possession.

v.4 *"These are they which were not defiled with a woman."* The word "not defiled" means celibate: pure, unmarried virgins. These men's primary focus will be their unique ministry. This statement does not speak out against the marital relationship.

It shows that there will be nothing to stand in their way or influence them from doing God's will. The Apostle Paul was zealous about doing the will of God (1 Corinthians 7).

Sexual perversion during the Tribulation period will run rampant and be worse than that of Sodom and Gomorrah. "As it was in the days of Noah, so will it be again in the coming of the Son of Man," (Matthew 24:27; Luke 17:26). The 144,000 male virgins will be obedient to the Lamb and will voluntarily remain chaste and not defile themselves with women. They did not compromise their chastity or fornicate with the Antichrist's religious system, nor will they defile themselves with the pleasures of this world.

Antichrist's philosophy of a woman.
"Neither shall he regard the God of his fathers, nor the desire of women, nor regard any god: for he shall magnify himself above all," (Daniel 11:37).

There is much debate over the Antichrist's sexual preference as a heterosexual or androgynous. Daniel 11:37 states, "...nor the desire of women." The Antichrist will be the opposite of the Messiah in character and behavior. He is the Man of Sin and the False Christ. The "nor the desire" (Hebrew *chemdah*) means to take no pleasure, delight of women.

It did not say "for" a woman but "of" woman. The context does not use the terms as "virgin or chaste." Although these verses in Daniel refer to the Old Testament Antichrist, "Antiochus IV Epiphanes," they suggest the New Testament Antichrist would take on the same traits in the future. Moreover, he is known as the first beast in chapter 13 and cast into the Lake of Fire alive (Revelation 19:20). It is possible the Antichrist may not be entirely human, and the scriptures tell very little about his genealogy and past. The only thing the Bible states about his origin is that he emerges from the sea of nations.

The *first-fruit* (Gk. *Aparche*) of God is the first one consecrated by God figuratively speaking. The 144,000 Jewish virgins are now present with the Lamb of God in Heaven. Their ministry campaign will be successful, and they will become the first fruits of the Great Tribulation and harvest of souls that are to come. They are redeemed as God's first fruit and deemed His property with a seal to show ownership. It suggests that after they are sealed and protected by God, they complete their service throughout first portion of the Tribulation period blameless and pure.

There are many arguments over the 144,000 Jews being of two different groups. However, the passages indicate that these are the same 144,0000 sealed in chapter 7. They are redeemed and are called the "first fruit" unto God and the Lamb.

"No fault," the 144,000 are virgin men, without guile (fault, lies), and pure. They will not speak lies of hypocrisy as the Antichrist's followers.

"The remnant of Israel shall not do iniquity, nor speak lies; neither shall a deceitful tongue be found in their mouth: for they shall feed and lie down, and none shall make them afraid." (Zephaniah 3:13).

The First Angelic Announcement: The Everlasting Gospel (v. 6-7) John writes that he saw another angel flying amid in the heavens, carrying announcements and warnings from God to the earth's inhabitants. Altogether, three angels flew in the heavens with three Gospel announcements: (1) the first angel proclaiming the everlasting gospel, v.6. (2) the second angel is announcing the fall of Babylon, v.8. (3) the third angel warns not to worship or receive the Mark of the Beast, or God's wrath will be upon them, vv.9-11.

"The Everlasting Gospel" The gospel is eternal because it was in the mind of the Father from the beginning of creation. The Bible says, "Jesus is the Lamb of God, slain from before the foundation of the world, a sacrifice for the sin of men who are all hopelessly ruined by sin." (cf. Leviticus 17:11; Matthew 25:34; John 17:24; Ephesians 1:3; Hebrews 4:2 ;1 Peter 1:17-21.)

The eternal gospel first touched humanity at the moment of Adam's fall in the Garden. God clothed the naked couple with animal skins of the first atoning sacrifice and promises them a "seed" in the future for humanity's salvation.

Finally, the everlasting gospel is the good news that Jesus will win the battle over evil; and the Antichrist and beast will be judged. This gospel focuses on the redemption through Christ and the coming of His kingdom,

v. 7 "Hour of His judgment is come" The last moment arrives to repent and believe before God's wrath is poured out. This verse first uses of the word: judgment," a term that has the same meaning as wrath (6:17, 12:12).

The Second Angelic Announcement: The Fall of Babylon (v. 8)
The second angel announces that *"Babylon is fallen, fallen,"* which indicates its impending fall but later or its end will be double destruction, both in this world and in the future world to come.

Babylon has not fallen yet in this chapter. The ecclesiastical Babylon fall in chapter 17, and political Babylon falls in chapter 18. The great Harlot riding on the beast makes the nations drink a cup of wrath. This is referring to immoral sexual practices, idolatry, and doctrines of demons. The Babylonian religious system will bring God's wrath on the nations and all that drink wine of her cup.

The Third Angelic Announcement: Warning Do not take the Mark of Beast (vv. 9-11)
The third angel announces a warning and a judgment on those who worship the Antichrist and receive the Mark of the Beast (Revelation 13:16). The heavenly host witness the apocalyptic destruction of fire and brimstone as it falls upon the worshippers of the Antichrist. Christ gives the order to execute judgment on the Antichrist's Kingdom and all the nations that defied the Living God's warnings.

"The cup of his indignation" describes as anyone loyal to the Antichrist and his evil kingdom will suffer the outpouring of God's collected wrath, done with the full force of His divine anger and unmitigated vengeance (cf. Psalms 75:8, Isaiah 51:17, Jeremiah 25:15-16).

"Fire and brimstone" These are two elements that are often associated in the Bible with the torment of divine punishment (Genesis 19:24-25, Isaiah 34:9-10). Here in context to hell, the lake of fire (Revelation 19:20, 20:10, 21:8).

We see that God once again sends a warning to humanity not to worship the image of the Antichrist. This warning also forbids acceptance of the Mark of the Beast. His judgment is imminent and followed by eternal punishment in the Lake of Fire. The Antichrist and the second Beast will force their religious system upon humanity. Those who refute his declaration will receive death by beheading. The laws will be changed, and worship of the Antichrist mandated to all. Many believers and newly converted believers will die as martyrs for rejecting the Antichrist's official decree of worship and his mark (Revelation 13:15).

No rest day or night references eternal damnation in the Lake of Fire. The unbelievers cast into the Lake of Fire with brimstone: physically resurrected body, soul, and Spirit. Christians take their rest beyond the grave in Heaven with God until a final resting place is in the new Heaven and the new earth (cf. 1 Timothy 5:24-25; Hebrews 6:10. Revelation 21-22).

Blessed are the Dead (v.13)
"And I heard a voice from heaven saying unto me, Write, Blessed are the dead which die in the Lord from henceforth: Yea, saith the Spirit, that they may rest from their labours; and their works do follow them."

Here, Jesus promises the believers that they will be resurrected from the dead as He was. He will ask that they be patient as their eternal rest is near. Resting from our labor indicates that the person dies in the Lord, then their soul and Spirit rests in Heaven until the first resurrection. The saints are rewarded for their labors, and their works will follow them to Heaven (cf. John 11:25-26,14:19, 20:17, Romans 6:5-6, Philippians 3:10, Revelation 20:6).

"Precious in the sight of the Lord is the death of his saints" (Psalm 116:15).

The Beatitudes of Revelation

1) Blessed is he that readeth, and they that hear the words of this prophecy, and keep those things which are written therein: for the time is at hand (Revelation 1:3).

2) Blessed are the dead which die in the Lord from henceforth: Yea, saith the Spirit, that they may rest from their labors; and their works do follow them, (Revelation 14:13).

3) Blessed is he that watcheth, and keepeth his garments, lest he walks naked, and they see his shame (Revelation 15:15).

4) Blessed are they which are called unto the marriage supper of the Lamb. And he saith unto me. These are the true sayings of God (Revelation 19:9).

5) Blessed and holy is he that hath part in the first resurrection: on such, the second death hath no power, but they shall be priests of God and Christ and shall reign with him a thousand years (Revelation 20:6).

6) Blessed is he that keepeth the sayings of the prophecy of this book (Revelation 22:7).

7) Blessed are they who do his commandments, that they may have right to the tree of life, and may enter through the gates into the city (Revelation 22:14).

The Fourth Angel: Reaping the Earth's Harvest (vv. 14-16)

John 5:21-23 states, "For just as the Father raises the dead and gives them life, even so, the Son also gives life to whom He wishes. For not even the Father judges anyone, but He has given all judgment to the Son, so that all will honor the Son even as they honor the Father. He who does not honor the Son does not honor the Father who sent Him."

John 5:27 states, "And he has given him authority to judge because he is the Son of Man, (John 9:39, Acts 10:42, Acts 17:31).

"A white cloud" symbolizes Christ's Second Coming and Judgment.

"Christ is taken out of their sight by a cloud, and he shall return to Earth in the same fashion with a cloud," (Acts 1:9-11).

"And then shall appear the sign of the Son of Man in Heaven: and then shall all the tribes of the earth mourn, and they shall see the Son of Man coming in the clouds of Heaven with power and great glory," (Matthew 24:30, 25:31, 26:64).

"Shekinah Glory" is the divine visitation of Jehovah's presence when on earth before an Israelite or a representative of His choosing.

Jehovah spoke to Moses from a pillar of cloud (Exodus 33:9-11). For forty years, the Divine presence guided His people in the desert as a pillar of cloud by day and a pillar of fire by night (Exodus 13:20-22).

- "Clouds are a hiding place for Him so that he cannot see, and He walks on the vault of Heaven," (Job 22:14).
- "...Clouds are the dust beneath His feet," (Nahum 1:3).
- "Clouds and thick darkness surround Him, righteousness and justice are the foundation of His throne," (Psalms 97:2).
- "And there was a cloud that overshadowed them: and a voice came out of the cloud, saying, this is my beloved Son: hear him," (Mark 9:7).

v. 14 *"Like unto the Son of Man"* identifies Jesus with the Lamb of God, the Messiah, the King, and the Judge. The phrase "Son of Man" describes Christ as a human being in His incarnate state. He is in the likeness of human flesh and fashioned as a man, but He is the Son of God. He is the epitome of humanity. Christ possesses a dual nature joined in the Hypostatic Union. He is fully God and man at the same time. In the four gospels, Jesus is often referring to Himself as the Son of Man (Matthew16:13, 27, Mark 14:21, Luke 7:34, John 3:13). In Daniel 7:13-14, denotes to Christ as the Coming Messiah as the "son of man." In Aramaic, the term "Son of Man" is *"Bar-Enash."* Ezekiel is also called the "son of man" by God in his human condition (Ezekiel 2:1, 3:1, 4:1, 5:1).

"Golden crown" - They crown Christ with a Stephano crown, a mockery from the Roman soldier who called him "the King of Jews," (John 19:2,5; Matthew 27:29; Mark 15:17-18). His second return, He will be wearing a diadem crown of majesty and glory. Christ, as sovereign ruler of the earth, will destroy all works of evil (Revelation 19:11-16).

"In His hand a sharp sickle." The sickle represents an instrument of judgment. This tool is used by farmers to cut down grapes in the

vineyard. Christ finishes judgment on humanity once and for all. This is the beginning of the end!

"And another angel came out of the temple, crying with a loud voice to him that sat on the cloud." The angel that comes from the Temple is only giving the cue for the judgment to begin. Christ proceeds with the judgment as planned. The Son of Man is more superior than all the heavenly hosts (Hebrews 1:5-14).

"God's Wrath" symbolizes the grape harvest by comparing the treading of the grape from the cluster with the unbelievers and worshippers of the beast being killed or destroyed.

The Fifth and Sixth Angels: Reaping the Winepress of the Wrath of God (vv.17-20)
The Scene in Heaven

The last two angels announce a woeful message to the world: another angel comes out of the Temple to announce the beginning of the end (Revelation 14:15). Another angel comes out of the altar, announcing that the time is ripe on earth to carry out God's wrath, purge the earth of sins and judgment on earth dwellers, and Dragon's kingdom.

The Two Reapers of the Harvest
According to Exodus 23:19, the first fruit of the harvest belonged to the Temple and was offered to God. The ripe fruit taken in baskets to the Temple and the priest would offer the first fruit on the altar to God (Revelation 14:14-16). The second reaper now examines the cluster of grapes that were harvested by the first reaper. Next, the grapes are cast into the winepress to extract the juice. The winepress was collected a large bin, located outside the city wall, where the workers trampled barefoot over the grapes until all the fresh juices flowed into a square distribution vat. The skin of the grapes burned in the fire.

The harvest: separation of the ripe/ overripe grapes.
"As the Lord reaps his harvest through preaching the gospel, judgment falls on all who reject it," (Revelation 14:14-16).

"While He will be gathering His harvest, the judgment of the wicked will continues. The analogy of the winepress portrays this idea rather than the final judgment at His second coming[31]." In Revelation 14:15 describes a great harvest at the end of the world in two segments: (1) gathering of the ripened grain (righteous) on the earth that was reaped (cf. Matthew 13:30).

v. 20 The winepress of blood from the wrath of God: The coming Battle of Armageddon.

There will be enormous bloodshed of the world's armies outside Jerusalem's city wall in the space of 1600 furlongs [approximately 200 miles]. There will be a river of blood from the bodies of dead soldiers and unbelievers that fought alongside the Antichrist at the beginning of the second advent of Christ (cf. Joel 3:12-14; Zechariah 14:4, Isaiah 63:1-6; Revelation 11:2, 19:17-19).

---

31   Hailey, p. 317

CHAPTER FIFTEEN

PRELUDE TO THE LAST SEVEN PLAGUES

Another Sign in Heaven (v.1)

John goes back to Revelation 14:20 and gives a concise explanation of the coming judgment of God. God's wrath started with the seven Seals in chapter 6 and finishes with the seven Bowls. The wicked world shall be no more, and the Antichrist and his kingdom shall have ended. Suggests this may be the end of the Dispensation of Grace shall cease to exist, and there shall be a new and final Dispensation of the Millennium Kingdom established under the iron rulership of Jesus Christ, our King of kings and Lord of lords.

"Seven angels, having the seven last plagues," John sees another sign in Heaven, great wonder, and marvel. John sees another sign for the third

time. (1) he saw a woman clothed with the sun (Revelation 12:1), (2) he saw the wonder of the dragon (Revelation 12:3), (3) Now, he sees the last sign of God's Wrath (Revelation 15:1).

Revelation 12:1 concluded the final portion of the seventh Seal Judgment near the end of the seven-year tribulation period preceding the seven vials Judgment. Many scholars argue that the last trumpet found in 1 Corinthians 15:52; 1 Thessalonians 4:16 and the last trumpet judgment found in Revelation 11:15; 15:1 is synonymous. The last trumpet in the Apostle Paul's writing and the blasting of the seven trumpets in Revelation are not the same. Why is this so important? It would place the rapture of the Church in one of these categories.

Revelation 15-16 gives the chronological order of events leading to the second advent of Christ. The seven angels prepare to inflict the seven vial Judgments of God on the earth. The term "vials" is used interchangeably with the word "bowl or bottle." In ancient Rome, a vial [flask] was used by women as a container for perfume or liquid aroma.

The Song of Moses and the Tribulation Saints (vv. 2-4)
v. 2 John sees *"a sea of glass mingled with fire,"* figuratively meaning those who had triumphed over the Beast of the Sea, the image of the Beast, and his numeral system. The Saints are seen standing on the sea of glass, with harps of God." The *glassy sea* mentioned in Revelation 4:6 is before God's throne, reflecting the majesty of God's glory (cf. Exodus 24:10; Ezekiel 1:22).

The sea is *"mingled with fire,"* suggesting God's severe judgment of the Beast and his kingdom without delay.

v. 3 This song is not about Moses or the Lamb of God.
John writes that this song is combined with Law and Grace "a new song." It is a new song about God Almighty and His tremendous power and justice on their oppressors. Moses and Miriam's songs and written lyrics give praise and testify how God delivered the Jews out of bondage in Egypt. God establishes the nations based upon His love for Israel.

The lyric in the new song of the Lamb of God also confirms how great and marvelous the Lamb delivery. God's master plan of redemption in the lyric of the song written. He provides a Lamb that will take away the world's sins. His plan delivered the Saints from the bondage of sins and will lead the redeemed to the promised land in Heaven. Moses credit for writing three songs (Exodus 15; Psalm 80; Deuteronomy 32).

"Miriam, the prophetess, Aaron's sister, took a timbrel in her hand, and all the women came out after her with timbrels and with dances.

Furthermore, Miriam called out to them, sing to the Lord, for very exalted is He; a horse and its rider He cast into the sea" (Exodus 15:20-21).

v. 3 (1) God works is "*Great and marvelous*" (2) God's ways are "just and true" (3) God is the "King of saints."

The Temple of the Tabernacle (vv. 5-7)
v. 5" *I looked, and behold!*" This phase introduces that something frighteningly is about to occur.

"*The temple of the tabernacle of the testimony in heaven was opened*" The Temple was the Holy of Holies where God would meet the High Priest once a year on the Day of Atonement (Exodus 25:1-2 and 8-9) describe the Tabernacle's layout and all the instruments given to Moses.

It was called the tent of testimony or covenant because it contained the Ark of the Covenant (Exodus 38:21, 40:34 and Acts 7:44).

Notice the Ark in the sanctuary is not mentioned here, but John recalls his Ark's vision in the sanctuary (Revelation 11:19).

"Who serve unto the example and shadow of heavenly things, as Moses was admonished of God when he was about to make the tabernacle: for, see, saith he, that thou make all things according to the pattern shewed to thee in the mount" (Hebrews 8:5).

The Ark of the covenant is a boxlike shape that houses the gold jar of manna, Aaron's staff that had budded, and the Ten Commandments (Exodus 32:15; Acts 7:44). The lid or atonement covers over the Ark of the Covenant contain a figure of two cherub angels with their wings touching. The Ark of Covenant rested in the Tabernacle and protected the history of the Israelites and God's relics.

v. 6 *"And the seven angels came out of the temple, having the seven plagues,"* the seven golden vials are full of God's Wrath and ready to avenge the forces of evil, the false trinity, and the wicked earth-dwellers on behalf of the martyred saints.

God delivers on His word to the martyred saints.

He has tolerated the sins of the wicked long enough. The outpouring of His wrath on the earth has finally arrived, and who shall be able to stand?

The Wrath of God: The End of the Beginning (v.8)
These four living beasts were around God's throne near the glass sea (Revelation 4:6-8). They were present at the opening of the first four seals (Revelation 6:1-8).

Seven angels were giving golden vials (bowls) full of the Wrath of God. The angels waited from the fall of Adam until this point to pours out vials on the earth. God's wages on sins dealt with once and for all (Romans 6:23).

"And when he had opened the fifth seal, I saw under the altar the souls of them that were slain for the word of God, and for the testimony which they held: And they cried with a loud voice, saying, How long, O Lord, holy and true, dost thou not judge and avenge our blood on them that dwell on the Earth?" (Revelation 6:9-11).

The term *"wrath"* (Gk. thumos) translates to "fierceness, anger or indignation" or (Gk. Orge) means anger from a settled disposition [1].

The (Gk. *Orge*) term is the more common use for God's anger in the New Testament.

Three Collections of Seven on God's Final Wrath:

(1) The seven seals on a scroll judgment (Revelation 5:1).
(2) The seven trumpets judgments (Revelation 8:6).
(3) The bowls or vials judgments, symbolically filled with the wrath of God (Revelation 15:5-8).

"At that time shall arise Michael, the great prince who has charge of your people. And there shall be a time of trouble, such as never has been since there was a nation till that time. But at that time your people shall be delivered, everyone whose name shall be found written in the book" (Daniel 12:1).

Isaiah describes the Wrath of God in his vision:
"Wail, for the day of the Lord is near; as destruction from the Almighty it will come! Therefore, all hands will be feeble, and every human heart will melt. They will be dismayed: pangs and agony will seize them; they will be in anguish like a woman in labor. They will look aghast at one another; their faces will be aflame. Behold, the day of the Lord comes, cruel, with wrath and fierce anger, to make the land a desolation and to destroy its sinners from it. For the stars of the heavens and their constellations will not give their light; the sun will be dark at its rising, and the moon will not shed its light. I will punish the world for its evil, and the wicked for their iniquity; I will put an end to the pomp of the arrogant, and lay low the pompous pride of the ruthless" (Isaiah 13:6-11).

"Terror and the pit and the snare are upon you, O inhabitant of the earth! He who flees at the sound of the terror shall fall into the pit, and he who climbs out of the pit shall be caught in the snare. For the windows of heaven are opened, and the foundations of the earth tremble. The earth is utterly broken, the earth is split apart, the earth is violently shaken. The earth staggers like a drunken man; it sways like a hut; its transgression lies heavy upon it, and it falls, and will not rise again. On that day the Lord will punish the host of heaven, in heaven, and the kings of the earth, on the earth. They will be gathered together as prisoners in a pit; they will be shut up in a prison, and after many days they will be punished" (Isaiah 24:17-22).

Jesus describes the last half of the Tribulation period in the Gospel "Immediately after the tribulation of those days the sun will be darkened, and the moon will not give its light, and the stars will fall from heaven, and the powers of the heavens will be shaken" (Matthew 24:29)

Aaron spoke to the whole congregation of the children of Israel, and they looked toward the wilderness, and behold, the glory of the LORD appeared in the cloud (Exodus 16:10, 40:34-38, 1 King 8:10-11, Matthew 17:5).

When the cloud filled the Temple, it represented the presence and protection of God. No one was allowed entrance to the Temple at this time because the cloud rested above it, and so His Glory filled the Temple (cf. Exodus 40:35).

Revelation 15:8 reads, *the temple was filled with smoke*" and not with "cloud." The "cloud" is associated with the Glorious Presence of God.

The *"smoke"* comes from the Glory of God and His power. The smoke represents judgment and calamity (Psalms 97:2).

The tolerance of sin will have reached a climax, and the seven vials will be unleashed. This segment indicates the sanctuary was filled with smoke during this time, preventing anyone from approaching God until the judgments finished.

Jesus says, "except those days should be shortened, there should no flesh saved: but for the elect's sake those days (1260 days) shall be shortened" (Matthew 24:22).

Now the time is up, and God will unleash His wrath upon the unbelieving earth dwellers.

"For we know him that hath said, vengeance belongeth unto me, I will recompense, saith the Lord. And again, The Lord shall judge his people. It is a fearful thing to fall into the hands of the living God," (Hebrews 10:30-31).

The unbelievers of the world refuse to take heed to the countless warnings of God. Their heart will harden from sin and rebellion. Now, they will taste the vials of His judgments.

A Summary of the Seven Vials/ Bowls Judgment Chapter 16:

1. **The First bowl** - "harmful and painful sore on the Antichrist followers" (Revelation 16:2).
2. **The Second bowl**- The remaining seas turn into blood kills the remaining life in the sea (Revelation 16:3). The second trumpet has already killed One-Third of sea life in (Revelation 8:8-9).
3. **The Third bowl** -The remaining fresh waters turns into blood kills destroying the freshwater source (Revelation 16:4). The Antichrist, the earth dwellers, shed the blood of believers; they will now drink that blood they spilled.
4. **The Fourth bowl**- the sun scorching heat temperature will soar with its fierce heat burn men. They curse God, but still do not repent and give Him glory. (Revelation, 16:8).
5. **The Fifth bowl**- "his kingdom was full of darkness; and they gnawed their tongues for pain" (16:10)—the Antichrist's kingdom in darkness and agonizing. Hell, conditions come to the prince of darkness kingdom on earth. Antichrist followers continue to curse God and not repent.
6. **The Sixth bowl**- "the great river Euphrates; and the water thereof was dried up, that the way of the kings of the east might be prepared" (16:12). The Dragon, Antichrist, and the false prophet deceive the world's armies to revolt against God's chosen people (Israel) and Christ at a place called Armageddon.
7. **The Seventh bowl**- "announces the end of the judgments on the earth" (16:17)

CHAPTER SIXTEEN

GOD'S WRATH RESUME WITH THE FINAL SEVEN BOWLS JUDGMENT

"The Fifth Parenthesis Period"[32]

The Pronouncement (v. 1)
The Scene on Earth

God answers the prayers of the martyrs as He calls the wicked in judgment and displays His fury. The angels are commanded to go and pour out the vials upon the earth. God's wrath begins on the land in

---

32   The fifth parenthesis is coming between the sixth and seventh vial judgment of the three unclean spirits pouring out on the earth in Revelation 16:13-16.

which the second Beast emerged and the ground in which Adam was made.

Ezekiel foresees the Wrath of God saying, "Therefore have I poured out mine indignation upon them; I have consumed them with the fire of my wrath: their own way have I recompensed upon their heads, saith the Lord God" (Ezekiel 21:31-32).

The word *"great"* occurs ten times in chapter 16. The idiom "Great" here means immeasurable. God answers the prayers of the martyrs and saints, avenging their murders.

Matthew 24:21 writes, "For then shall be great tribulation, such as was not since the beginning of the world to this time, no, nor ever shall be."

The First Bowl Judgment: Sores (v. 2)
A horrific judgment falls upon men who receive the Mark of the Beast and partake of the wine of the Great Whore of Babylon. They worshipped the Beast, intentionally disregarding God's warning and plagues. The Mark of the Beast symbolizes a covenant and alliance with the Beast of the Sea.

v. 1 The first vial "fell a noisome and grievous sore" The sores are like a blister, bump, lesion, or ulcer occurring all over the body. The sore may be painful, itchy swollen

A remarkable similarity exists between the first bowl (sores) and the sixth plague (boils) of Egypt. The magician and Egyptians could not stand before Moses' God, Exodus 9:11. Those who receive the Mark of the Beast will fall before the plague.

The Second Bowl Judgment: The Sea Turns to Blood (v. 3)
Some scholars believe the second bowl judgment is limited to the Mediterranean Sea. This plague may not affect any other seas. All forms of life in the sea will die as the blood spreads as far as the tide can carry it. There is the possibility that meteorites or comets will strike the sea

and adversely affect marine life. The second vial is a reminder of the saints' bloodshed and those slain for the word of God.

The sea business will collapse and all activities at sea along with it. All will witness the power of God's wrath on land and sea. Babylon will lose profitability, and its economic power will begin to diminish as God's wrath escalates. The Planet earth from space would appear reddish because the bodies of water turn to blood.

"Every living soul died in the sea." "Soul" (Gk. psuche) is "the vital force which animates the body and shows itself in breathing."

The third part of sea life dies under the second Trumpet judgment (Revelation 8:8-9).

The Third Bowl Judgement: Turns the Fresh Waters to Blood (vv. 4-7) v. 5 "And I heard the angel of the waters say, Thou art righteous, O Lord, which art, and wast, and shalt be, because thou hast judged thus."

The third vial Judgment is similar to that of Egypt. "Thus saith the Lord, In this thou shalt know that I am the Lord: behold, I will smite with the rod that is in mine hand upon the waters which are in the river, and they shall be turned to blood," (Exodus 7:14-25).

The third vial continues to target the earth's dwellers' freshwater supplies—the wicked will recall the bloodshed they inflicted on the saints and prophets of God

They defamed the name of God Almighty and followed the Beast. In Hebrews, Paul writes, "And almost all things are by the law purged with blood; and without shedding of blood is no remission," (Hebrews 9:22). The wicked men brought God's judgment upon themselves, and now they deserve to be punished for their unjust deeds. In Revelation 16:6-7, the earth dwellers are reaping what they have sown.

Moses writes a song in Deuteronomy 32:36-42 that reads, "I will make mine arrows drunk with blood, and my sword shall devour flesh; and that with the blood of the slain and of the captives, from the beginning of revenge upon the enemy."

"Be not deceived; God is not mocked: for whatsoever a man soweth, that shall he also reap. For him that soweth to his flesh shall of the flesh reap corruption, but he that soweth to the Spirit shall of the Spirit reap life everlasting. And let us not be weary in well doing: for in due season we shall reap if we faint not" (Galatians 6:7-9).

The Fourth Bowl Judgment: Celestial Body under Judgment (vv. 8-9)
Although men knew who was responsible for these plagues, their heart was hardened like Pharaoh's and repented with insincerity. The vials were poured out on the "sun and not the earth." The vials may have caused a solar storm on the sun to wipe out the earth's ozone layers, allowing sun flares to scorch the planet. The heat will soar to an unbearable temperature that will torment people day and night. The climatic change causes many to die from dehydration and drinking unclean [contaminated] water to quench their thirst.

"Blaspheme" means to "slander or revile" the name of God. The word "blaspheme" occurs three times in this chapter (Revelation 16: 9, 11, 21). The two Beasts "blaspheme" God (Revelation 13: 1, 5, 6).

The Fifth Bowl Judgment: Targets the Antichrist Headquarters and Kingdoms (vv. 10-11)
John may be referred to the judgment falling upon the throne or headquarter of Beast and his kingdoms. Probably the Beast's throne as a reference to his entire kingdom. Some see this as the city of Babylon, but his kingdom will be global. In Revelation 12:7-14, we told that the Archangel Michael had cast Satan and spiritual forces down to the earth. The earth dwellers submit unto powers of the God of this world, and their gods cannot deliver or protect them from the wrath of God Almighty.

God will change the length of time that sunlight will provide light on the earth. The Beast and his followers will be in much pain from the sores, the lack of freshwater, and temperatures soaring to incredible heights. The earth dwellers will become angry with God until their hearts become like calluses, and they defame His name.

"Woe to you who long for the Day of the Lord! Why do you long for the day of the Lord? That day will be darkness, not light" (Amos 5:18; Zephaniah 1:15; Nahum 1:6, 8, John 1:5).

The darkness of days is literally, and it will be darkness upon the entire earth. The daily and total length of night upon the world is unknown (Revelation 8:12).

The Sixth Bowl Judgment: The Euphrates River Dries Up (vv. 12-16) The fifth parenthesis Period

The Euphrates River is one of the greatest rivers in the Middle East and occurs in Genesis 2:14. It is about 1,750 miles long and begins in Turkey. It flows down through Syria and Iraq, joining the Tigris River before ending at the Persian Gulf.

v. 12 *"The Euphrates River drying up prepares the path of the King of the East to cross"*

The sixth vial comes in two divisions:

(1) the river will dry up, allowing an army to cross for the last war in human history;
(2) the demonic force of darkness will influence the East and North's rebellious troops to join the armed forces in the Valley of Megiddo to oppose the Lord.

The Kings of the East

If an imaginary line crossed the Euphrates in Syria and went east, it would pass through Iraq (ancient Babylon), Iran, Afghanistan, Pakistan (ancient Persia), India, and China. If one draws an imaginary line eastward to Jerusalem, it will intersect (32 parallel) and pass through the same countries (Ezekiel 38:2-5, Daniel 11:44). Many scholars say that China is the King of the East. China has the most massive army in the world. The Kings of the Far East are the Asian nations.

The Kings of the North
Kings of the North: (1) Kings of the North - Russia (Gog is the leader) and its allies: Upper Mesopotamia (Northeast Syria, ancient name "Assyria"), Turkey "Meshech and Tubal," Iraq "Babylon"), and other Islamic countries. (2) The Kings of the East - Asia and nations North of the Euphrates and the Tigris river (3) Kings of the South - Egypt "Mizraim," Libya "Phut/Put" (Northern Africa).

The False Trinity
v.13-15 John saw three unclean spirits, like frogs, come out of the mouth of the (1) Dragon [Satan], (2) the Beast of the sea [Antichrist], and (3) the Beast of the earth [false prophet]. Frogs are a symbol of uncleanliness, unclean spirits, or demons (cf. Exodus 8:5; Leviticus 11:10-11, 41). Perhaps, the Beast and the False Prophet controlled by demons or Satan himself. However, the false trinity is identified as unclean spirits, like frogs. Satan led the fallen angels to rebelled against and fight wars with God's heavenly armies. Here Satan influences the Antichrist, the world leaders, kings, and the world armies to assemble for battle against God's chosen people Israel. This Battle usher in the Second Coming of Christ, and He comes quickly without delay.

v. 16 "And he gathered them together into a place called in the Hebrew tongue Armageddo" God strategy is to gather the armies into one located and decimates them.

"Armageddon" (Gk. Harmagedon) occurs only one time in the New Testament (16:16).

The Hebrew phrase of origin is Har Megiddon or "Mountain of Megiddo." It symbolizes war and defeat. Satan's evil strategy is to destroy Israel and oppose God Almighty. He uses all of his power, principalities, demonic influence, and deception to deceive the nations into revolting against God. The final war of human history will happen: Good versus Evil! This campaign is called "The Battle of Armageddon."

Satan has already caused one-third of the angels in heaven to revolt against God, and now he deceives the nations of the world as well to defy God Almighty.

The Antichrist will mustard an army of 200 million soldiers to invaded God's most possession "Israel" is surrounded and back against the Mediterranean Sea. The white horsemen of the first seal in Revelation 6:2, with the intention to slaughter Israel and wiped them off the earth.

The Egyptians armies pursue Israel on dry land through the Red Sea, and once Pharaoh reaches midway, they drowned (Exodus 14:15-31). The armies the world will follow the same pattern crossed the Euphrates River on dry land into Megiddo Valley and be destroyed by Jesus Christ.

Jesus says "… behold, I come quickly; and my reward is with me, to give every man according as his work shall be" (Revelation 22:12).

The Seventh Bowl Judgment: Great Earthquake; the Great City Divided and Babylon Remembered; Cataclysmic Events (vv. 17-21)

v. 17 "And the seventh angel poured out hid vial into the air" Satan is the prince of the air around the earth and the invisible realm of the air where he rules (Ephesians 2:2). In Ephesians 6:12 states "For we wrestle not against flesh and blood, but against principalities, against powers, against the rulers of the darkness of this world, against spiritual wickedness in high places." The Kingdom of Satan is under judgment.

"It is done" in Greek was written in the perfect tense. The phrase *"It's finished"* occurs three times in scripture (1) "Thus the heavens and the earth were finished, and all the host of them" on the sixth day, Genesis 2:1-2. (2) Jesus' last words on the Cross "I have glorified thee on the earth: I had finished the work which thou gavest me to do" (John 17:4) (3) When Jesus died on the cross at the sixth hour, He said, "it is finished," (John 19:28-30). (4) "And he said unto me; It is done" (Revelation 21:6).

The final act of God precedes the second coming of Christ. It signifies the fulfillment of the Tribulation period, the end of God's Wrath on the sacrilegious, the completion of Jacob's troubles, and the closure of sin in the world. It is finished!

"*It is done*" God's Wrath on the wicked, enemies of the cross, and the kingdom of Satan will be complete. The last enemies are death and Satan.

Fulfillment of Psalms 8:6: "Thou madest him to have dominion over the works of thy hands; thou hast put all things under his feet," (cf. Psalms 101; 1 Corinthians 15:22-28; Ephesians 1:21-23; Hebrews 2:2-9).

v. 18 "*And there were voices, and thunders, and lightnings; and there was a great earthquake* " In the Scriptures earthquakes symbolize the divine presence of God and His splendor Glory, Earthquakes occurs many times in the Old Testament in the Exodus from Egypt to the Wilderness as a shadow of future events. (1) God presence on Mount Sinai: Thick darkness, Great quake (Exodus 19:18). (2) Thousands Israel adversaries dies by earthquake, hailstones, fire and plagues (Exodus 7-10), (3) Korah swallow up by a great earthquake (Number 16; 12-13)

v. 19 "*The great city will be divided into Three Parts*" if the Jerusalem spilt into three part by the great earthquake maybe Mount Olives, Mount Zion and Mount Moriah would also be destroyed because they are with 2 miles radius of Jerusalem. The great city will split into three parts, and the cities of the nations will collapse. The Great earthquake will swallow up a portion of the 200-million-man army

The three primary purposes for a biblical earthquake:

(1) Divine judgment
(2) Communication
(3) Deliverance.

The City of Jerusalem is Divided by the Religions

    (1) Christianity
    (2) Judaism
    (3) Islamic

"Babylon" is known as the city of Satan, and Jerusalem is the Holy city of God. Babylon occurs in the Bible over 260 times.

"And their dead bodies shall lie in the street of the great city, which spiritually is called Sodom and Egypt, where also our Lord was crucified." The location where the two witnesses were the martyr (Revelation 11:8).

"Then the Lord will go forth and fight against those nations, as when He fights on a day of battle. And in that day His feet will stand on the Mount of Olives, which is in front of Jerusalem on the east; and the Mount of Olives will be split in its middle from East to West by an enormous valley, so that half of the mountain will move toward the north and the other half toward the south. And you will flee by the valley of My Mountains, for the valley of the mountains will reach to Azel; yes, you will flee just as you fled before the earthquake in the days of Uzziah, King of Judah" (Zechariah 14:3-5)

"Awake, awake! Rise up, Jerusalem, you who have drunk from the hand of the LORD the cup of his Wrath, you who have drained to its dregs the goblet that makes people stagger" (Isaiah 51:17).

"For thus saith the Lord of hosts; Yet once, it is a little while, and I will shake the heavens, and the earth, and the sea, and the dry land; And I will shake all nations, and the desire of all nations shall come: and I will fill this house with glory, saith the Lord of hosts" (Haggai 2:6-7).

"The earth shall quake before them; the heavens shall tremble: the sun and the moon shall be dark, and the stars shall withdraw their shining" (Joel 2:10).

v. 20 There is the suggestion that the islands will flee away, and the mountains will remove by a powerful earthquake that causes tsunamis and records high tidal waves throughout the earth.

Severe topographic and geologic changes on earth by the seventh vial:

- The most powerful earthquake known to humanity, 16:18. The "Armageddon earthquake," is associated with the return of Christ to Jerusalem (Zechariah 14:1-11 and Acts 1:9-11).
- The earth is possibly knocked off its axis by this great earthquake, which causes tidal waves and tsunami.

v. 21 *"Hailstorms"* are made of ice and snow and usually fall in the springtime or summer in Syria and Israel. A great hail out of heaven weighing about a talent [100 lbs. rock] will fall on them, and they will slander God for allowing this catastrophe to happen on the earth. Their heart will be hard and opposed to God's sovereignty.

Hailstones and lightning are frequently tools of judgment against God's enemies, as seen against Egypt (Exodus 9:24), the Canaanites (Joshua 10:11), Judgment on Ephraim (Isaiah 28:2) A Prophecy against Gog and Magog (Ezekiel 38:22).

Job 38:22 states, "Hast thou entered into the treasures of the snow? Or hast thou seen the treasures of the hail?"

Natural disasters are tools of judgment against the invading armies as they attempt to annihilate Israel. After the last plagues against the Egyptians' firstborns, Pharaoh pursued Israel's children to the Red Sea, and God drowned the Egyptian armies (Exodus 9:22-23, 14:7-31).

Ezekiel foretells of a similar event occurring with the armies of the world against Israel. "And I will plead against him with pestilence and with blood; and I will rain upon him, and upon his bands, and upon the many people that are with him, an overflowing rain, and great hailstones, fire, and brimstone," (Ezekiel 38:22).

CHAPTER SEVENTEEN

THE DESTRUCTION OF BABYLON THE GREAT: ECCLESIASTICAL

The Angel Revealed the Great Whore Judgment (vv. 1-2)
Religious Babylon arises on the scene in the first three and half years of the Tribulation era and later destroyed by her ten kings. These kings grow to hate her and become an instrument of God at this moment in history.

One of the seven angels told John to follow him and said he would show John the judgment of the Great Whore that controls many people, including dignitaries, kings, and Presidents of many nations. She seduces the kings of the earth until they comes intoxication and submit to her corrupt system. The wine they drink is the blood of innocent believers killed in wars and martyred because they refused to compromise.

Purpose of her Punishment: Spiritual Fornication
The Great Whore will become the most influential Church on earth. She will become the Apostate Church and will persecute the Tribulation believers as she did in her past. She is "great" because of wealth and influence over world leaders.

Historically, she has had a notorious track record of persecuting Christians during the Middle Ages.

The kings of the earth revealed
As John marvels at the vision and an angel says, "I will tell you the mystery of the woman, and of the beast with seven heads and ten horns that carry her" (v. 7). The Angel tells John that the seven heads symbolize seven kings, five of whom have fallen, one is, the other has not yet come, and when he does come, he must remain only a little while (compare v. 10). The identity of these "king" has been disputable by scholars.

"Drink with wine of her fornication" applies to a person who fornicates spiritually by worshipping other gods, idols, who is not the Creator God. The earth dweller turns to worship the Antichrist and Satan. The World leaders would be drunk from seeking guidance from false religion and her deception.

"Who changed the truth of God into a lie, and worshipped and served the creature more than the Creator, who is blessed forever. Amen" (Romans1:25).

Fornication" (Gk. *"porneuo"*) means to indulge in unlawful lust of either sex. A harlot is one who commits adultery or incest. Someone who engages in illegal sexual acts between two heterosexuals, not in a covenant relationship, bestiality relations, androgynous relations, or any sexual relationship outside of the covenant of marriage between a male and female.

This "fornication" refers to spiritual, sexual immorality, or a compromise with the world system. It is a person who is unfaithful to Christ while posing as His faithful follower and bride.

> Paul says, "Flee fornication. Every sin that a man doeth is without the body, but he that committeth fornication sinneth against his own body. What? Know ye not that your body is the Temple of the Holy Ghost which is in you, which ye have of God, and ye are not your own? For ye are bought with a price: therefore, glorify God in your body, and in your spirit, which is God's" (1 Corinthians 6:19-20).

Old Testament: Spiritual Adultery

The children of Israel are in a covenant relationship with the God of their fathers. The agreements they made with God are honored concisely, and they were blessed as a result. If Israel failed to keep its promise to God, a curse would fall upon the nation (Leviticus 26, Deuteronomy 28).

"And it shall come to pass after the end of seventy years, that the Lord will visit Tyre, and she shall turn to her hire, and shall commit fornication with all the kingdoms of the world upon the face of the earth" (Isaiah 23:17).

Spiritual adultery is when a covenant relationship with God is breached. The promise keeper habitually transgresses against God's laws and follows the abominable customs and practices of the pagan and heathen nations.

Israel's acts of spiritual adultery:

- She deserted God for false gods such as Molech, Dagon, Baal, Asherah, etc.
- God is the husband of Israel (cf. Jeremiah 3, 31; Isaiah 54).

New Testament: Spiritual Adultery
Spiritual adultery has the same meaning as the Old Testament physically, and the New Testament is both physical and spiritual.

> "Ye adulterers and adulteresses, know ye not that the friendship of the world is enmity with God? Whosoever, therefore, will be a friend of the world is the enemy of God" (James 4:4).

Jezebel, the false Prophetess in the Church of Thyatira, typified a "system" similar to the "Papal Church." The Papal Church introduces statues and images of saints as a symbol and bows down to it. The Roman Catholic Church teaches that the Virgin Mary is "Co-Redemptress," with Jesus the Redeemer. The practice of Syncretism is a form of spiritual adultery or fornication.

What John Saw in the Wilderness (vv. 3-6)
John was carried away in the vision to different locations and a new scene in the wilderness. Suppose the woman sitting upon the beast is in modern Iraq. In that case, there are only two deserts that would fit the wilderness that the Apostle John is referencing: the Syrian or Arabian deserts. The *"wilderness"* may refer to *the world*. The word "scarlet" symbolized royalty, power, and wealth, both religiously and politically. The Roman soldier's mockery Christ placed a scarlet robe on Him (Matthew 27:28; Luke 23:11).

The woman represents the great city [Rome] that is surrounded by seven hills. "The woman you saw is the great city that rules over the kings of the earth" (17:18). The Roman Catholic church is the most powerful and has global influence over world leaders today.

Scarlet is associated with the woman in verse 4. She is clothed in "scarlet and purple," symbolizing a one-world religion. The word *"sit"* signifies the position of influence or dominance; biblical terms usually means *"rule."* Perhaps, her sitting on the beast indicates where her power comes from (Revelation 18:2).

The vision shows that she has control of the beast, but it is the beast that controls the woman as a puppet. "Babylon the Great" is the Mother of all Harlots.

"*Many waters*"- indicates many "nations" around the world. The inhabitants of the earth, which represent humanity as a whole. The woman dominates over the world with false religious beliefs and doctrines of devils.

The color purple represents "*godliness.*" Since the woman was wearing both colors, it suggests that she has an ungodly trait. The passage here states, "since the woman is on top of the beast, she must guide it," but what is the real truth? She receives support from the beast, and theoretically she is not in control of the political situation or the beast. The beast is in command and demands worship from the world (Revelation 13).

"*Having seven heads*" - The number seven (7) represents perfection and completeness in a spiritual context.

"*Ten Horns*" - the number Ten (10) represents the world empires or governments and the power of the beast.

A harlot decked herself with gold, costly pearls, earrings, and seductive attire to lure her prey to spiritual immorality and idolatry (cf. Proverbs 7:10; Jeremiah 4:30; Matthew 23:7;1 Timothy 2:9; 1 Peter 3:3). She appears to be glamourous and beautiful externally, but she is superficial, corrupt, and rotten within.

Gold in the Bible signifies the purity of God. The "*Golden Cup*" is a relic that belonged to the Temple of God. The golden cup has been removed from the Temple and will be defiled by the ungodly. John's vision of the golden cup also suggests the debauchery of banquets in which drunkenness and sexual immorality occurred, Revelation 13:1.

"Babylon hath been a golden cup in the hand of the LORD, intoxicating all the earth. The nations have drunk of her wine; Therefore, the nations are going mad" (Jeremiah 51:7).

The "*forehead*" the marking on the forehead symbolizes ownership or allegiance to the stamp's authority.

The Apostle Paul says, "Let this mind be in you, which was also in Christ Jesus" (Philippians 2;5-11; Romans 12:2; 1 Corinthians 2:14-16; 1 Peter 1:13).

"And upon her forehead was a name written." The context yields no clues of who inscribed the name on her forehead.

God has chosen 144,000 Jews and sealed His name into their foreheads. There is no condition for the elect because they were all hand-picked by God Almighty, our Creator (cf. Revelation 7:3,14:1).

In Revelation 13:16, the Antichrist's servants "receive the beast mark, or the name of the Beast, or his number 666."

The word "Mystery" (Gk. *musterion*) refers to the counsels of God, once hidden but now revealed in the Gospel. The mystery shows Satan's secret power and gives a clearer picture of how he operates behind the scenes through both the woman and the beast. "In whom the god of this world has blinded the mind of them which believe not" (2 Corinthians 4:4). The Man of Sin is "the mystery of iniquity" until God chooses to reveal his true identity (2 Thessalonians 2:1-7).

The word "Babylon" derives from "Babel," which means confusion (Genesis 10-11). Nimrod built the city and a tower in the land of Shinar (Genesis 10:10). He made a tower that attempted to reach heaven. God came down confused their language and scattered them upon the face of all the earth (Genesis 11:1-6). The ruins of modern-day Babylon are located in Iraq along the Euphrates river and Shinar's city approximately 535 miles East of the Holy City of Jerusalem. Babylon is in the (East) and Jerusalem in the (West).

"Babylon the Great is the Mother of Harlots" "The Mother of Harlots" It suggests that she represents herself as the originator of all harlots, beginning at the Tower of Babel. She represents a form of spiritual

adultery, fornication, and a false religious system. She gives birth to the ideology of false religious practices and all idolatrous worship.

Babylon the Great is (1) Origin of Idolatry (2) Location near Garden of Eden, where the first sin occurred (3) Babylonian empire conquer Israel (4) The Seat of the Antichrist Headquarter (5) The symbol of all false religion.

"And I will render unto Babylon and to all the inhabitants of Chaldea all their evil that they have done in Zion in your sight, saith the Lord" (Jeremiah 51:24).

Ancient cities that are describes as a harlot:

Nineveh: associated with Babylon and Nimrod (Genesis 10:11-13).

- Nineveh was known for "the multitude of the whoredoms of the well-favored harlot, the mistress of witchcrafts, that selleth nation through her whoredoms, and families through her witchcraft" (Nahum 1:1; 3:1, 4, 7).
- Daughter of the Chaldeans, [Babylon], who is called the Queen of the Kingdoms. She bewitches "with the multitude of sorceries, multitude of counsel through soothsayers for hire" (Isaiah 47:1, 5-15).

Tyre and Sidon: A wealthy, trade city, Tyre "committed fornication with all the kingdoms of the world" (Isaiah 23:1,14-17).

Jerusalem: She committed spiritual adultery. "She went upon every hill and under every green tree thou wanderest, playing the harlot" (Isaiah 1:1, 2:1; Jeremiah 2:1-2, 20).

The Queen of Heaven is a pagan deity "Ishtar" suggests this idolatrous, pagan worship of the Queen of Heaven was carried over into Mary's Catholic worship as the Virgin Mary as the Queen of Heaven.

- The son of the Queen of Heaven and Nimrod, (Ezekiel 8:14-15).
- Offering cakes unto the Queen of Heaven (Jeremiah 7:18).
- Burning odor to the Queen of Heaven, Jeremiah (44:17-19, 25).

"And I saw the woman drunken with the blood of the saints, and with the blood of the martyrs of Jesus," The woman in verse 6 is drunk with the aspiration to persecute the Tribulation believers and a desire to kill those who oppose her evil practices. The true believers are willing to be persecuted for their beliefs and make a stand for Christ. The Harlot slaughtered the saints and celebrated in their blood bath of the saints as drunken revels in wine.

"And I will feed them that oppress thee with their own flesh; and they shall be drunken with their own blood, as with sweet wine: and all flesh shall know that I the LORD am thy Saviour and thy Redeemer, the mighty One of Jacob" (Isaiah 49:26).

Her golden cup overflows with the blood of millions of saints who refuse to compromise their faith and follow the beast. This will be the worst slaughter of all ages. The saints have been persecuted and martyred by the Dragon, who disguises himself as an angel of light since the falls man and Abel's death. The woman's religious system is like a wolf in sheep's clothing and a counterfeit (Galatians 1:7; 2 Corinthians 11:13-15; 2 Timothy 3:1-5, 4:3-4).

The Mystery of the Woman Revealed (vv. 7-8)
The Angel explains the meaning of the woman's secret (vv.15-18). The beast is connected to the woman's power, and later the beast turns on the rider. The seven heads and ten horns are explained by the Angel (vv. 9-14)

"Ten horns" are mention in (Daniel 7:7, 20, 24 and Revelation 12:3, 13:1, 17:3, 7, 12, 16). Daniel interprets it to represent ten kings and ten kingdoms. The kingdoms are associated with the kings (Daniel 7:24).

"And the ten horns out of this kingdom are ten kings that shall arise: and another shall rise after them, and he shall be diverse from the first, and he shall subdue three kings" (Daniel 7:24).

The beast from the sea [Antichrist] mimics the ministry of Jesus Christ and tries to steal His identity to deceive the world. The angel describes the beast in similar terms as Christ.

"John to the churches which are in Asia: Grace be unto you, and peace, from him *which is, and which was, and which is to come;* and from the seven spirits which are before his throne" (Revelation 1:4).

Antichrist terms: the beast that thou sawest *"was"* and *"is not"* and shall *ascend out* of the bottomless pit, and go into perdition, *"which is to come."*

"Was" - he *was* the seventh king of Revelation 13 and 17 and *"is not"*-in existence now because of his "deadly wound to the head." *"Yet is"* - the Antichrist, the seventh king, will be the first beast that ascends out of the bottomless pit in restoration form as the eighth king. The eighth king will go into perdition after a short reign (vv. 9-14).

The Angel Explained the Vision (vv. 9-14)

"And here is the mind which hath wisdom. The seven heads are seven mountains on which the woman sitteth. And there are seven kings: five are fallen, and one is, and the other is not yet come; and when he cometh, he must continue a short space. And the beast that was, and is not, even he is the eighth and is of the seven, and goeth into perdition. And the ten horns which thou sawest are ten kings, which have received no kingdom as yet; but receive power as kings one hour with the beast. These have one mind, and shall give their power and strength unto the beast."

"The seven heads" the Angel now explains the meaning of "the seven heads" revealed to John. The seven heads symbolize the seven kings. Five of the kings have fallen, and one of these kings was in existence in John's Day, ca. 99 A.D. The seventh king has not come yet, but he will be described as the eighth king, which is the beast (Antichrist). The seven heads also reference the church government's successive forms related to the kings seated in Rome. The final form of world government will be the eighth beast (Antichrist), which manifests as the Great Tribulation's one World Empire.

The revived Roman Empire will reoccur in history after the Church's rapture, as indicated by the seventh beast. King Jesus will cast the eighth beast into the Lake of Fire alive at His second coming.

Two Groups of Kings:

1. The seven heads are seven mountains of government and the seven ruling Kings.
2. The ten horns are the ten Kings without a Kingdom to rule simultaneously at the end time (Revelation 13, 17).

In Bible prophecies, God only deals with the kingdoms that affect Israel as a nation. There are many Gentile kingdoms and countries in the world, but we will focus our attention on the kingdoms or empires that persecuted God's people throughout Israel's history.

Five Kings are Fallen

1. Assyria- conquers Northern kings of Israel.
2. Egypt- enslaves the nation of Israel for over 400 years
3. Babylon- carries the Southern Kingdom off into captivity for 70 years.
4. Medo-Persia- exile ends and is released to rebuild the walls and Jerusalem.
5. Greece- occupancy of Philistine

Last two kings

1. *"One is in John's days,"* Roman Empire - Persecutes the Jews and the Church.
2. *"The other is not yet come, but will in the future,"* Revived Roman Empire.
3. *"The Beast even he "is" the eighth, and is of the seven, and goes into perdition.* The seventh Beast "is" The resurrected Antichrist.
4. Also, the eighth and re-emerges into power over all the previous pagan, idolatrous empires. The Antichrist is the last world leader of the revived Roman Empire.

In Revelation 13, the ten kings relinquish their power and authority over to the eighth beast. The beast has a short space of time to make war with the Lamb. The Antichrist and the world's armies will serve as Satan's instrument to attack and surround Israel. Suddenly, the "Lord of lords" and "the King of kings" will appear in the clouds and defeat the Beast and his mighty Empire. His kingdom will be utterly destroyed at the second coming of Christ, and he will be thrown into perdition [cast into the Lake of Fire].

Perdition means "loss of eternal life and eternal misery" (Thayer). Wickedness will lead to being expelled from Heaven and God's presence for eternity.

The *"son of perdition"* is found twice in the New Testament in John 17:12 and 2 Thessalonians 2:3. The phrase here means *"man is doomed to destruction."* John describes Judas Iscariot as the "Son of Perdition" and the Antichrist, who emerges from the sea before the Tribulation period as the "Man of Lawlessness."

Some think the last world leader will be the resurrection of Judas Iscariot or Nero, the emperor of Rome in 66 A.D. referencing back to Chapter 13, the form of Roman government just proceeding the world empire. The ten horns rule as Kings, and they are subject to the beast himself. They share the same intent as the beast, which gives them power for a short time.

(1) The ten toes on the statue's feet in Daniel 2:41-44 represent the revived Roman Empire. (2) The first Beast in Revelation 13:1 and 17:3 resembles the vision in Daniel 7:7-24, "the fourth Beast with ten horns."

It will exist as a significant power only for a short while since it will give its authority to the beast (13:7). This authority is handed over to make war with the Lamb, fulfilled in Chapter 19, during the second coming of Jesus Christ.

V. 14 *"These shall make war with the Lamb, and the Lamb shall overcome them"* This war started in Genesis 3:15, The enmity between the seed of woman [Jesus] and the seed of the serpent [Satan]. After the death and resurrection of Jesus. Satan sought to destroy the true believers in Christ throughout the church age and the saints during the tribulation period and those associated with Christ. V. 12 "one hour with the beast..." Satanic power and evil influence make war with the elects of the Lamb. The Lamb will destroy his enemies at the battle of Armageddon in Revelation 16:16 (cf. Psalm 2:2; Daniel 2:44).

The phrase "Lord of lords and King of kings" is used six times in scriptures related to Jesus (cf. Deuteronomy 5:4, 10:17, Psalms 136:3, 1 Timothy 6:15-16, Revelation 17:14, 19:16). Jesus Christ is the supreme power of heaven and earth; Creator.

The Climax of the Vision: Antichrist Allies Turn on the Harlot (vv. 15-18) The ten horns (kings) shall destroy the woman riding on the beast. The angel gives John an explanation of the vision in verses 15-18. The meaning of the water is peoples, multitudes, nations, and tongues. The ten horns hate the great whore and shall make her desolate and naked, destroying her and bringing an end to her religious system. The destruction of the Harlot reduces all her false splendor to nothing. The kings will be the downfall of the Apostate Church in the future. God will allow the earth's kings to turn over their kingdoms to the Antichrist until His divine will is completed.

The Antichrist's religious system is destroyed, and the Apostate Church bylaws are abolished. The Antichrist's true identity is revealed as the Man of Sin. The second beast continues new operations that demand worship of the Antichrist and his image. He will enter into the third Temple and require the world to worship him as their God (Daniel 11:36).

"The woman, which thou sawest is that great city". The great city here in context refers to Babylon as the woman who reigns over the earth (cf. Revelation 14:8, 18:10, 18:16, 18, 21). Satan's kingdom is associated with Babylon, and God's Kingdom refers to Jerusalem as "the City of God. The focus is on Satan's Kingdom and subordinate leaders that rule the world with the first beast.

CHAPTER EIGHTEEN

THE DESTRUCTION OF BABYLON THE GREAT: COMMERCIAL

The Announcement by a Mighty Angel: Fall of Great Babylon (vv. 1-3)
The Scene on Earth

John said, "After these things." The event happens in chapter 17. The Ten Kings of the Earth destroy the Mother of Harlots and her corrupt system. The Antichrist quickly moves his seat or headquarters to Jerusalem (Daniel 11:45). The Antichrist desecrates the temple and now demands to be worshiped as a God. The second Beast erects an image of the first Beast, and power is given to the idol statue to hear, see, and talk to the worshippers.

Jesus' prophecy mentions in Matthew 24:15, "When ye, therefore, shall see the abomination of desolation, spoken of by Daniel the prophet, stand in the holy place (whoso readeth Daniel 9:27, let him understand." The Antichrist will make a seven-year peace treaty with Israel's nation: (1) Isaiah, in his writing, called it the covenant. "The covenant with death and hell. A Great agreement" (Isaiah 28:14); (2) Daniel called the covenant "a strong and firm covenant with many" (Daniel 9:27).

According to Flavius Josephus, "In 167 B.C., a Grecian by the name Antiochus Epiphanies set up an altar to Zeus over the burnt offerings in the temple in Jerusalem.

Additionally, he sacrificed an unclean animal [pig] on the altar of God in Jerusalem."[33] This is a double reference prophecy that the Antichrist may duplicate in the future.

John saw another angel (different from the one in chapter 17) coming down from Heaven. He said, "the great angel's splendor and glory shone upon the Earth." This angel was great in his glory, suggesting that he plays a significant role in God's divine plans.

"Babylon the Great is Fallen, is Fallen" the destruction of Commercial Babylon occurs at the end of the Great Tribulation period, before the Second Coming of Christ in Revelation 19. The phrase *"Is fallen, is fallen"* means a sudden event or swift destruction of both systems. Hence, Babylon the Great (Religious) is fallen, Babylon the Great (Commercial) is fallen! The cause of Babylon's fall is moral corruption, and her accumulation of sins continually comes before the LORD. The word "fallen" is mention twice; it comes from Babylon's prophecy falling as cited in Isaiah 21:9. Also, it suggests Babylon felt in the past under the hand of the Persian and again in the future. Finally, fallen twice could mean double punishment for her sins.

Babylon will reap what she has planted! Moreover, portions of God Wrath will fall on her work with a double dose, and all who partakes in her sin will be punishment (cf. Jeremiah 50:15, 29; Galatians 6:6-9).

---

33 Josephus, Flavius, V2:87

Babylon's judgment will come in one day and will be utterly destroyed and burned to the ground by her former allies [ten horns and the Beast] (cf. Isaiah 13:6, 9-11; Jeremiah 51:8).

In her heart, she said, "I" [self-pride] sit as the queen of Babylon forever. God remembers the arrogant boast of the Queen of Babylon.

"And, behold, here cometh a chariot of men, with a couple of horsemen. And he answered and said, is fallen; and all the graven images of her gods, he hath broken unto the ground," (Isaiah 21:9).

There is a similarity in the context of Revelation 18:3 and 17:2. "For all nations have drunk of the wine of the wrath of her fornication, and the kings of the earth have committed fornication with her." Suggests that God pictures two different Babylonian empire systems: (1) religious and (2) commercial.

"Become the habitation of devils" - This refers to a dwelling or a holding place [Babylon] of evil and wickedness. A cage of every unclean and hateful bird is used to hold all sorts of birds. This cage becomes the haven of "demons, principalities, powers, and rulers of the darkness of this world, and spiritual wickedness in high places," (Ephesians 6:12). The cage could be an observation post where those that are caged may closely watch and examine the observed movement.

"Hateful birds" - Birds always indicate demons or evil spirits. The name of Babylon in Revelation 17:5 is "the Abominations "of the whole Earth destroyed by the Kings of the Earth. Here in Revelation 18:2, she is "mystery, Babylon the Great, the Mother of Prostitutes." The judgment of God destroys her. The only thing they held in common was they are both connected to Babylon. The Antichrist and the False Prophet now set their sights on the third Jewish Temple in Jerusalem. Afterward, the devastation of the Babylon religious system occurs.

The Harlot convinces the nations of the world to put their trust in the Antichrist and the Beast. She leads them in worshipping the Dragon and Beast until they become drunk with the wine of her fornication.

"Delicacies" (Gk. *streniao*) refers to "living in sensual, lustful behavior, in self-indulgence and wanton luxury." Babylon was a wealthy and arrogant city. The merchants and travelers wanted a blessing for hire but at a high cost. The merchants purchased salvation at any cost (indulgences), paid for spiritual blessings and false religious rituals.

Strong Warning from Heaven: Repent and Come Out of Her Sins (vv. 4-8)
John heard a different voice than that of the mighty angel. Perhaps, this was the voice of God Almighty. He warns His people [believers] living in the corrupt society of the Antichrist not to compromise and partake in the sins of the woman that rides on the Beast (Revelation 17:4). He issues this warning because His Wrath is imminent, and her sins have spilled over into Heaven (Matthew 24:26-29).

The Signs of Warning:

- His judgment will fall suddenly on all those who receive the Mark of the Beast (Jeremiah 51:6, 45).
- God sends angels to warn Lot and his family of the destruction of Sodom and Gomorrah (Genesis 19:15).
- Diseases: seventh vial (Revelation 16).
- Babylon's sins continue to accumulate before God Almighty, and He takes action.
- In the days of Noah, God warns the earth dwellers of His impending judgment. Destruction comes after 120 years of warning (Genesis 6:11-22).
- Approximately 107 years after the flood, under the leadership of Nimrod, the Tower of Babel was built. The earth's inhabitants rebelled, and out of pride, they built a tower that would "reach Heaven." God came down to see the Tower; He brought judgment against them and scattered them across the earth, causing many languages (Genesis 11:1-9).

Isaiah 47:9 says, "But these two things shall come to thee in a moment in one day. The loss of children, and widowhood: they shall come upon thee in their perfection for the multitude of thy sorceries, and for the great abundance of thine enchantments."

Jeremiah 51:8 says, "Babylon is suddenly fallen and destroyed: howl for her; take balm for her pain, if so may she be healed."

Isaiah 47:7-8 states, "And thou saidst, I shall be a lady forever: so that thou didst not lay these things to thy heart, neither didst remember the latter end of it. Therefore, hear now this, thou that art given to pleasures, that dwellest carelessly, that sayest in thine heart, I am, and none else beside me; I shall not sit as a widow, neither shall I know the loss of children."

The Fall of Babylon Mourned (vv. 9-20)

vv. 9-10 Mourning: The Kings of the Earth
The kings, the merchants of the earth, and tradespeople by the sea will lament their profitability and clients' loss. All their hopes will burn up in flames. The evil practices will no longer be available in the city. They will have suffered a significant loss and will be outraged with the one responsible for her destruction. Many scholars believe that Babylon will be restored or revived during the end (Revelation 14:8, 16:19, 17, 18).

The Lord gives warning in Matthew 6:24, "No man can serve two masters: for either he will hate the one, and love the other; or else he will hold to the one, and despise the other. Ye cannot serve God and mammon.

In the Old Testament, Ezekiel foretold a similar prophecy. In Ezekiel, there is a prophecy about the fall of Tyre. Many countries profit by doing business with Tyre. The city was the same as Babylon in that it thrived in all trades, imported foreign goods had great wealth, and maintained splendor as a beautiful and luxurious place. Tyre was a one-stop-shop where all the people would purchase their merchandise. Tyre smirked at the fall of Jerusalem "because she was a gateway to God for the people.

"When thy wares went forth out of the seas, thou filledst many people; thou didst enrich the kings of the earth with the multitude of thy riches and of thy merchandise" (Ezekiel 27:33).

This "great city" of Revelation 11:8 is not synonymous with the city of Jerusalem. It refers to the city of Babylon. However, the city of Jerusalem becomes spiritually mourning, like "Sodom and Egypt."

"Alas, Alas" (Gk. *ouai*) "an expression of grief or denunciation of woe."

"one hour is thy judgment come" Babylon's wealth and economic power disappeared rapidly and gone up in smoke. Her annihilation properly did not occur within an hour but is a figure of speech. Suggests that the *"one hour"* mean it happens so quickly. Babylon was destroyed economically through rapid change in commerce. Her great city left in ruin and smoke by God's judgment. The Old Testament predicts Babylon destruction will come in the Day of the Lord (cf. Isaiah 13:6-11, 13;1, 14:1-3; Jeremiah 50:1-6).

After the Babylonian empire was conquered by the Persian kings Darius and Xerxes in 597 B.C., most of Babylon's impressive buildings were destroyed. On that same night or one hour of receiving the interpretation of king Belshazzar's dream, "he was slain and Babylon siege by Darius and Median took the kingdom" (Daniel 5).

vv. 11-17 Mourning: The Merchants of the earth
The merchants will stay far off at sea in disarray and be horrified as the city goes up in smoke. How quickly she fell from fame and affluence to wasteful state.

"The pleasures of sin would only last for a season, and the end is dissatisfaction" (Hebrews 11:25).

vv. 17b- 19 Mourning: The Shipmasters and sailors on the sea.
The Shipmasters and sailors were in extreme mourning over Babylon's obliteration. We can imagine those upon the ships approaching great Babylon's seaport with high hopes and indulges in lustful sins at Babylon

but finding the city in ruin and smoke. How disappointed they have felt after being at sea for a long time and disbelief her fall quickly. In fear of sharing in Babylon's fate, they stand afar off.

v. 20 Rejoicing in Heaven: Martyrs, Tribulation saints, and heaven hosts God answers the prayer of the saints, "And they cried with a loud voice, saying, how long, O Lord, holy and true, dost thou not judge and avenge our blood on them that dwell on the earth?" (Revelation 6:10)

Babylon has Fallen (v. 21)
v. 21 The *"great millstone"* is a huge boulder. The millstone has a form like a wheel and uses it as a grinder. The stone does not burn but causes an explosion once it strikes any flammable things in its path.

"But whoso shall offend one of these little ones which believe in me, it were better for him that a millstone were hanged about his neck, and that he were drowned in the depth of the sea" (Matthew 18:6).

"Come down, and sit in the dust, O virgin daughter of Babylon, sit on the ground: there is no throne, O daughter of the Chaldeans: for thou shalt no more be called tender and delicate. Take the millstones, and grind meal: uncover thy locks, make bare the leg, uncover the thigh, pass over the rivers (Isaiah 47:1-2).

Babylon is Desolate and Powerless (vv. 22-23)
All the inhabitants of Babylon who didn't take heed to the warning of God. Drink from her cup of wrath by the holy decree of God. All life forms in that great city die, and the city is silent in her shame and smoke.

"Sorceries" (Gk. Pharmakeia) is how all nations will be deceived. It "means to administer drugs related to sorcery, like the practice of black magical arts, often found in connection with deceptions and seductions of idolatry.

The Reason for Her Destruction (v.24)
"And in her was found the blood of prophets, and of saints, and of all that were slain upon the earth."

The Destruction of Religious Babylon (Chapter 17)	The Destruction of Commercial Babylon (Chapter 18)
Papal or Apostate Church destroyed by the ten kings. The ecumenical system is destroyed ushing in the new world order and worshipping of the Anitchrist image.	The announcement of the fall of Babylon "After these things" fulfilled in chapter 17. Babylon the Great (the city) is destroyed by God suddenly.
Events of Chapter 17 were introduced by "one of the seven angels who had the seven bowls," (Revelation 17:1).	"I saw another angel coming down from Heaven." The angel referred to in (18:1) is, of course, not the same as the one who introduced the events of Chapter 17:1.
The names in both chapters are different: "Mystery, Babylon the Great, the Mother of Prostitutes and the Abominations of the whole earth" (17:5). The only similarity is the location of Babylon.	The name in Chapter 18 is simply "Babylon the Great." (18:2).
Babylon, the prostitute of Chapter 17, will be destroyed by the ten kings of the earth, (17:16).	The Babylon of Chapter 18 will be destroyed by the cataclysmic judgments of God (18:8)
The was no lamenting over the destruction of the woman in Chapter 17.	The kings and merchants lament over the destruction of Babylon (18:9-11).
If chapter 17 and 18 take places during the last days of the Tribulation, there will be no place for the Antichrist and the False Prophet to do away with all religions and substitute the worship of the Antichrist's image as described in Chapter 13. Chapter 17 take place at midpoint of the Tribulation and Chapter 18 at the end of the Tribulation period.	The prediction of the final destruction of Babylon (Jeremiah 50:35, 39-40; Isaiah 13:1, 19-22).

Figure 13: The Comparison of the Two Babylonian Systems

CHAPTER NINETEEN

THE TRANSITION OF POWER: THE BATTLE OF ARMAGEDDON AND THE SECOND COMING OF CHRIST

The Sixth "Parenthesis Period"
Christ is prepared to return with His saints.

Heaven Rejoices over the Fall of Babylon (vv. 1-5)
The Scene in Heaven

"And after these things," John referring to the destruction of Religious and Commercial Babylon in Revelation 17- 18. Next on God's agenda is to defeat His enemies: Antichrist, all the power of darkness and armies of the world.

"And it shall come to pass in that day, saith the Lord, that I will cut off thy horses out of the midst of thee, and I will destroy thy chariots: And I will cut off the cities of thy land, and throw down all thy strong holds: And I will cut off witchcrafts out of thine hand, and thou shalt have no more soothsayers: Thy graven images also will I cut off, and thy standing images out of the midst of thee; and thou shalt no more worship the work of thine hands. And I will pluck up thy groves out of the midst of thee: so will I destroy thy cities. And I will execute vengeance in anger and fury upon the heathen, such as they have not heard" (Micah 5:10-15).

The word *"Alleluia"* or Hallelujah (Heb. *"Praise Yahweh"*), which means "Praise Yahweh" and often rendered as "praise ye the Lord" (Psalms 149:4-9). Alleluia is found only here in Revelation 19:1, 3, 4,6, a total of four times.

"Salvation" signifies deliverance. Salvation may refer to saints' deliverance of Satan power during the tribulation period. God makes provision for us through His Son Jesus Christ.

"Glory and honor" imply God's righteous Judgment in His Glory. God is the only deliverance from the saints' enemies and sin; The glory and honor ascribed to Him.

"Power" implies that God is omnipotent and almighty in authority to execute judgment upon the Harlot. His judgment is declared to be righteous.

v. 2 *"For true and righteous are his judgments: for he hath judged the great whore, which did corrupt the earth with her fornication, and hath avenged the blood of his servants at her hand"* John indicates that he heard one great voice in unison with all the inhabitants in heaven. In his vision, they were shouting with praise and honor to God for destroying Babylon and avenging His servants' blood.

The Great Whore has finally judged; again, they shout "Alleluia." God executes judgment on the earth through truth and righteousness.

Her cup will overflow with indignation and sin. She will lead the world to rebel against God Almighty and refuse to repent. The LORD's act of judgment will be swift; He will destroy the works of pride, leaving her city in ruin, and the smoke will rise forever and ever.

v. 4 *"The four living creatures and twenty-four elders"* first introduced in Chapter 4, prostrate before God Almighty and worship Him. They say, *"So be it,"* praising God the Most Highest for His righteous judgment upon sin. All of the human histories

It has been over two thousand years since Christ ascension to heaven, and humanity, we are told to wait for His Second Coming. Christ's return to earth is imminent and heavenly hosts are rejoicing.

v. 5 *"And a voice came out of the throne, saying, Praise our God, all ye his servants"* The word "servants" in this verse in Gk. *"douloi"* signifying "in bondage" or bondservants. Apostle Paul refer to himself as a servant of God who does the will of God in their heart (Ephesian 6:6).

Heaven Rejoices in Preparation for The Marriage of The Lamb
(vv. 6-10)
The Scene in Heaven

"The voice from the throne room," maybe that of Jesus Christ or a mighty angel. The great voices of the multitude collectively sound like many waterfalls and mighty thunderings when heard together, saying "Alleluia." The first time in the Bible, the word *"omnipotent"* occurs in v. 6. The word "omnipotent" means Almighty God is unlimited in His power, *"For the Lord God omnipotent reigneth."*

A voice from the throne room calls upon the saints and inhabitants of heaven to praise their God, the Supreme Ruler, and revere Him. God is worthy of all the praise and honor. All will reflect on what the Creator has done for them. He is the source of existence, and He made provision for all of humanity. He sustains the believers, and He provides residence for them in heaven. It was His plan and His doing that rescued humanity from the debt of sin. God Almighty is worthy of praise: "Alleluia."

The Fourteen Worship Hymns in the Book of Revelation	
Jesus made us Kings and priests unto God and His Father.	Revelation 1:5,6
Holy, holy, holy, LORD God Almighty, which was, and is and is to come.	Revelation 4:8
Thou art worthy, O Lord, to receive glory and honor and power.	Revelation 4:10-11
Thou art worthy to take the book, and to open the seals thereof…	Revelation 5:8-10
Worthy is the Lamb that was slain to receive power, and riches, and wisdom, and strength, and honour, and glory, and blessing.	Revelation 5:11-12
Blessing, and honour, and glory, and power, be unto Him that sitteth upon the throne, and unto the Lamb for ever and ever.	Revelation 5:13
Salvation to our God which sitteth upon the throne, and unto the Lamb	Revelation 7:9-10
Amen: Blessing, and glory, wisdom and thanksgiving, and honour, and power, and might, be unto our God forever and ever. Amen	Revelation 7:11-12
Great and marvelous are thy works, Lord God Almighty; just and true are thy ways, thou King of saints. Who shall not fear thee, O Lord, and glorify thy name? For thou only art holy: for all nations shall come and worship before thee; for thy judgments are made manifest	Revelation 15:2-4
Thou art righteous, O Lord, which art, and wast, and shalt be, because thou hast judged thus.	Revelation 16:4-5
Even so, Lord God Almighty, true and righteous are thy judgments.	Revelation 16:7
Alleluia, Salvation, and glory, and honour, and power, unto the Lord our God.	Revelation 19:1-2
Alleluia: for the Lord God omnipotent reigned.	Revelation 19:5-6

Figure 14: The Fourteen Worship Hymns in the Book of Revelation.

The Marriage of the Lamb (vv. 7-8)
Here in the passage, there is a claim of ownership on His bride [the Church]. In Revelation 21 and 22, a great city describes as "the bride, the wife of the Lamb," The city is coming down from Heaven, chapter 19, the wedding of the Lord, and His bribe take place. It is evident in the Old Testament that Israel is the bride of God (Hosea 2:19-20; Ezekiel 16:8-14; Isaiah 54:1-6). God's bride was conceded through the seed of Abraham. However, Christ's bride was formed by faith.

The Process of an Ancient Jewish Marriage Contract:
First, one should examine the Jewish marriage customs that lead to the wedding feast. (1) Betrothal: this is the marriage covenant that binds the man and woman together as husband and wife (Malachi 2:14; Matthew 1:18-19). (2) The marriage ceremony: betrothal commonly lasts for one year, and then the groom takes his wife or bride from her residence at night to his Father's house (Matthew 25:1-8).

The marriage consummation occurs on the first night at the groom's Father's house (Matthew 22:2-13, 25:10). (3) Marriage supper or feast: all the guests are invited and gather at the designated location to celebrate the bride and groom's marriage consummation.

The wedding guests would feast and be merry for seven days (Genesis 29:21-23, 27-28; Judges 14:1-2, 10-17).

The correlation of the Jewish marriage custom and the Marriage of Christ and the Church:

(1) betrothal of Christ and the Church takes place during the church age after Jesus paid the dowry for man's sin. The Holy Spirit sealed them until the day of redemption (2 Corinthians 11:2).
(2) The Marriage of the Lamb happens when the Church is raptured at night and taken to the Father's house in heaven (John 14:2-3; 1 Thessalonians 4:13-18). The Marriage of Christ and the Church will be consummated in heaven.

Arrayed in *"Fine linen, clean and white,"* righteousness will have been bestowed upon the saints by their faith in Christ Jesus.

The believers enter into a relationship with Christ dirty and filthy, with no righteous of their own, because of sin (Isaiah 64:6; 2 Corinthians 5:21).

"But of Him are you in Christ Jesus, who of God made unto us wisdom, and righteousness, and sanctification, and redemption" (1 Corinthians 1:30).

"Jesus is called the Lord our Righteousness" (Jeremiah 23:6).

"I will greatly rejoice in the Lord, my soul shall be joyful in my God; for he hath clothed me with the garments of Salvation, he hath covered me with the robe of righteousness, as a bridegroom decketh himself with ornaments, and as a bride adorneth herself with her jewels" (Isaiah 61:10).

Every believer is given fine linen, an inner garment of white to represent that they have washed their sin-stained robe in the blood of the Lamb. The outer garment with the adornment of gold, silver, and precious stones is an award given at the BEMA seat of Christ (cf. Romans 14:10-11; 1 Corinthians 3:11-15; 2 Corinthians 5:9-10; 1 John 2:28; Revelation 3:11-17).

The Marriage Supper of the Lamb (vv.9-10)
There are two views of the location and time of the marriage supper.

The first view: the marriage supper takes place on earth. It will happen after the Second Coming of Christ on earth and after the destruction of Babylon. All evil on earth has been destroyed. The nations will be separated, and He will be setting up His earthly kingdom (John 3:29; Romans 7:2; 2 Corinthians 11:2; Ephesians 5:25-33; Revelation 19:21:1- 22:7).

The second view: the marriage supper takes place in heaven after the rapture of the Church because the wedding guests have already been called and gathered. The rapture of the Church takes place before the Tribulation period begins. The marriage supper lasts one week. The one-week period is the Tribulation period. Sixty-nine weeks of the seventy weeks of Daniel's prophecy fulfilled in John's days.

It seems that the marriage feast of the Lamb takes place in heaven just before Jesus descends with His bride [the Church] to take His place as King of kings and Lord of lords. When He reigns, His bride will reign with Him.

John was so awed with the vision and all that he had witnessed. He fell at the feet of the angel, and immediately the angel told him to stand. This was because the angel felt that only God should be worshipped. Therefore, he asked John not to kneel before him again. Satan may desire to be worshiped but not a faithful servant of God.

"The testimony of Jesus is the spirit of prophecy" The Old Testament prophesies of Jesus coming to humanity. Jesus is the fulfillment of all given prophecies in the volume of books (Psalm 40:7). Jesus also speaks the truth of Himself to all that will hear and His disciples in the four Gospels. His apostles testify of Him in their Epistles.

John writes in Revelation 1:1-3, "The Revelation of Jesus Christ, which God gave unto him, to shew unto his servants things which must shortly come to pass; and he sent and signified it by his angel unto his servant John: Who bears record of the word of God, and of the testimony of Jesus Christ, and of all things that he saw. Blessed is he that readeth, and they that hear the words of this prophecy, and keep those things which are written therein: for the time is at hand."

Hebrews 10:7 runs parallel with Psalms 40:7: "Then said I, Lo am, I come in the volume of the book it is written of me, to do thy, will O God."

The Descriptions of the White Horseman: The Word of God" (vv. 11-13) *"I saw Heaven opened."* This may be a literal doorway to heaven that transports the spirit through a portal from time to heaven. It is possibly a door from a heavenly dimension to an earthly reality. The Bible does not give a more in-depth insight into this open the door passage. In Jesus' ascension to heaven, he ascended to heaven in a cloud (Acts 1:9-12).

"Who coverest thyself with light as with a garment: who stretchest out the heaven like a curtain" (Psalm 104:2).

"And Jesus, when he was baptized, went up straightway out of the water; and lo, the heaven were opened unto him, and he saw the Spirit of God descending like a dove, and lighting upon him" (Matthew 3:16).

Before his death, Stephen says, "Behold, I see heaven open and the Son of Man standing on the right hand of God" (Acts 7:56).

Jacob said, "dreamed, and behold a ladder set on the earth and the top of it reached to heaven and behold the angels of God ascending and descending on it" (Genesis 28:12).

Psalm 78:23 states, "Though he had commanded the clouds above and opened the door of heaven."

"*White horses*" symbolizes the armies of God who follow Christ riding on white horses and wearing white linen (symbolizes the righteousness of God armies).

In Revelation 6:2, the Antichrist also rides "a white horse: and he that sat on him had a bow; and a crown was given unto him: and he went forth conquering, and to conquer." He uses speech and Satanic deception to deceive the nations.

John described the names and character of the white horseman as the Lord Jesus Christ. Jesus Christ has many names to describe His characters and a new divine role in future events. The names God uses here, "*Faithful and True, and righteousness,*" highlight specific attributes of Christ. Specifically, they show His absolute faithfulness and commitment to carry out what He promises (cf. Psalm 33:4-5, 111:7-8, 119:75,128, Proverb 30:5, Matthew 24:35).

v. 12 "His eyes were as a flame of fire" The figure's eyes match the description John saw in his first vision of the glorified Christ in Revelation 1:14 and 2:18. Which denotes the omniscience of Jesus to look into the soul and the spirit of man. His eyes discern the secret of men sins and conspiracies, schemes of their wickedness behaviors.

"Many crowns on his head" Christ is wearing "diadems" or crowns of royalty. Christ's rival, the Antichrist, wore ten crowns, and Satan wore seven diadem crowns (Revelation 12:3, and 13:1).

"Unknown name" Jesus' real name is a mystery and unknown to humanity. His actual name identifies the mystery of His nature and character as God (cf. Deuteronomy 29:29). Jacob asks the "man" [God] his name and receives no answer (Genesis 32:22-32).

Moses asks God in the burning bush for His name, and the LORD replied, "I am who I am," (Exodus 3:13-15).

"And without controversy great is the mystery of godliness: God was manifest in the flesh, justified in the Spirit, seen of angels, preached unto the Gentiles, believed on in the world, received up into glory" (1 Timothy 3:16).

"He's clothed with a vesture dipped in blood." Vesture is an outer or inner garment, robe, or cloak. His garment dipped in blood indicates a blood stain from war or blood-shedding (Isaiah 63:1-6.) His second return begins the bloodshed of the world's armies, the "Battle of Armageddon." Every eye will see Him as He descends to Mount Olives as He promised. Mount Olives will split in half because of Christ's presence (cf. Zachariah 14:3-7; John 18:2).

v. 13 *"The Word of God"* He is also known to the saints as "The Word of God." John confirms Christ's name the first time, in John 1:1-3. "In the beginning was the word, and the word was with God, and the Word was God. The same was in the beginning with God. All things were made by Him, and without him was not anything made that was made."

The Second Coming of Christ (vv. 14-16)

The terms the Nation of Israel must meet before the return of Christ: Jesus says, "Behold, your house is left unto you desolate: and verily I say unto you, *Ye shall not see me, until the time come when ye shall say*, blessed is he that cometh in the name of the Lord" (Luke 13:35).

"And I will pour out on the house of David and the inhabitants of Jerusalem a spirit of grace and pleas for mercy, so that, when they look on me, on him whom they have pierced, they shall mourn for him, as one mourns for an only child, and weep bitterly over him, as one weeps over a firstborn" (Zechariah 12:10).

Daniel describes the Christ coming, "I looked, and there before me was one like a son of man, coming with the clouds of heaven. He approached the Ancient of Days and was led into his presence. He was given authority, glory and sovereign power; all nations and peoples of every language worshiped him. His dominion is an everlasting dominion that will not pass away, and his kingdom is one that will never be destroyed." (Daniel 7:13-14).

Hosea prophecy "I will go and return to my place, till they acknowledge their offence, and seek my face: in their affliction they will seek me early" (Hosea 5:15).

Jeremiah speaks of the Messiah "The days are coming, declares the Lord, when I will raise up for David a righteous Branch, a King who will reign wisely and do what is just and right in the land (Jeremiah 23:5).

The Old Testament prophecies foretell the final destruction of the last empire on earth (cf. Joel 3:9; Jeremiah 51:27-36; Zephaniah 3:8).

"Our God comes; he does not keep silence; before him is a devouring fire, around him a mighty tempest" (Psalm 50:3).

"I myself have commanded my consecrated ones, and have summoned my mighty men to execute my anger, my proudly exulting ones. The sound of a tumult is on the mountains as of a great multitude! The sound of an uproar of kingdoms, of nations gathering together! The Lord of hosts is mustering a host for battle. They come from a distant land, from the end of the heavens, the Lord and the weapons of his indignation, to destroy the whole land" (Isaiah 13:3-5).

"The sun shall be turned to darkness, and the moon to blood, before the great and awesome day of the Lord comes. And it shall come to pass that everyone who calls on the name of the Lord shall be saved. For in Mount Zion and in Jerusalem there shall be those who escape, as the Lord has said, and among the survivors shall be those whom the Lord calls" (Joel 2:31-32)

"And ye shall flee to the valley of the mountains; for the valley of the mountains shall reach unto Azal: yea, ye shall flee, like as ye fled from before the earthquake in the days of Uzziah king of Judah: and the LORD my God shall come, and all the saints with thee" (Zechariah 14:5).

For I would not, brethren, that ye should be ignorant of this mystery, lest ye should be wise in your own conceits; that blindness in part is happened to Israel, until the fulness of the Gentiles be come in. And so all Israel shall be saved: as it is written, There shall come out of Sion the Deliverer, and shall turn away ungodliness from Jacob: For this is my covenant unto them, when I shall take away their sins" (Romans 11:25-27).

Jesus, His bride, and the angelic hosts will return to earth. The armies of the world will have Israel surrounded and outnumbered. The kings of the east and his allies will cross the Euphrates River. The king of the north will have destroyed the king of the south.

God will exterminate the king of the north and its allies. So, that leaves the king of the west and the king of the east. Satan, the Prince of darkness, influences the world's armies to campaign with the Antichrist against Christ and the heavenly armies.

According the prophet Enoch, "And Enoch also, the seventh from Adam, prophesied of these, saying, Behold, the Lord cometh with ten thousands of his saints, To execute judgment upon all, and to convince all that are ungodly among them of all their ungodly deeds which they have ungodly committed, and of all their hard [speeches] which ungodly sinners have spoken against him" (Jude 1:14-15)

"For as the lightning cometh out of the east, and shineth even unto the west, so shall also the coming of the Son of Man be. For wheresoever the carcass is, there will the eagles be gathered together. Immediately after the Tribulation of those days shall the sun be darkened, and the moon shall not give her light, and the stars shall fall from heaven, and the powers of the heavens shall be shaken: And then shall appear the sign of the Son of Man in Heaven: and then shall all the tribes of the earth mourn, and they shall see the Son of Man coming in the clouds of heaven with power and great glory. Moreover, he shall send his angels with a great sound of a trumpet, and they shall gather together his elect from the four winds, from one end of heaven to the other" (Matthew 24:27-31).

"The armies of Heaven" - John describes an enormous number of horsemen following their Leader to the earth to liberation Israel from the 200 million-man armies. Ancient battles were fought and led by their king in the Old Testament period (cf. 1 Samuel 4:3-5, 15; 2 Kings 3:1-27; 2 Chronicles 20:1-37). God does not need an army, but He chooses to have one. He is God and can do as He pleases. The armies may be speaking of a group of Hosts such as angels and redeemed saints. God does not need angels or redeemed saints to fight for Him. God is the Creator of all living things, all existence. Life in the universe is subject to the Almighty God. Jesus is the LORD of Hosts (1 Samuel 1:3; Psalm 24:10; Isaiah 37:16).

> "Then shall the Lord go forth, and fight against those
> nations, as when he fought in the day of battle. And his
> feet shall stand in that day upon the mount of Olives,
> which is before Jerusalem on the east, and the mount
> of Olives shall cleave in the midst thereof toward the

east and toward the west, and there shall be a very great
valley; and half of the mountain shall remove toward
the north, and half of it toward the south. And ye shall
flee to the valley of the mountains; for the valley of
the mountains shall reach unto Azal: yea, ye shall flee,
like as ye fled from before the earthquake in the days
of Uzziah king of Judah: and the Lord my God shall
come, and all the saints with thee" (Zechariah 14:3-5).

The Divine will not show any mercy to those who refuse to repent and
decide to continue in their sins (Revelation 19:15; Isaiah 63:1-6). During
the time of judgment, it is too late to ask for mercy. He will rule with a
rod of iron; Christ will govern all nations and destroy all His enemies
(Psalms 2:8-9, 1 Cor. 15:24-25).

"clothed in fine linen, white and clean," the redeemed saints are clothed
in the garments of salvation and wearing the robes of righteousness. The
heavenly hosts all wear white linen, which represents purity.

Isaiah declared, "I will greatly rejoice in the Lord, my soul shall be joyful
in my God; for he hath clothed me with the garments of salvation,
he hath covered me with the robe of righteousness, as a bridegroom
decketh himself with ornaments, and as a bride adorneth herself with
her jewels" (Isaiah 61:10).

*"And out of his mouth goeth a sharp sword, that with it he should smite the
nations"* referred to in scripture is a metaphor for the "Word of God."
Jesus will conquer the forces of darkness in the Battle of with truth and
with His Word.

"He shall rule them with a rod of iron" a rod of iron is a shepherd tool
that was used to protect the flock from wolves and other predators.
Jesus will rule His kingdom like a good shepherd and not as a dictator.
The *"rods"* were used as symbols of authority as well as for correction
and punishment. Jesus' kingdom will be a theocratic kingdom and not
a dictator.

When the Lord comes *"He treadeth the winepress of the fierceness and wrath of Almighty God"* denotes God will trample over the armies of the Antichrist with His fiery Wrath like grapes in the winepress.

"And the winepress was trodden without the city, and blood came out of the winepress, even unto the horse bridles, by the space of a thousand and six hundred furlongs" (Revelation 14:20).

"A name written, King of kings, And Lord of lords."

The title "King of Kings" occurs in scripture six times:

1. *The King of kings, and Lord of lords" v. 16.*
2. Title of Artaxerxes (Ezra 7:12).
3. King Nebuchadnezzar, (Ezekiel 26:7; Daniel 2:37).
4. God the Father, (1 Timothy 6:15).
5. Jesus Christ, (Revelation 17:14, 19:6).
6. Jesus Christ is an absolute ruler over all the governmental authority in heaven and earth (Mark 13:6).

v. 15 Christ will smite the nations with the words from his mouth. *"The sword from His mouth"* illustrates the Judgment through His spoken Word (cf. Isaiah 11:4; 2 Thessalonians 2:8; Revelation 1:16; 2:12-16). Christ strikes down as inflicting a heavy or fatal blow. If Christ literally and physically slays His enemies at His Second Coming (Revelation 19:21). It represents the sword of the spirit, the Word of God: that which God has set forth as His spoken will (Ephesians 6:17). Christ's enemies were slain and judges by the Word of God (Revelation 20:12- 15).

The Jews believe that God's Throne of Mercy is located in heaven. However, when He descends to earth, He sits on the Throne of Judgment. The rider's name is called "Faithful and True," going forth to judge and make war in righteousness. King Jesus' will be victorious over the Antichrist, false prophet, and the armies of the world.

Isaiah writes, "But with righteousness shall he judge the poor, and reprove with equity for the meek of the earth: and he shall smite he earth: with the rod of his, and with the breath of his lips shall he slay the wicked," (Isaiah 11:4).

"Do ye not know that the saints shall judge the world? And if the world shall be judged by you, are ye worthy to judge the smallest matters? Know ye not that we shall judge angels? How much more things that pertain to this life," (1 Corinthians 6:2-3).

The Battle of Armageddon (vv. 17-19)
The angel John sees may be the same angel linked to the fourth Bowl Judgment (Revelation 16:8-9, 16). Perhaps the angel stood in the path of the sun with its rays in the background. The birds are not called to participate in Armageddon's campaign but are invited as a guest to feast on the flesh of kings, mighty men, and soldiers of all levels and ranks. Suggests that all levels of humanity will be enlisted in the Antichrist's armies to fight against the Messiah, who will come to the rescue of the surrounded and besieged Israelites.

The Creator does not need to fight a conventional war on man's terms. God does not need a strategic and tactical plan to defeat mortal armies. Christ's battles is not of modern warfare or the use of primitive weaponry. He will tramp over those rebellious armies by the "Word of God" and with the brightness of His glory.

"The world was framed by the Word of God," (Hebrews 11:3).

The Vision of the Battle of Armageddon in Zechariah
God dried up the Euphrates River and lured the armies into the city of Jerusalem, and there they would be destroyed the Word of God.

"Behold, I will make Jerusalem a cup of trembling unto all the people round about, when they shall be in the siege both against Judah and against Jerusalem. And in that day will I make Jerusalem a burdensome stone for all people: all that burden themselves with it shall be cut in pieces, though all the people of the earth be gathered together against it" (Zechariah 12:2-3).

Israel is the key to Christ's Second Coming.

"In that day shall the Lord defend the inhabitants of Jerusalem; and he that is feeble among them at that day shall be as David; and the house of David shall be as God, as the angel of the Lord before them. And it shall come to pass in that day, that I will seek to destroy all the nations that come against Jerusalem. And I will pour upon the house of David, and upon the inhabitants of Jerusalem, the spirit of grace and of supplications: and they shall look upon me whom they have pierced, and they shall mourn for him, as one mourneth for his only son, and shall be in bitterness for him, as one that is in bitterness for his firstborn. In that day shall there be a great mourning in Jerusalem, as the mourning of Hadadrimmon in the valley of Megiddon. And the land shall mourn, every family apart; the family of the house of David apart, and their wives apart; the family of the house of Nathan apart, and their wives apart; The family of the house of Levi apart, and their wives apart; the family of Shimei apart, and their wives apart; All the families that remain, every family apart, and their wives apart" (Zechariah 12:8-14).

The casualty of the Armageddon Campaigns

"And it shall come to pass, that in all the land, saith the Lord, two parts therein shall be cut off and die; but the third shall be left therein. And I will bring the third part through the fire, and will refine them as silver is refined, and will try them as gold is tried: they shall call on my name, and I will hear them: I will say, It is my people: and they shall say, The Lord is my God" (Zechariah 13:8-9).

The war in the city of Jerusalem

"Behold, the day of the Lord cometh, and thy spoil shall be divided in the midst of thee. For I will gather all nations against Jerusalem to Battle; and the city shall be taken, and the houses rifled, and the women ravished; and half of the city shall go forth into captivity, and the residue of the people shall not be cut off from the city. Then shall the Lord go forth, and fight against those nations, as when he fought in the day of Battle. And his feet shall stand in that day upon the mount of Olives, which is before Jerusalem on the east, and the mount of Olives shall cleave in the midst thereof toward the east and toward the west, and there shall be a very great valley; and half of the mountain shall remove toward the north, and half of it toward the south. And ye shall flee to the valley of the mountains; for the valley of the mountains shall reach unto Azal: yea, ye shall flee, like as ye fled from before the earthquake in the days of Uzziah king of Judah: and the Lord my God shall come, and all the saints with thee" (Zechariah 14:1-5).

"And the angel thrust in his sickle into the earth, and gathered the vine of the earth, and cast it into the great winepress of the wrath of God" (Revelation 14:19).

Rev. Billy Graham has stated, "The Bible plainly forecasts the coming of yet another great war. It will be a war to eclipse anything the world has ever seen. It will embrace most of the nations of the world; and its focal point will be in the Middle East, where the armies of the world will someday deploy themselves, centering at Mount Megiddo. This great war has been called the Battle of Armageddon. In the midst of this terrifying war that could destroy civilization the Lord Jesus Christ will return to this earth in glory and power to judge the nations of the world and set up His own glorious kingdom."

The Judgment of Antichrist and the False Prophet (vv. 20-21)
vv. 20-21 "And the beast was taken, and with him the false prophet that wrought miracles before him, with which he deceived them that had received the mark of the beast, and them that worshipped his image. These both were cast alive into a lake of fire burning with brimstone. And the remnant were slain with the sword of him that sat upon the horse, which sword proceeded out of his mouth: and all the fowls were filled with their flesh."

The world's armies will have such resentment against the LORD because of the judgments brought to earth. They will be under demonic influence to join with the Antichrist and the second Beast to fight against the white horsemen (Jesus Christ). This Battle is parallel to Ezekiel 39:17-20 and Matthew 24:28.

It is clear that if they are fighting against the Creator, the Battle ended before it started. Jesus, the Word of God, speaks words, and war end rapidly. All the participants die, and all the air's fowls are invited to the great feast to eat man's flesh after the Battle of Armageddon (Matthew 24:28; Luke 17:37).

The Antichrist and the false prophet cast into the Lake of Fire alive. Satan summons into chain 1,000 years and is parole for a short season at the end of the 1,000 years. Finally, Satan, the fallen angels, all of Satan forces of darkness, all whose names not recorded in the Book of Life cast into the Lake of fire for eternality.

The false trinity of Satan:

- The Dragon - Satan (Revelation 12).
- The first Beast from out the sea – Antichrist (Revelation 13).
- The second Beast from out of the earth - False Prophet (Revelation 16:13, 19:20, 20:10).
- The Scarlet Beast on which the Harlot sits - Religious system or an Apostate Church (Revelation 17).

CHAPTER TWENTY

THE MILLENNIAL KINGDOM ON EARTH: THE REIGN OF THE SON OF GOD

The Seven Parenthesis Period[34]

---

34   The Last parenthesis comes between the fourth and the fifth episodes: (1) Satan cast into a bottomless pit for 1,000 years (vv. 1-7), (2) the completion of the first resurrection (vv. 4-5); (3) The Millennium reigned of Christ (v. 6); Satan loosed for a short season (v.7).

Satan is Bound in the Hell/ The Millennial Reign of Christ (vv.1-6)
The Scene on Earth

vv. 1-3 Satan is Incarcerate for 1,000 years
"having the key of the bottomless pit," John sees an anonymous angel from heaven coming down to earth with the key to the bottomless pit and a chain in his hand. The key refers to the authority given by God to bound and loose Satan. We are told that the messenger shut the Dragon into the Abyss and set a seal upon it him. Chapter 19 describes the defeat and judgment of the two Beasts and cast into the Lake of Fire (Revelation 19:20-21).

Next, God authorizes a special mighty angel to apprehend Satan and confine him to the Abyss for 1,000 literal years without a possibility of parole. For added security, God will place a sealed on the pit. Christ has established the Millennium kingdom without interruptions of the Dragon, and all his works will cease for a short season. Satan no longer has access to Heaven and Earth for a thousand years.

"A great chain in hand"- Satan is a spirit to bind him intangible chains that must be figurative. Perhaps the great chains depict imprisonment and restricting the movement of Satan to the bottomless pit. If this chain is literal, then the material is made of a heavenly substance used to bind a spiritual being. However, Satan will be subdued and bound in the bottomless pit by an angel. The scriptures allude to heaven's spiritual materials such as robes, crowns, rivers, trees, fruits, the sea, and a great chain.

The bottomless pit is also called *the Abyss*, which is believed to be in the earth's core. The angel that binds Satan is not just an ordinary angel because Satan is a mighty angel.

The Archangel Michael did not insult Satan (Jude 9). In Revelation 9:1, the angelic being has the *"keys"* [of authority] to open and close the bottomless pit. This angel may work near the Throne of God and was given great power by Christ to bind Satan in the bottomless pit.

"Satan" is also known as *"The Devil, Serpent, and Lucifer."* Satan is not just an idea or a source of influence in the world. He is known as the god of this world (2 Corinthians 4:4).

He is the ruler of the power of darkness (Ephesians 6:11-12, 2:2). So, who is this angel that is capable of binding Satan in heavenly made chains? He is the fifth angel in Revelation 9:1. Satan is not omnipotent. When God speaks, it becomes the perfect law, and nothing can stop the righteousness of God's judgment.

Satan described in four titles:

1) *"The Dragon"* (Gk. drakon) properly "seeing one," derived from the mythical Dragon (giant serpents) known for seeing their prey from far away or subtlety."
2) *"The Old Serpent"* (Heb. nasash; Gr. ophis), the serpent's character, is alluded to in the narratives of Eve and the Serpent in the Garden of Eden (Genesis 3:1-4, 13). The Old Serpent character and the behavior are crafty and shrewd (cf. 2 Corinthians 11:3; Revelation 12:9, 15, 20:2). Satan uses a real serpent as an agent of temptation.
3) *The Devil"* (Gk. diabolos) means to accuse falsely or slander (Matthew 13:19, 38)
4) *"Satan"* (Heb. Satanas) means "adversary or accuser." He was the accuser in the narrative of Job (Job 2:1-6).

"Set a seal upon him" Satan's confined in the Abyss for a thousand years, closed and seal by the authority of God. The seal prevents Satan from leaving or escape his confinement without God's approval. God seals on Satan to guarantee full terms of his imprisonment and will be eligible for a pardon for a short time after his term served.

The king signet makes a deep impression in clay, forming an official seal. The stamped seal carries the king's full authority or emperor in office, and no one can tamper with the seal. The king mark indelibly declared the authority of royal ownership. There is a death penalty for those who violate it.

"And a stone was brought, and laid upon the mouth of the den; and the king sealed it with his own signet, and with the signet of his lords; that the purpose might not be changed concerning Daniel" (Daniel 6:17).

Matthew writes, so they went, and made the sepulcher sure, sealing the stone, setting a watch" (Matthew 27:66).

"Do not work for the food which perishes, but for the food which endures to eternal life, which the Son of Man will give to you, for on Him the Father, God, has set His seal" (John 6:27).

vv. 4-6 **The Millennial Kingdom**

"I saw thrones" John saw more than one throne present at the judgment. Jesus promises his disciples thrones to judge Israel's house (Matthew 19:28-29; Luke 22:28-30). Jesus promises the saints will reign with Christ and judge the world and fallen angels (Daniel 7:22; 1 Corinthians 6:2-3). The symbolism of twenty-four elders in Revelation 4:4 sitting on thrones or maybe the twelve or thirteen assigned Apostles of Jesus. Their task is to judge Israel and the Gentile nations before they may gain access into the Kingdom of Christ (cf. Matthew 25:31-34; Luke 22:28-30). However, Judas Iscariot will not be present and replaced by Matthias or Paul or both.

Future Judgments in Scriptures:

1. BEMA Seat Judgment of the saints: The judgment seat of Christ (cf. Matthew 25:21; 1 Corinthians 3:12-15; 2 Corinthians 5:10).
2. The Judgment of Israel: The Time of Jacob's Trouble (cf. Jeremiah 30:7; Zechariah 13:1; Romans 11:15).
3. The Judgment of the Gentile Nations: The Millennium Kingdom separation (cf. Matthew 25:32-34, 35-40; Galatians 6:10).
4. The Judgment of Fallen Angels (Jude 6, 1 Corinthians 6:2-3).
5. The Judgment of Wicked Dead: The Great White Throne (Hebrews 7:25; Revelation 20:11-12, 15).

Five classes of people during Millennium Age: The Reign of Christ on earth

1. Immortal: Old Testament Saints (Daniel 12:1-4; Isaiah 25:8).
2. Immortal: The Bride of Christ [the Church] (Revelation 5:10, 2:26-28; 1 Thessalonians 4:15-18).
3. Immortal: Tribulation Saints and Martyrs (Revelation 6:9).
4. Mortal: The surviving believers (sheep) of the Tribulation period (Matthew 25:31-46).
5. Mortal: The surviving unbelievers (goat nations).

The Millennium kingdom: A theocratic government that will rule, and the laws of righteousness is mandated. Jesus Christ will rule as King and Lord over the world. Jesus' co-regent will be King David (cf. 2 Samuel 7:15-17; Psalms 89:20-38; Isaiah 9:6-10, 24:23; Jeremiah 33:15-17; Ezekiel 34:23-24. 37:24-25; Daniel 7:13-14; Hosea 3:14; Luke 1:30-33).

The Millennial age is the time Jesus will rule on earth in righteousness and fulfilling all the covenant promises made to the Old and New Testament saints:

1. Abrahamic covenant (Genesis12:1-3, 13:14-17, 17:2-6 and 22:18).
2. Palestinian covenant (Deuteronomy 30:1-10).
3. Davidic covenant (2 Samuel 7:12-16).
4. The new covenant (Jeremiah 31:31-34).

The Millennium Kingdom will be similar to the Garden of Eden before the fall of man. Adam and Eve lived in a perfect world free from sin, and the citizens of the kingdom will live in an ideal world under perfect and excellent conditions. All temptations, accusations, and the presence of evil is eliminated during the 1,000 years reign. There will be perfect peace and harmony on earth among all life forms (cf. Isaiah 11:6-9; Zephaniah 3:15; Jeremiah 23:5-6; Habakkuk 2:14).

The curse of illness and death will be removed (cf. Isaiah 33:24, Ezekiel 34:16). Death and sin will still exist for the natural man (Isaiah 65:20).

Isaiah describes the living conditions during the Millennium age: (Isaiah 65:20-25).

"There shall be no more thence an infant of days, nor an old man that hath not filled his days: for the child shall die an hundred years old; but the sinner [being] an hundred years old shall be accursed. And they shall build houses, and inhabit [them]; and they shall plant vineyards, and eat the fruit of them. They shall not build, and another inhabit; they shall not plant, and another eat: for as the days of a tree [are] the days of my people, and mine elect shall long enjoy the work of their hands. They shall not labour in vain, nor bring forth for trouble; for they [are] the seed of the blessed of the LORD, and their offspring with them. And it shall come to pass, that before they call, I will answer; and while they are yet speaking, I will hear. The wolf and the lamb shall feed together, and the lion shall eat straw like the bullock: and dust [shall be] the serpent's meat. They shall not hurt nor destroy in all my holy mountain, saith the LORD."

The Old and New Testament gives us a panorama glimpse of the reign of Christ on earth (cf. Isaiah 2:1-4, 11; Psalms 72, Jeremiah 23:5-8, 31:31-30; Ezekiel 47, Daniel 2:44-45, 7:13-14, Micah 4:1-8, 5:2-5, Zechariah 14.

"*Resurrection*" (Gk. Anastasis) means to "*raise up, or rise up*" from the dead or "referring to the physical resurrection of the body." The believers are raised from a spiritual rest and given a glorified body comparable to Jesus' resurrection. The wicked are also raised from the dead and given an immortal body suitable for eternal damnation in the Lake of fire. Their resurrected bodies' immortal and not made from corruptible dirt or dust, but its essence is similar to the incorruptible soul and spirit.

"For this corruptible must put on incorruption, and this mortal must put on immortality. So when this corruptible shall have put on incorruption, and this mortal shall have put on immortality, then shall be brought to pass the written statement, death is swallowed up in the victory. O death, where is thy sting? O grave, where is thy victory" (1 Corinthians 15:53-55).

"For we know that our Earthly house of the tabernacle [flesh] was dissolved, we have a building of God, a house [spiritual body] not made with hands, eternal in Heaven" (2 Corinthians 5:1).

The First Fruit of the Resurrection:

1. Christ and Old Testament saints (cf. Matthew 27:52-53;1 Corinthians 15:23; Ephesians 4:8).
2. The resurrection of the living: the church age (cf. John 14:3; 1 Thessalonians 4:13-17; 1 Corinthians 15:50-53).
3. The two witnesses: killed by Satan (Revelation 11:11-12).
4. The remaining Old Testament saints will be resurrected (cf. Daniel 12:2; Isaiah 26:19; Ezekiel 37:13-14).
5. The Tribulation martyrs: reward and reign with Christ (Revelation 20:4-5).

The unbelieving dead summons from Hell and appears before the Great White Throne Judgment. Jesus Christ is the Presiding Judge (Revelation 20:11-15).

"The rest of the dead" denotes the unbelievers whose names are not written in the Book of Life. from Adam to the end of the Millennium.

The Bible does not mention what happens to the living saints and those who die during the Millennium.

The Final War in Humanity History: *"The Battle of Gog and Magog"* (vv. 7-10)

"Satan will be loosed for a short season" Satan will continue where he left off, which is his final attempt to lead the unbelievers to their doom and

rebellion against God. Humanity has lived in a perfect world of peace and righteousness under the leadership of Jesus Christ.

"*Gog*" is name of a man and "*Magog*" is location of land.

"The sons of Joel; Shemaiah his son, *Gog his son*, Shimei his son" (1 Chronicles 5:4).

"Son of man, set thy face against Gog, *the land of Magog*, the chief prince of Meshech and Tubal, and prophesy against him" (Ezekiel 38:2-11).

Magog describes the land or nation.
"*The four quarters of the earth*" Nations of the four corners of the earth signify a global context. Satan himself will lead a worldwide campaign against God in the final war. A global frontal attack from the North, East, South, and West will be launched against the kingdom of Christ.

Satan release for a short season and finally defeat by God and cast into the Lake of Fire. The goat nations would have replenish over the 1,000 years, and their depraved heart will be without repentance. They will once again revolt against their Creator and join forces with Satan. God destroyed the rebellion armies, which leads to a new era and a new beginning. The White Throne Judgment, new heaven, and a new earth.

Last Three Wars in Revelation:

1. The Battle of Michael and the Dragon - Satan and the fallen angels cast out of heaven for good (Revelation 12:7-17).
2. The Battle of Armageddon – Sixth Vial Judgment, After Jacob's Trouble (Ezekiel 39:4-17; Revelation 16:12-20).
3. Gog and Magog War- After the Millennium (Ezekiel 38:2-22; Revelation 20:7-10).

The Old Testament mentions "Gog" and "Magog" in the Book of Ezekiel as an antagonistic force to come against Israel. Ezekiel 38:1-4 prophesies the LORD's decisive triumph over Gog and Magog. "Gog" is the title of a leader and not a king or second in command; but a "chief prince." Gog was "killed and buried" (Ezekiel 38:11-12; 39:11).

Most scholars argue that "Russia" represents the land of "Magog," which "Gog" will emerge from. (Vos) identified "Gog" with "Gyges," a Lydian King of Assyria" (Circa 680-645 B.C.). Magog's land could be referring to modern-day "Turkey," what was once the ancient Lydia. Magog is included in the *"Table of Nations"* in Genesis 6:10 as one of Japheth's sons after Noah's flood. Japheth's descendants settled in Europe. Japheth's descendants included (14 Nations): Gomer, Magog, Madai, Javan, Tubal, Mesech, and Tiras (Genesis 10:2). "Gog" could be another name of Satan as a leader of "Magog," the multitudes of nations that revolt against God.

The world would have been at peace for over 1,000 years. A millennium earlier, the Antichrist and second Beast led the armies the world in the Battle of Armageddon was destroyed by the Word of God. Both beasts were cast alive into the Lake of Fire in Revelation 19:20. After the Golden Ages, Satan will lead the armies of the world into the final war of the "Battle of Gog and Magog," an invasion of the Kingdom of God. Almighty God will call fire out of heaven and devour the armies, casting Satan into the Lake of Fire.

The fulfillment of Genesis 3:15, "And I will put enmity between thee and the woman, and between thy seed and her seed; it shall bruise thy head, and thou shalt bruise his heel."

Satan is finally defeated and placed under the feet of Jesus. The fallen angels will be put on trial and judged at the White Throne Judgment.

The Great White Throne Judgement: Presiding Judge of Righteousness (vv. 11-15)

v.11 *"The Judge on the Great White Throne"* John describes the horrific scene of the Great White Throne Judgment. He sees all of the accused who did not believe in God's Son. Jesus sitting on the Bench at the White Throne prepares to judge humanity in righteousness (John 5: 22,27).

> "For God shall bring every work into judgment, with
> every secret thing, whether it be good, or whether it be
> evil" (Ecclesiastes 12:14).

Paul speaks how "the day of God righteous judgment will be revealed" (Romans 2:5-6).

"Now we know that what things soever the law saith, it saith to them who are under the law: that every mouth may be stopped, and all the world may become guilty before God," (Romans 3:19).

"Who shall give account to him that is ready to judge the quick and the dead" (1 Peter 4:5).

"Great White Throne" is known as "the Great" because all created beings will be judged: the fallen angels and men from Cain to the end of the ages. "White Throne" signifies the righteousness of Christ as Judge (cf. John 5:22-27, Acts 17:31; Romans 2:5-6, 2 Corinthians 5:10). The Last Judgement will occur after the Millennium Age and after the final war of Good vs. Evil. The scriptures are silent on the location of the White Throne Judgment and the Lake of Fire. All secret things belong to God, including the final judgment location.

"I saw the dead" refers to the unbelievers and unsaved that rejected God and His plan for salvation.

vv. 12-13 **The Judgment of all the Dead**
"Small and great" refers to the unimportant people and dignitaries that stand before God (Jesus) to be judged for their sins and deeds of the flesh.

"The books were opened" The book of Life, the Lamb's book of Life, the book of deeds, and the book of conscience will be opened.

The Book of conscience and deeds will judge Their works. The angels verify all names in the Book of Life. The individual guardians' angel will testify the truth as recorded in each book (cf. Luke 8:17; Romans 2:6-16, 3:9-19, 23, 6:23; 1 Corinthians 5:10).

"The sea will give up the dead bodies that die at sea" before the new heaven, and the new earth emerge, the old world and the sea will surrender the bodies of those who died at sea.

"Death" the graves will give up the material dust of the physical bodies.

"Hell" the place of torment that holds the soul and spirit of man after death will deliver up the soul and spirit of man. (cf. Luke 16:19-31). The resurrected body will stand up and reunite with its soul and spirit into an immortal body designed for an eternal realm known as "the Lake of fire" (Daniel 12:2; John 5:29).

vv. 14-15 The Lake of Fire
"The wages of sin is death, but the gift of God is eternal life" (Romans 6:23).

"Spiritual death" refers to spiritual separation from God.

The walking dead without any connection with God spiritually. The spiritual lost in Adam's sinful state (cf. John 3:16, 36; 1 John 5:12; Romans 5:12-15; Ephesians 2:1-3;2 Thess. 1:9).

The first death is a separation of the body from the soul and spirit. The corpse returns to dust in the grave, and the soul/spirit of the unbelievers immediately goes to "Hades" after death and waits for the second resurrection (2 Corinthians 5:6-8, James 2:26). The believers' soul/spirit goes directly to "paradise" to wait until the resurrection and the BEMA Judgment (Luke 23:43). The body is the material part of man. The soul is the incorporeal essence of a living being: psyche, intellect, spirit, consciousness, and the seat of emotions. These attributes are all used interchangeably with the spirit or the breath that comes from God. All departed spirits still would the full capacity of their five senses and full consciences at death (Luke 16:19-31).

"The second death" The body in the grave and the soul/spirit in Hades are resurrected to an immortal state, judged, and eternally separated from God in the Lake of Fire (Isaiah 25:8; 1 Corinthians 15:26, 55).

CHAPTER TWENTY-ONE

THE ETERNAL AGE: A NEW HEAVEN, A NEW EARTH AND A NEW JERUSALEM

God Made All Things New (vv. 1-2)
Location is unknown

v. 1 *"A new heaven and a new earth"* The person on the throne is "the Word of God." He will make all things "new" (Gk. *kainos*), its primary meaning newly made, fresh, or recent. The use of the word *new* (Gk. Neos) is compared with the former (cf. Matthew 9:17; Mark 2:22; Luke 5:38).

"A New Heaven" (Gk. *ouranon*) in the singular form means "the atmosphere, the sky, the starry heavens," (Genesis 1:1). The Universe is comprised of galaxies, stars, and planetary systems. The Universe is part of the second heaven, and God's throne resides in the third heaven.

The first heaven- Genesis indicates the first heaven refers to the expansion or the firmament (cf. Genesis 1:6, 8,14, 17, 2:19, 7:3, 23; Psalms 8:8; Lamentation 4:19).

The second heaven - This begins from the outer horizon of the earth's fifth atmospheric layers between the heavenly body or space (cf. Deuteronomy 17:3; Jeremiah 8:2; Psalm 19:4-6; Isaiah 40:22; Matthew 24:25).

The third heaven refers to "The Heaven of heavens," the "Throne of God" or "Paradise," (cf. Deuteronomy 10:13-14; 1 Kings 8:26-27; Psalms 2:4, 115:16, 148:4; 2 Corinthians 12:4).

It is God's dwelling place and the angelic hosts, where the souls and spirits of the righteous go after death (2 Corinthians 5:8, 12:2).

A New Creation: God's new creation of man consists of a new universe as it is written. The earth was in a chaotic condition in Genesis 1:2 and called dry land earth after it emerged from water (Genesis 1:7-10). The sea overflowed from the incessant rain, and the waters of the deep brought judgment on the world as in the flood of Noah. New earth rises from the flood (Genesis 7:11).

The earth once again is in chaos conditions because of judgment in Revelation 20-21. A new heaven and new earth emerge from the fire, and God creates all things new as His originated plans from the beginning.

Isaiah prophesy, "For, behold, I create new heavens and a new earth: and the former shall not be remembered, nor come into mind, But be ye glad and rejoice forever [in that] which I create: for, behold, I create Jerusalem a rejoicing, and her people a joy.," (Isaiah 65:17-18).

What is meant by "passing away" of the first heaven and earth? The word (Gk. *"Parerchomai"*) Most scholars agree that the "passing away" indicates a new state or condition for the world that God originally intended in the beginning.

The phrase "passing away"- metaphorically speaking in scriptures:

"Therefore, if anyone is in Christ, he is a new creation. The old has *passed away*. Behold, the new has come! "(2 Corinthians 5:17; cf. Matthew 5:17; Galatians 6:15; Ephesians 2:15).

"And the world *passeth away*, and the lust thereof: but he that doeth the will of God abideth forever" (1 John 2:17).

"Yet we do speak wisdom among those who are mature; a wisdom, however, not of this age nor of the rulers of this age, who are passing away" (1 Corinthians 2:6).

"Therefore if anyone is in Christ, he is a new creature; the old things passed away; behold, new things have come" (2 Corinthians 5:17).

"And those who use the world, as though they did not make full use of it; for the form of this world is passing away" (1 Corinthians 7:31)

"But the day of the Lord will come like a thief, in which the heavens will pass away with a roar and the elements will be destroyed with intense heat, and the earth and its works will be burned up" (2 Peter 3:10)

"Heaven and earth will pass away, but My words will not pass away" (Luke 21:33).

"And to Him was given dominion, glory and a kingdom, That all the peoples, nations and men of every language Might serve Him. His dominion is an everlasting dominion. Which will not pass away; And His kingdom is one. Which will not be destroyed" (Daniel 7:14

The former heaven and earth are where Satan dwelled and ruled. Paul writes, "Satan is the god of the world," (2 Corinthians 4:4; Ephesians 2:1-3).

The dry land will emerge from the fires like lava from a volcano developing new land and islands. A new heaven and new earth will emerge from the smoke. God will probably create a new atmosphere on earth, and all bodies of water will diminish. The old earth surfaces us water-covered, and the oceans hold about 96 percent of all earth's water.

The new earth's surface will have more land than water sources. The new earth conditions would have more rivers or fountains of Living water. All life forms on the new earth are immortal men and women. No need for oxygen, drinking, or anything the former world supply for moral men needs.

The scriptures indicate that the earth "will abide forever," (cf. Ephesians 3:21; Ecclesiastes 1:4, Psalms 78:69). The ecosystems of the planet will change during the acts of God's judgment. The new earth will become the righteous dwelling place of all ages (2 Peter 3:10-13).

In the beginning, Adam fell out of fellowship with God and lost his rest in the Garden of Eden. At the end of the ages, the Creator provides man with a better Covenant of "eternal rest and fellowship" in a new and perfect environment. The whole new earth would be paradise and a place of eternal rest. The Sabbath day constituted a day of rest, and God fulfilled His promise. The new earth survivability depends not on the sun or moon, for God's glory, and the Lamb of God would illuminate the earth.

The Old Earth Conditions:

- The dirt or ground from which man was made causes the decay of mortal bodies that had become sinful.
- God gives humanity an immortal, glorified body, free of decay and sin.
- The influence of the two Beasts that emerge from the sea and the earth causes havoc on humanity and rebellions.
- The evil kingdoms and corrupt leaders that led to the destruction of the earth.
- All evil's influence of sin and sinners will be removed as they are judged and cast into the Lake of fire.

"No more Sea." Isaiah associating *"the Sea"* with the wicked. He writes, "But the wicked are like the troubled sea when it cannot rest, whose waters cast up mire and dirt" (Isaiah 57:20).

The Judgment on the Sea and the Old Earth:

- The sea drowns the Armies of Pharaoh (Exodus 14:28).
- The Leviathan beast controls the sea in ancient days (Isaiah 27:1).
- The four great beasts that came out of the sea (Daniel 7:3-11).
- The first Beast [Antichrist] emerges from the sea (Revelation 13:1).
- The sea will give up the dead in it (Revelation 20:13).

The LORD reserves the heavens for future judgment (cf. Isaiah 34:4, 51:6; Zephaniah 1:18; Haggai 2:21; Matthew 24:49; Luke 12:49; 2 Peter 3:7; Revelation 20:11).

All Celestial Bodies Judge:

- The moon shall not reflect light on the earth.
- The stars will fall from their fixed locations.
- The sky will be on fire.
- The sun shall become darkened.
- The heavens will be shaken like a fig tree.
- God is the source of light for the new heaven and the new earth (Revelation 22:5).

Most scholars are divided on "the new heaven and the new earth" passages. If the scriptures refer to new earth being created within a *"new heavens"* [Universe], this is unsupported by scriptures. However, if our Creator desires to create a new earth and a new heaven, God's word is final and truth. The world was frame by the Word of God, and He is fully capable of creating or make a new heaven and earth if He chooses.

" For as the new heavens and the new earth, which I will *make,* shall remain before me, saith the Lord, so shall your seed and your name remain" (Isaiah 66:22).

v. 2 New Jerusalem
"And I John saw the holy city, new Jerusalem, coming down from God out of heaven, prepared as a bride adorned for her husband."

The old Jerusalem city allegorically compares to "Sodom and Egypt," (Revelation 16:19). Jerusalem also becomes polluted with immoral acts, and demonic activities will desecrate the holy temple throughout the world by the Antichrist and his administrators.

"The New Holy City" is a real eternal city of the redeemed (John 14:2-3). The New Jerusalem is described as "coming down from God out of heaven, prepared as a bride adorned for her husband. John says, "I saw" a new act of creation, the old heaven and earth pass away. Many scholars would argue that the New Jerusalem is a satellite city or a cube city that hovers over the earth during the Millennium reign of Christ. It would then return to the new earth permanently.

God Dwells Among Men (vv. 3-4)
John heard a voice calling out from heaven, "Behold, the tabernacle of God is with men." The word "Tabernacle" means the dwelling place of God. God will no longer be alienated from His people or "veiled" in a Temple.

The Tabernacle: God's Transition of the Tabernacles throughout History
In the construction of the Tabernacle, God gives Israel a picture of who He is and His expectations from them as sinners when they approach Him.

(1) the first tabernacle was a pattern of the dwelling place of God in heaven on earth. It was first established in a tent among the children of Israel when they wandered in the wilderness. It was where God spoke to Moses and Aaron, giving His instructions or guidance. "The tabernacle served as a meeting place between God and men and was thus known as the "tent of meeting" (Exodus 25:40, 36:8-39:43).

"Moreover, I will make a dwelling among you and My soul will not reject you. I will also walk among you and be your God and you shall be my people," (Leviticus 26:11-12).

(2) The second tabernacle is described in John 1:14, "God became a man and dwelled among His people in the form of a child." The first tabernacle was a shadow of the second tabernacle to come.

"Behold! The virgin shall be with child and shall bear a son, and they shall call His name Immanuel." Immanuel translated means, "God with Us," (Matthew 1:23).

(3) The third tabernacle is described as God dwelling in His people's hearts and minds through the Holy Spirit (cf. 2 Corinthians 13:5; Galatians 2:20; Ephesians 3:17).

"Know ye not that ye are the temples of God and that the Spirit of God dwelleth in you? If any man defiled the temple of God, him shall God destroy; for the temple of God is holy, which temple ye are" (1 Corinthians 3:16-17

(4) The final Tabernacle is God Almighty and the Lamb of God dwelling with immortal men and heavenly hosts in the new earth, new Jerusalem, and new heaven for eternally. In our eternal state, we will not only enjoy fellowship with our loved ones but will also have genuine fellowship with God Himself face to face (Revelation 21:3).

"Those who are pure in heart shall see God. The believers will see God as He is," (Matthew 5:8).

The Announcement from the One Who Sat on the Throne (vv.5-8) The person on the throne is *"the Word of God"* [Jesus]. He will make all things "new" (Gk. *Kainos*) "newly made, not impaired by time or use, spoken of new skins, used as a container" (Matthew 9:17; Mark 2:22; Luke 5:38).

God assures us that there will be (1) no more sea, (Revelation 21:1) (2) no more death, neither sorrow, nor crying, neither shall there be any more pain, (Revelation 21:4) (3) No Temple is there, (Revelation 21:22) (4) No more curse, (Revelation 22:3) (5) No night there, (Revelation 22:5).

Moreover, "He said unto me, 'It is done" indicates completion. Closely examining the scriptures could yield an interpretation that God consummated all things new. These words mark the end of redemptive history. God's announcement heard by John, "It is done" (Gk. *gegonan*), means the divine finality of God's wrath.

What was fulfilled by Christ after his finished work in His revelation?

- All enemies are under Christ's foot.
- The 144,000 Jewish evangelists reach uttermost parts of the world with the good news.
- God's Righteous Judgment on the unbelievers.
- The restoration of Israel back to God and their Messiah,
- The two Beasts are cast alive into the Lake of Fire.
- Satan cast into the Lake of fire.
- The unbelievers of all ages judged at the Great White Throne and cast into the Lake of Fire.
- Christ conquered Satan's influence of sin and death on humanity.
- He made all things new.
- All promises in the Old and New Testament fulfilled.
- The promise of "the Sabbath day" has been fulfilled, and humanity would enjoy eternal rest with God and the Lamb.
- God wipes away the tears from their eyes.
- He said unto me, "It is done."

What did Jesus have in mind when He said: *"It is finished"*?

"It's done" (Gk. *tetelestai*) in layman's terms means "paid in full." Jesus uttered those words on the cross to the Father. He was affirming to humanity that the debt of sin owed to His Father was paid in full and wiped away finally and forever. The obligation of sin was eliminated by the Son of God (John 19:28-30).

John describes the journey before the Tribulation saints and Millennium saints. The trial of temptation will determine their fate. The victors that put their faith in the Lord will gain eternal life at the end of the ages and drink from the fountain of living water.

He that overcomes shall inherit all things – this is a reference to all the promises listed in Revelation 21:4. God gives the inheritance to the overcomers of the Tribulation, the martyrs, and the adopted "sons' [and daughters] of Israel.

"The fearful" denotes to become afraid or cowardly during persecution and lose faith. It may refer to the apostate unbelievers.

"Abominable" refers to the vile, detestable things, the reprobate mind, and to live a sinful life.

"The Murderer" a pre-mediated or intentional murder (Genesis 9:6, Joshua 20:3) and the hatred of a brother or sister (1 John 3:15).

"The whoremongers" a person who is a monger of whores and has illegal sexual intercourse outside of marriage. Their soul and spirit will become one with the ungodly through sex. Sexual sins bring a severe penalty among God's people. This immoral behavior shows the lack of discipline and self-control over the flesh.

"Sorcerers" will use drugs and religious incantations to entice people into living by their illusion. Using satanic supernatural powers, they will manipulate people through deception and magic.

"Idolaters" are the ones who forsake God to worship an image made with their hands or from nature. It is honoring any created object or material thing on earth in the place of our Creator.

"Liars" refers to people who use words to deceive or distort their true intentions through deception and malice.

While the old Heaven and the old Earth are passing away, the dead's second resurrection is being judged somewhere in the cosmos.

These mysterious questions are difficult to answer because the Bible doesn't reveal that information.

1. Where is the location of the White Throne Judgment?
2. What and where is the Lake of Fire?
3. Where will the saints be during the White Throne Judgement and the passing away of the old Heaven and Earth?

The Bride of Christ: The New Jerusalem (vv. 9-21)
John sees the seventh angels he met early in Revelation 16:17, which shown him the bride, the Lamb wife. We were already told about the Lamb's marriage has come, and now the bride is ready. The New Jerusalem infrastructure and the bribe are linked together with God the Lamb for eternally. New Jerusalem is the permanent residence for the bride of Christ. The most dominant feature of the holy city is the manifestation of God's glory.

Ezekiel 8:11 states, "Reestablished to the new Jerusalem in the hereafter." At this point, the union has already taken place in Revelation 19:7, and the city is now referred to as "the Lamb's Wife." This city didn't materialize on earth, nor was it made with human hands. It is a new city that graciously comes down from heaven as a bride comes to her husband.

"The Glory of God" The majesty and glory of God will illuminate the city. The metropolis will have no need for sunlight or the moon. Therefore, words cannot describe the beauty of the gemstones, clear crystal sea, or the gold streets reflecting the brilliant colors from God's glory through the new city.

The Description of the City and Wall.
Numerical values of twelve is used 187 times throughout the Bible and found 22 times in the Book of Revelation, especially concerning new Jerusalem. The number twelve relates to God's divine authority and

government, according to Biblical numerology used by scholars. In Revelation 7, twelve thousand Jews were chosen from each of twelve tribes of Israel for services. In the book of Restoration (Nehemiah), the city of Jerusalem had 12 gates. Each gate had a spiritual signification of the reality to come [Jesus] (Hebrews 8:5).

The Infrastructure of the wall and city of Jerusalem:

I. The Wall Around the City

The wall of the city had twelve foundations inscribed with the names of the twelve apostles of the Lamb.

II. The Gates Around the Walls

- Twelve angels at each gate.
- The twelve gates each had one pearl.
- The names written on the twelve gates are the twelve tribes of the children of Israel
- Three gates on each side of the four walls. [Old Jerusalem on earth has eight gates, names]

> "And the gates of the city shall be after the names of the tribes of Israel: three gates northward; one gate of Reuben, one gate of Judah, one gate of Levi. And at the east side four thousand and five hundred: and three gates; and one gate of Joseph, one gate of Benjamin, one gate of Dan. And at the south side four thousand and five hundred measures: and three gates; one gate of Simeon, one gate of Issachar, one gate of Zebulun. At the west side four thousand and five hundred, with their three gates; one gate of Gad, one gate of Asher, one gate of Naphtali" (Ezekiel 48:31-34).

III. The Foundation of the wall

There were twelve foundations of the wall garnished with all manner of gemstones.

"And thou shalt put in the breastplate of judgment the Urim and the Thummim; and they shall be upon Aaron's heart, when he goeth in before the Lord: and Aaron shall bear the judgment of the children of Israel upon his heart before the Lord continually" (Exodus 28:17-20, Ezekiel 28:13).

The Foundation wall compared to the High Priest's Breastplate			
Foundation Level	Gemstone	Gemstones color	Tribes Name
1st	Jasper	Fire Opal	Benjamin
2nd	Sapphire	Blue	Issachar
3rd	Chalcedony. Agate	Sky Blue	Gad
4th	Emerald	Green	Judah
5th	Sardonyx	Red &White	Dan
6th	Sardius	Fiery Red	Reuben
7th	Chrysolite	Yellow Gold	Joseph
8th	Beryl, Onyx	White Diamond	Zebulon
9th	Topaz	Transparent Green	Simeon
10th	Chrysoprasus	Yellow-Green	Naphtali
11th	Jacinth	Red	Levi
12th	Amethyst	Violet Purple	Asher

Figure 15 The Twelve stones foundation and colors

IV. The Dimension and the Splendor Glory of the City

- A golden reed to measure
- Shape of a cube like City
- 12 thousand furlongs. Estimate 1500 miles in Width [x] distance [x] height
- The length and the breadth and the height of it are equal size.
- Walls 144,000 cubits in honor of the 144,000 Jews sealed for services in the Tribulation.
- The building of the wall of it was of Jasper [like a diamond].
- The city was pure gold [like unto clear glass].
  The street of the city was pure gold, as it were transparent glass.

V. Activities in the City having the Glory of God present.

The Glory of the Holy City (22-27)

1.   No temple, The Lord God Almighty and Lamb are the Temple
2.   Two sources of Light: No need for the sun, the moon. The glory of God did lighten it, and the Lamb is the light.

These brilliantly colored stones refract the shining splendor of God's glory into a spectrum of beautiful colors that will flash from New Jerusalem throughout the new earth. At times, the Jews believe that God conceals His light or glory, but we will see God unconcealed in His full Glory.

The perfect city from heaven will be the most beautiful view to the human eye, and words won't be able to describe the beauty of this New Jerusalem or Heaven. The streets of the metropolis will be paved with pure gold or translucent glass.

"But as it is written, Eye hath not seen, nor ear heard, neither have entered into the heart of man, the things which God hath prepared for them that love him" (1 Corinthians 2:9).

Paul quoted from the writing of Isaiah: "For since the beginning of the world men have not heard, nor perceived by the ear, neither hath the eye seen, O God, beside thee, what he hath prepared for him that waiteth for him" (Isaiah 64:4).

No Temple in the City
John notices, while in the vision, that there was no temple in the city. The temple was the place of priestly sacrifices, where God's people regularly gathered for prayer and worship.

There will be no more night, *"no need"* for the sun or the moon because the Triune God presence will illuminate the city and infuse the entire Earth with His glory.

In Revelation 21:23, the phrase "no need" suggests that the new earth doesn't depend upon the sun and the moon for its light source. The Almighty God and the Lamb are the city's temples and the lights of the new earth. There is no temple because God's shadows to man are replaced with the reality of God in person.

Isaiah writes, "The sun shall be no more thy light by day; neither for brightness shall the moon give light unto thee: but the LORD shall be unto thee an everlasting light, and thy God thy glory," (Isaiah 60:19).

The Sixth Seal Judgment causes a cosmic disturbance in the Heavens; "the sun darkened, the moon turns to blood, and the stars falling," (Revelation 6:12). The scriptures are unclear on all the details of the sun and the moon's continual existence and whether or not the sun and the moon fully recover during the Millennium or if the conditions will be permanent (cf. Job 9:7; Isaiah 13:10; Joel 2:10, 30-31, 3:15; Amos 8:9-10; Matthew 24:29; Mark 13:24; Acts 2:18-21).

The new heaven and earth become the Holy of Holies because God and the Lamb will dwell among man. There are no boundaries to God's glory and His presence. Men of the old earth were rebellious as they did not recognize God.

vv. 24-25 John sees nations of people on the new earth and the new Jerusalem from all walks of life. Maybe John sees all nations of saints from Adamic age through Millennial age in the new city and presents on the new earth in fellowship.

The Tenants of the New earth: Immortal human

1. Names recorded in the Book of Life.
2. Old Testament Patriarchs and saints from Adam to the closing of Millennium age
3. The nation of Israel.
4. The sheep nation [the Church].
5. The Gentile nation, who overcame by the blood of the Lamb.

6. The great multitude from the Great Tribulation period.
7. The Goat Nations (Gentile) which will comes to faith during the Millennial age.

The Heavenly gates are open to all God's people. The Redeemed from every nation, tribe, and tongue will be welcome (Matthew 5:8, 1 Corinthians 15:50). Every immortal believer will be equal and spread out over the new earth as nations. The resurrected saints won't require sleep because of their eternal state and will reside with the Creator. The days will be endless in the presence of God and the Lamb of God, Hallelujah!

"The gates shall not be shut." The twelve gates around New Jerusalem will be accessible to all Heavenly citizens forever. There will be no need to shut them because all God's enemies will have been cast into the Lake of Fire and will never again invade earth.

v. 26 They shall bring the *"glory"* (Greek *Doxa*) means "honor, renown, glorious splendor." All the saints, believers of all ages, kings, princes, the wealthy, and the poor will give GOD Almighty glory. He is worthy of being praised and honored.

v. 27 All sins will be eradicated forever, and only the redeemed saints will enter into eternal rest and abide with God forever (cf. Ephesians 3:21; Psalms 78:69).

The last enemy [death] destroyed, and all things will be under the feet of Christ. All forms of wickedness and evil have been judged.

Warning of the works of abomination or liar.

The Lord is sending a strong warning to all that hear this book's prophecy to come to Him while there is time. Here what will happen to all names not recorded in the "Lamb's Book of Life." They will not enter into eternal rest but will encounter the second death. Warning to future believers who are reading the letter of John in this book.

CHAPTER TWENTY-TWO
EPILOGUE: WARNINGS AND PROMISES

The Description of the New Jerusalem (vv. 1-5)
The Apostle Paul writes, "But as it is written, eye hath not seen, nor ear heard, neither have entered into the heart of man, the things which God hath prepared for them that love him," (1 Corinthians 2:9, Isaiah 64:4), fulfilled in Revelation 22.

"The Pure River of the Water of Life" John sees the New Jerusalem and the river of living water flowing from the throne room of God and the Lamb. The river of living water supernaturally supplies the spiritual thirsty of the soul and spirit of man. The water is free to drink and the Lord desires to satisfied the thirsty soul of all for eternity. The Living water flows down the main street of the city with Trees of Life on both

sides of the river producing twelve manners of fruits monthly. John was unable to describe the majesty of the city in words. "The Tree of Life and Knowledge in the middle of Eden near the four Rivers (Genesis 2:9-14).

"In the last day, that great day of the feast, Jesus stood and cried, saying, If any man thirst, let him come unto me, and drink. He that believeth on me, as the scripture hath said, out of his belly shall flow rivers of living water. (But this spake he of the Spirit, which they that believe on him should receive: for the Holy Ghost was not yet given; because that Jesus was not yet glorified.)" (John 7:37-40

God commanded Adam, "of every tree of the garden thou mayest freely eat, except the tree of knowledge" (Genesis 2:16-17). In the new earth, "there shall be no more curse," and all the inhabitants may drink and eat freely, having fellowship with God Almighty and the Lamb of God forever. If they can recall their former life of the old earth and what all the Lord has done for them, they will shed tears of joy and happiness. God will wipe them away from their eyes. The redeemed saints will see God face to face and have fellowship with Him without the fear of death because God's name shall be in their spirit.

Many scholars argue that the pure River Life is synonymous with the Millennium Temple River in mentioned Ezekiel (cf. Ezekiel 47:1-12; Zechariah 14:8 -9; Joel 3:18; Psalm 46:4).

Ezekiel 47	Two Different Rivers	Revelation 21
Millennium Temple River	New Jerusalem River	
"The river comes from under the east side of the house [temple], south of the altar," 47:1.	"I saw no temple therein, 21:22.	
The river flows down into the desert through the Dead Sea and into the Mediterranean Sea. Healing the land, the sea and all things in it path, 47:8-9.	"I saw a hew heaven and a new earth: for the first heaven and the first earth were passed away; and there was no more sea," 21:1.	

The river in Ezekiel 47 will exist for a thousand years during the reign of Christ on the old Earth.	The new Heaven and the new earth were created first, the River of Life came down to the earth within the city of New Jerusalem, Revelation 22.

Figure 16 The Millennium River and the New Jerusalem's River.

vv. 3-4 *"And there shall be no more curse"* The curse mention in Genesis 3:17-19, removed forever. The curse on Adam covers the ground and physical death. God gives man a glorified body and eternal life. Humanity suffers consequences for sin, but God wipes away the tears from their eyes. Adam and Eve banished from the Garden of Eden, and Paradise ceases to exist on the old earth. God gives man new Heaven and new earth with paradise amenities, trees of life, Living water, and much more.

- No more thorns or thistles
- No more child-bearing
- No more sickness or sorrow or death.
- The blessing of God will replace the curse of sin.

"They shall see His face." God is light, and in Him is no darkness. No man can approach God in his fleshly form, or they would be consumed by His Glory and die. The fleshly body is not designed for the spiritual realm because men were made a little lower than the angels. Humankind's body was designed for existing on the earth, and his soul and spirit created spiritual realms after death. Only the righteous and redeemed saints will see God's face in His full Glory on the new earth and in the New Jerusalem as He is (1 John 3:2). However, men have seen God and walked with Him, but not as He is. To see God's face is prohibited by Jewish belief and death (Exodus 33:20). The Jews believe that seen God face to face death would occur and forbidden.

"But He said, "you cannot see My face, for no man shall see Me, and live" (Exodus 33:20).

"No one has seen God at any time..." (John 1:18, 6:46,1 John 4:12).

- When Adam was created, he would fellowship with God in the cool of the day. This suggests Adam may have seen God face to face, but not in His full Glory because Adam was mortal flesh and blood. After the fall of Adam, he lost fellowship with God.
- Enoch walked with God and was taken to Heaven in flesh and blood (Genesis 5:22-24).
- Noah walked with God (Genesis 6:9).
- Jacob says, "he has seen God face to face, and my life is preserved," (Genesis 32:30).

"His name shall be in their foreheads" In Revelation 7:18, God seals the 144,000 Jews.

John indicated that God would write His name on their foreheads. This suggests that God will write His laws into the minds of the redeemed saints whom He has already purchased (cf. Psalms 37:31, 40:8; Jeremiah 31:33; Hebrews 8:10, 10:16).

v.5 *"And there shall be no night there."* There be no more night but Light for eternal because God Almighty and Lamb is the Light. Man's immoral body does not require rest or sleep.

Epilogue (vv. 6-21)
vv. 6-7 "And he said unto me, These sayings are faithful and true" This angel seems to be the angel in Revelation 1:1-3, confirming the complete divine Revelation of Jesus to John. The words are "faithful and true" and verified by the angel of the "Lord God of the holy prophets" to show his servant [John] the things which must shortly come to pass. The Lord's return is imminent, and the readers of John's letter in the Church communities (past, present, and future) are warned to keep this book's sayings. Worship God and believe in Him with your whole heart. It is not God's desire that anyone should perish, but all come to repentance and believing faith in Jesus Christ (2 Peter 3:8).

The phrase *"the words of the prophecy of this book"* is found four times in this chapter in (vv. 7, 10, 18, 19). Five times *"This book"* is mentioned in (vv. 7, 9, 10, 18 19).

"Unjust" (Gk. *adlikeo*) means to do wrong (moral, socially or physically)[1].

Every human has a choice of their eternal condition. They may choose to be righteous or continue with a filthy, sinful heart.

If they die in a sinful state, they will remain that way for eternity; their estate becomes permanent, whether it is an unjust, filthy garment, or righteousness and holiness. They will stay in that eternal sinful estate and be judged at the Great White Throne. The fallen angels who left the first estate will be judged as well (Jude 1:16).

vv.8-9 John is rebuked again by the angel or the same angel in Revelation 19:10 for trying to worship him. The angel informs John that he is also a fellow servant of God. They are also required to worship and serve God. All honor and glory belong to God alone.

vv. 10-11 A Warning is Given by the Same Angel

The angel instructs John not to seal the book of prophecy, for the time is at hand. He allows the scroll's prophecy to be read by the church community, and all that will read and obey the warnings in this book would be blessed. Daniel was told just the opposite, "to seal up the vision and prophecy," (cf. Daniel 9:24; 12:4-9). Daniel's prophecy was closed and concealed until the appointed time to be revealed.

"He that is unjust, let him be unjust still, and he which is filthy, let him be filthy still: and he that is righteous, let him be righteous still and he that is holy, let him be holy still" This is a warning to all those who read this book. Since Jesus is coming suddenly, there will not be any time for repentance. Whatever the status you are found in will seal your fate until judgment. Take heed to the warning written in this book because our eternity is depending upon it.

vv. 12-17 An Invitation to the World: Free Salvation Through Jesus
v. 12 "I come quickly" is a phrase spoken by Christ that occurs six times in (Revelation 2:5, 2:16, 3:11, 22:7, 12, 20). Jesus states that He will fulfill his promises and reward the saints for their work and dedication.

The works and deeds present in the mortal body will follow them after this life (1 Corinthians 3:13).

v. 13 Christ identifies Himself with the Father at the beginning and the end. The phrase "I am the Alpha and Omega, the beginning and the end, the first and the last" occurs four times in John's vision (cf. Revelation 1:8, 1:11, 21:6, 22:13). "Alpha" is the first letter of the Greek alphabet, and "Omega" is the last. Jesus was the only person within human history who was present from the beginning of creation and will remain present at the end of civilization. What was initiated by God at the beginning of man's history (Genesis 1-3) is finished at the end of Revelation.

John writes, "Christ at the beginning was with God. He made all things, and without him was not anything made that was made," (John 1:1).

Jesus said to them, "Truly, truly, I say, before Abraham was, I am," (John 4:58).

v. 14 The last Beatitude in the Bible is found in (v.14) Jesus said, "Whoever shall keep his commandment is blessed and will be a rewarded openly. He gives them entry to the new city and the Tree of Life."

The lists of sins mentioned herein (v. 17) are similar to Revelation 21:8.

v. 15 *"For without are Dog"* is a metaphor for false prophets, unbelievers, and those who are morally unclean.

v. 16 Jesus Christ Himself endorses and authentication the entire book of John. This message is to be circulated throughout the Church as an inspiration to all men and believers. The only time the word *"churches" resurface in* the Book of Revelation is after Chapter 3. The Church is absent from Revelation 4-22:16.

"I'm the root" Jesus is the root of David's existence and all life on earth as the Creator. All forms of life blossom from the root of Adam and Eve, whom he created in Genesis 2.

John writes, "I'm the vine; you are the branches" (John 15:5).

"The offspring of David" Jesus identifies His from the lineage of King David in human form through the virgin birth of Mary. David is the progenitor of the woman's seed (Genesis 3:15; Jeremiah 30:9; Hosea 3:5).

"The bright and morning star" Refers to Christ Messianic title (Numbers 24:17; Revelation 2:28). Christ as the Morning Star is a picture of promise and blessing of another day. The Morning star announces the beginning of a new day and all things new.

v. 17 The invitation to come to God

1) *"The Bride"* (The Church) offers an invitation to come to Christ through the preaching of the Gospel and be saved, receiving eternal life.
2) *"The Holy Spirit"* responds to those that hear the Gospel's message and saved through redemption.
3) This extended invitation to the unbelievers that thirst for the righteousness of God and lost in sin may also come freely. They may drink freely and wash their sinful robes in the blood of the Lamb. Jesus is that Living Water that men desire to drink (Isaiah 12:3; John 4:14 and John 7:37-38). The Holy Spirit is a symbol of water.

Warning to the Readers and Hearers of the Book (vv. 18-21)

"Every man that heareth the words of the prophecy of this book..."

The Book of Revelation shouldn't be taken lightly by its readers and hearers. The Book of Revelation was authenticated by God and Jesus, and given to John to propagate the message to the world as the angels conveyed it.

Now, there's a warning to the readers not to add to or take from the word of this prophecy (cf. Deuteronomy 4:2, 12:32, 28:27, 60; Proverbs 30:5-6; Jeremiah 26:2; Galatians 1:6-9).

God will plague all violators who diminish His words. This warning applies not only to the Church communities in John's days but all translators and teachers through the ages.

This strictly pertained to those who intentionally tried to pervert the word of God, i.e., false teachers, false leaders, and those who modify the word of God for personal gains.

Peter writes, "Knowing this first, that no prophecy of the scriptures is of any private interpretation, for prophecy never came by the will of man, but holy men of God spoke as they were moved by the Holy Spirit," (2 Peter 1:20-21).

v. 20 The Lord Jesus Christ confirms John's testimony written in this book is genuine. He encourages all believers to wait in preparation and readiness for that day to come. His return is imminent. All believers throughout ages desire the Lord's return would occur in their lifetime. However, the Lord assured us that He would return and fulfilled all His promises written in this book.

v. 21 The phrase *"Grace"* is only mentioned twice in the Book of Revelation: (1) once during the Church age (Revelation 1:4); (2) in closing remarks of the His Revelation (Revelation 22:21). The dispensation of grace comes to a close after the removal of the Church, (Revelation 4:1). The Book of Revelation reveals God's plans of judgment on the world and the unbelievers.

The words "Love, hope, belief, goodness, joy, and mercy" never appear in the Book of Revelation outside of the Church.

BIBLIOGRAPHY

Anker, John, and Dillons. *Middle East Meltdown*. Eugene: Harvest House, 2007.

Bauder, Walter. *Greek-English Lexicon of the New Testament*. Williams F. Arndt, Theodore Danker, and F. Wilbur Gingrich, trans. And rev., 3rd ed. Chicago: University of Chicago Press, 2000.

Benware, Paul. *Understanding End Times Prophecy*. Chicago: Moody, 2006.

Blomberg, Craig L., *From Pentecost to Patmos*. B&H Publishing Group, 2006.

Bury, J.B.;S.A. Cools. And F.E. Adcock, eds. *The Cambridge Ancient History*, 12 vols. 2nd ed.Reprinted. Cambridge: University Press, 1928.

Buswell, James. *A Systematic Theology of the Christian Religion*. Grand Rapids: Zondervan, 1979.

Duff, Paul B. *Who Rides the Beast? Prophetic Rivalry and the Rhetoric of Crisis in the Churches of the Apocalypse*. Oxford and New York: OUP, 2001.

Encyclopedia Britannica. *Nero: Christianity*. Encyclopedia Britannica Premium Service. 2005.

Furtick, Odell. *An Exposition of the Book of Revelation*. Westbow Press, 2018.

Geisler, Norman. *Systematic Theology*. Minneapolis: Bethany House, 2005.

Hailey, Homer. Revelation: An Introduction and Commentary. Grand Rapids, MI: Baker Book House, 1979.

Hitchcock, Roswell D. *Entry for 'Jehovah-tsidkenu*: "An Interpreting Dictionary of Scripture Proper Names". New York, N.Y., 1869.

Josephus, Flavius. *The works of Flavius Josephus (3 Volumes)*, Trans. William Whiston. New York: A. L. Burt, 1907 (Original 1737).

Kaiser, Walter C. and Duane Garret, eds. *The Archaeological Study Bible*. Grand Rapids: Zondervan, 2005.

Kenneth Scott Latourette, *A History of Christianity*, Volume I: Beginnings to 1500, rev. ed. (Prince Press, 2000), p. 81.

Koester, Craig R. *Revelation and the End of All Things*. Grand Rapids and Cambridge: Eerdmans, 2001.

LaHaye, Tim, and Ed Hindson, eds. *The Popular Bible Prophecy Commentary*. Eugene Harvest House, 2006.

Metzger, Bruce M., *Breaking the Code: Understanding the Book of Revelation*. Abingdon Press, 1993.

Mounce, Robert H. *The Book of Revelation*. rev. ed. The New Testament International Commentary on the New Testament. Grand Rapids, MI: Eerdmans, 1997.

Pate, C. Marvin, ed. *Four Views on he Book of Revelation*. Grand Rapids: Zondervan, 1998.

Pentecost, J. Dwight. Things to Come. Grand Rapids: Zondervan, 1964.

Ryrie, Charles. *Basic Theology Wheaton*: Victor, 1986.

Rhodes, Ron. *The End Times In Chronological Order.* Eugene Harvest House, 2012.

Steven Gregg, *Four Views of Revelation* (Nashville: Thomas Nelson Publishers, 1997), 31, 217, 309, & 399).

Thomas, Robert L. *The Chronological Interpretation of Revelation 1-7: An Exegetical Commentary.* Chicago: Moody Press, 1992.

Vos, Howard. *Wycliffe Historical Geography of Bible Lands.* Peabody, MA: Hendrickson. 2003

Walvoord, John F., *Every Prophecy of the Bible.* Chariot Victor Publishing. 1999.

Walvoord, John F., *Revelation.* Chicago: Moody Publishing. 2011.

All Scripture quotations, are taken from The Holy Bible, English King James Version. By Bible Gateway.

FIGURES

Figure 1 Comparison of Jezebel of Thyatira and the Phoenician Queen Jezebel 27

Figure 2 Other Genre Books 32

Figure 3 Jesus Assessment of the Seven Churches. 40

Figure 4 The Seven Churches Compared to Matthew Parables........41

Figure 5 Comparison of John and Ezekiel visions............................45

Figure 6 The Order of the Camp assemble in the Wilderness. 49

Figure 7 Comparison of Revelation 1 and 4 52

Figure 8 A Comparison of The Sixth Seal Judgment and the Olivet Discourse...70

Figure 9 The Family Tree of Jacob's sons (12 Tribes of Israel)..........77

Figure 10 The Marking order of the 144,000 Jewish's Servant 78

Figure 11 The Trumpets and Bowls Judgment: Foreshadow the ten Plagues of Egypt...86

Figure 12 Moses and Elijah's Work Correlated with The Judgment in Revelation 11... 105

Figure 13: The Comparison of the Two Babylonian Systems 184

Figure 14: The Fourteen Worship Hymns in the Book of Revelation. 188

Figure 15 The Twelve stones foundation and colors 225

Figure 16 The Millennium River and the New Jerusalem's River...231